Linguistic Studies
in
Medieval Spanish

Edited by

Ray Harris-Northall
Thomas D. Cravens

Madison, 1991

To the memory of
Dennis Paul Seniff
(March 5, 1949 - November 24, 1990),
indefatigable worker in the
field of Old Spanish philology,
these studies are affectionately dedicated.

Contents

vi

Preface

Dennis P. Seniff was a friend of the Hispanic Seminary of Medieval Studies, which he had often visited in the course of his work. Upon learning of his death, the Seminary decided to publish a volume of studies in his honor. There will undoubtedly be other commemorations containing papers more closely associated with Dennis's primary field of research, Medieval Hispanic literature, and those of his colleagues whose work falls within the realm of linguistics wished to express their esteem in an equally appropriate manner. Given Dennis's enormous interest in, and fascination with the Spanish language, it seemed fitting to offer a collection of linguistic studies devoted to the same period.

The result is a somewhat eclectic collection, reflecting, however, the variegated yet entirely complementary interests of a number of highly-respected historians of Ibero-Romance. Thus the chronological range of the studies collected here stretches from Hispanic Latin through the expansion of Ibero-Romance outside the geographical limits of the Peninsula, while the scope of topics spans numerous aspects of linguistic endeavor: text editing, syntax, phonology, dialectology, lexis, morphology, pidgins and creoles, and etymology.

We hope that this volume will stand as a fitting homage to the life and work of our colleague, remembered not only for his considerable scholarly achievement, but also for his warm-hearted and generous nature.

Thomas D. Cravens
Ray Harris-Northall
Madison, July 1991

Squeezing the Spanish Turnip Dry:
Latinate Documents from the Early Middle Ages

Robert Blake

University of Rochester

In charting the evolution of the Spanish language, nothing is of more value than consulting primary source materials. Primary sources are the only firm evidence that can be pointed to when formulating a chronology of language change; every bit of linguistic information, then, must be diligently squeezed out of the texts.[1] Ironically, the Early Middle Ages (roughly the 8th to 11th centuries) — a crucial period for the development of Spanish — provides records written exclusively in Latin, and a rather inferior-looking brand of it at that. Yet no one has ever doubted that Hispano-Romance, in some form or other, was in full development and actively being spoken during this period, despite the lack of direct proof until the relatively late appearance of the glosses from San Millán and Silos. To make matters worse for the historical linguist, a wholesale proliferation of Hispano-Romance texts does not commence until the early 13th century. Before that, researchers are left anxiously 'champing at the bit' for more raw data, especially after having surveyed the tantalizing but sketchy attestations of linguistic change that filter down from the 9th-century *jarchas* and 11th-century glosses. In short, it is agreed that Romance must be the principal medium for social intercourse before the 13th century, but the texts are silent.

Serious argument arises, however, with respect to how much and what type of Latin was employed during the same time period, again owing to the nature of available textual evidence. Two viewpoints vie for center stage. On the one hand, the traditional view states that Spain was diglossic, speaking both Latin and Romance, but writing only the former with varying degrees of proficiency. Various names have been devised to refer to the peculiar type of non-standard Latin found in Peninsular

---

[1] See Craddock (1970) and Blake (1987) for more elaborate pleas to exploit primary source materials.

notarial documents, adding to the confusion: Low Latin, Vulgar Latin, Popular Leonese Latin, Notarial Latin, among others (see Wright, in press, for a more complete list).

An alternate interpretation, championed most prominently by Wright (1982), claims that Spain spoke only Romance in the Early Middle Ages, with registers ranging from the most colloquial to the most formal, but writing superficially continued to follow Latinate spelling conventions. Many have charged Wright with overstating his case (Walsh 1986, Penny 1984, Marcos Marín 1984), especially with respect to texts written by and for clerics of high rank (Walsh 1991). The charge is not without merit, because some writers clearly demonstrate a sophisticated knowledge of Classical Latin grammar and style. The vast majority of notarial scribes, however, did not enjoy this classical training and their 'Latin' shows it. Walsh (1991:207) has described their knowledge of Latin as being restricted to stock legal phrases, which are typically invoked at the beginning and end of the text; the rest of it is 'shot full of errors'.

The dilemma seems intractable: Romance must have been the primary spoken language but we have no textual proof of it, while spoken Latin, on the surface of it, appears to have limped along in a degenerate form for five centuries only to disappear virtually all at once by the turn of the 13th century.[2] Where is the missing link for Hispano-Romance? The link is, of course, the realization that writing attends more to the dictates of propriety and long-established traditions than those of phonemic accuracy. Writing systems naturally tend to display an uninterrupted scribal tradition which continues to represent the language as though it had not changed (Hoenigswald 1960:7). The case of Hispano-Romance is no different, except for the fact that its scribal tradition is based on Latin, a separate language as seen through modern eyes, lending the appearance that Latin was generally understood right up to the 13th century. In reality, only the very educated, in particular, the clerics, were capable of this, and for most of them, I would wager that Latin was probably a purely written not spoken form of communication, as it was for the scientific expressions of Sir Isaac Newton or Roger Bacon.

---

[2] According to Bastardas y Parera (1953), there are no Peninsular Vulgar Latin texts before the 8th century.

In this study, then, I will summarize the arguments in favor of interpreting Peninsular Latinate texts of the Early Middle Ages as a written expression of the Romance vernacular or 'Older' Old Spanish.[3] In what follows, I will illustrate with examples from the San Millán Chartulary (Ubieto Arteta 1976) some of the phonological, lexical, and syntactic benefits that accrue when these Latinate texts are squeezed for all they are worth, like turnips cooked in a well-simmered stew. In other words, I claim that Latinate documents are a primary source of data for Old Spanish. They have long been overlooked, given the mistaken but persistent belief that people always read words aloud phonetically, exactly as they write them down (cf. Cravens 1991:56-62 on the dangers of this). Linguists should know that very few writing systems are ever closely phonemic, much less phonetic.

The diglossia model has always had to fly in the face of a set of strong contradictory facts. Most disconcerting among them is the observation that Latinate writing shows no unidirectional orthographic evolution from the 8th to the 13th century. Taken as a whole, Latinate texts are discontinuous, with some 12th- or 13th-century texts appearing more Latinate in style than 9th- or 10th-century ones. These observations suggest the existence of a spelling continuum, with texts varying from highly Latinate to barely Latinate styles, according to each scribe's knowledge of Latin and/or the formality of the event. Undoubtedly, the various bills of sale and property donations to the church that make up the bulk of the notarial documents were meant to be performed by a scribe but understood by the community at large. They are records of a verbal act, as is often acknowledged in the discourse itself. The implication being that if Latin and, in turn, diglossia were so firmly entrenched in the speech community, as is traditionally believed, why did these Latinate texts vanish overnight at the start of the 13th century? A diglossic community which has demonstrated five centuries of linguistic stability shouldn't do that. But if Latinate writing were merely an outdated and, by then, awkward formalism for expressing speech, its catastrophic demise amounts to no more than the final triumph of spelling reforms (cf. Wright 1982).

The aberrant nominal and verbal morphology common to Latinate texts constitutes another troublesome detail for the diglossia model. In the San Millán chartulary, some documents use traditional case endings

---

[3] For an elaboration of this thesis see Blake (1991).

(correctly or incorrectly), others use prepositions, and still others combine both strategies (Blake 1991). Pulgram (1987:193 n.3) has summarized it best:

> The seemingly totally wrong and arbitrary use of case-endings in medieval 'Latin' texts is not due to the writers' ignorance of proper syntactic employment or to morphological errors, but rather to their progressive ignorance of what exactly a declension is: their native speeches, of one or the other early Romance variety, simply no longer operated with cases, and such forms as appear in writing are senseless and vague remembrances of school grammar.

In other words, the target language of Latinate documents was not Latin, but rather, Romance. Is it any wonder that notarial scribes frequently didn't get the Latin morphology right?

Perhaps the most telling contradictions to the diglossia model can be found in the frequent Romance spellings of toponyms, proper nouns, and professional terms that are routinely intercalated into the body of Latinate texts, as shown below in an 11th-century repopulation record (#175, 1022).[4] (Also notice the appearance of the Castilian article *el* in line 4 and the correct Romance preterite *popularon* in line 8.)

Et populavit in Sancti Georgii Aita Pascuale regero.
Et populavit in Sancti Georgii Felices de Pazongis
Et populavit in Sancti Georgii Scemeno Longo de Canales.
Et populavit in Sancti Georgii Eita Ziti el castellano.
Et populavit in Sancti Georgii Vincenti ollero.
Et populavit in Sancti Georgii Teillo tornero.
Et populavit in Sancti Georgii Iohannes de Izlavarra.
Et in diebus Sancio rex populavit in Sancti Georgii Maria
        Lavandera et suo marito Monio Alaves.
Et populavit in Sancti Georgii Salvator Zahato, cum sua uxore.
Et populavit in Sancti Georgii domna Ander.
Et populavit in Sancti Georgii Iuliani pelligero.

If one adheres to the traditional stance that Latinate writing was read aloud phonetically, then this text would suggest not only the

---

[4] The sign '#' refers to Ubieto Arteta's numbering of the documents in his edition of the *Cartulario de San Millán de la Cogolla* (1976). The documents' dating follows.

presence of diglossia but also code-switching — an absurd position to have to argue for regarding a formal repopulation record. But if word recognition — regardless of the accepted orthographic conventions — suffices for reading aloud, there is no reason why Latinate writing would not serve Romance pronunciation as well as ideographs do for Chinese. In the case of proper names, places, and professions, scribes would not always have access to Latinized equivalents; in the name of notarial accuracy, they would have no other choice than to invent a best-effort notation for the spoken word. This accounts for the jolting appearance of *regero, ollero, tornero, el castellano*, and *pelligero* [sic] sandwiched in among the other more proper Latinate forms.

Place names, in particular, exhibit well-formed Romance forms from the very earliest documents, complete with palatalization, assibilation, vowel inflexion, and diphthongization, as shown in the following examples culled from a mid 9th-century text (#8, 867).

palatalization:
Orbanianos [orbañanos],
assibilation:
Ferruzu (FERRUTIO > [ferrudzo])
diphthongization:
Fontaniella (-ELLA > [-jeλa])[5]
Loperuela (-ROLA > [-rwela]
vowel inflexion:
Ferrera (-ARIA > [-aira] > [-eira] > [-era]).

Ironically, a more generic term like *terra* never appears diphthongized in the entire chartulary. The toponyms clearly establish the productivity of a diphthongization rule for this period, but the *terra* example simply proves that traditions die hard.

If the diglossia model seems implausible, what factors speak in favor of a monolingual model? If Latinate writing were not phonemically-based, neither spellings nor morphology would expose beyond a shadow of doubt its Romance nature — only a study of syntactic patterns can accomplish that. To this end, consider the word order displayed below in a 10th-century text (#99, 986) patterned against the Romance translation.

---

[5] The earliest example of diphthongization in this corpus occurs in a document dated 800 (#2): *ziella, ripiella, valliciella*, the latter coexisting with its nondiphthongized form, *vallicella*.

A word by word translation results in well-formed medieval Spanish (and Modern Spanish, for that matter).

Ego Ionti presbiter de Sancti Felicis de Auca illo die
(Yo Jonti presbítero de San Felices de Oco el día)

quando me saccaron de captivitate de terra de
(cuando me sacaron de captividad de tierra de)

mozlemes, abbates et fratres de Sancti Felicis
(musulmanes, los abades y frailes de San Felices)

dederunt in mea redemptione C.L. solidos argenti.
(dieron en mi redención 150 sueldos de argento.)

Et ego Ionti presbiter sic roboro duos meos agros
(Y yo Jonti presbítero así roboro dos de mis agros)

in territorio de villa Domino Assur ad Sancti Felicis.
(en territorio de Vill[dueño]asur a San Felices)

Uno agro est iuxta villa, latus serna de
(Un agro está junto a la villa, lado de la serna de)

Sancti Felicis; de alia pars, carrera. Alio agro
(Santelices; de otra parte, la carrera. Otro agro)

in lomba, iuxta limite de Amuna.
(en la loma, junto al límite de Amuna)

Similar passages which mirror the syntactic patterns of Old Spanish abound in the San Millán chartulary, if one disregards the typically formulaic portions that occur at the opening invocations and closing condemnations of each legal transaction (e.g., *Si quis vero homo extraneare voluerit, sit anathematizatus* ...).

Could the same type of direct syntactic conversion be accomplished for the texts glossed by the now famous *Glosas emilianenses*? No, as those texts are truly composed in Latin and do not follow Romance syntactic patterns. That explains why some of them are accompanied by superscript letters to direct a vernacular performance. When reordered alphabetically (e.g., b e d c a > a b c d e) along with their corresponding words, these glosses provide a conversion to Romance syntax (Stengaard 1991). Using this syntactic aid, and the other lexical and grammatical clues supplied by additional glosses, a reader could painstakingly construct a Romance reading, but not a spontaneous one. The notarial texts of the chartulary, however, have no need of such syntactic reordering because no significant syntactic scrambling is required to read them aloud directly as Romance.[6]

Royal charters, as might be expected, were written in much more formal or Latinate styles than the type of minor land donation cited above. Charters were drafted by the best scribes of the day and demanded someone of equal training to read them. Nevertheless, they are not incomprehensible when properly read aloud by a skilled scribe possessing a sophisticated lexical knowledge, especially the central parts which refer to the specific land and property claims.[7] Consider the 10th-century charter given below, which was conferred by García II Sánchez el Temblón to the monastery of San Millán (#77, 959):

... concedimus et confirmamus vobis quinque heremitas
(... concedimos y confirmamos a vos cinco ermitas)

vobis vicinas, id est Sancti Martini et Sancte Marie et
(para vos vecinas, esto es San Martín y Santa María y)

Sancti Sebastiani et Sancti Johannis et Sancte Marie,
(San Sebastián y San Juan y Santa María)

quod vulgo dicitur Cella Alfoheta, cum exitis et
(que en el vulgo diz Cella Alfoheda, con exidas y)

introitis, terris, vineis, molinis, ortis, rivulis,
(entradas, tierras, viñas, molinos, huertos, ríos,)

---

[6] Minor stylistic changes would still be necessary, such as converting *manus suas* to *sus manos*. These types of stylistic reorderings are also tackled by the glosses (Stengaard 1991). Both expressions, nevertheless, are grammatical.

[7] While Royal charters are relatively 'rough going' to transpose into Romance, the difficulties should not be exaggerated. See Walsh (1991:206) for an opposing viewpoint.

montibus ac defessis et pastum, ... damus ad Sanctum
(montes y dehesas y pastos . . . damos a San)

Emilianum sine ullo fuero malo, ut liberos et ingenuos
(Millán sin ningún fuero malo, libres e ingenuos)

ab omni servicio regali vel senioris serviant vobis
(a todo servicio real o señorial sirviendo a vos)

per omne seculum, amen.
(por todo sieglo, amen.)

What are the benefits, then, of considering Peninsular Latinate
texts as the first textual manifestation of the Hispano-Romance
vernacular? With respect to the phonological development of Old
Spanish, any and all sporadic changes in spelling should be treated not
as vacillations in pronunciation (which was Menéndez Pidal's approach),
but rather as experimental 'attempts to readapt the script to the changed
state of the spoken language' (Hoenigswald 1960:8). For instance, *modios*
'a measure of grain' (#19, 899) is recast fifty years later as *moios* (S.
Millán #53, 949), confirming the completed change from -DY- to a voiced
palatal fricative [-y-], [moyos]. The same result obtains for initial G-
before front vowels, as seen in document #273 (1050) where *germana*
coexists with *iermana* [yermana] (< GERMANA).

These types of attestations are often chronologically reversed: the
Romance form appears before the traditional form, as in the case of
puteum (#198, 1033) > *pozo* [podzo] (#29, 942). The phonetic consequences remain clear: the cluster -TY- has undergone assibilation under
the influence of yod, [-ts- ~ -dz-].

These spelling reversals stem from the unpredictable cross
between a conservative writing system and a particular scribe's
innovations, nothing more. Slavishly interpreting these spelling
discontinuities from within the framework of a continuous model of
gradual linguistic change only leads to more confusion. Propriety, above
all else, mandates that medieval scribes make their writing *look like* Latin,
quite apart from their actual oral performances of the same texts. The
occasional spelling innovation which does filter down must be seen as a
linguistic bonus, making explicit (from the modern point of view) the

vernacular pronunciation. But orthographic vacillations found in Latinate texts bear no resemblance to the type of statistically significant speech variation that sociolinguists normally find in synchronic research.

The consonant cluster -CT- provides another striking example of this phenomenon. Words like *nocte* or *octo* maintain -CT- unaltered throughout the entire corpus. Yet the medieval word *pechar* < PACTARE 'to pay' surfaces in an 11th-century document first as *pectare* (#145 1012), and then as *peitare* (#145 1012). Finally, another scribe employs a clearer annotation, *peggare*, a few years later (#231 1044). Vocalization ([-ait-]),inflexion ([-eit-]), and palatalization ([-etʃ-]) have all become a reality of the spoken language, but the written language still awaits the introduction and acceptance of the French grapheme *ch* in order to consolidate written usage. Until that moment, any one of these three forms will do because they all successfully trigger word recognition and, hence, the correct vernacular pronunciation for the reader. But no phonetic variation is implied by these orthographic vacillations.

The dating of initial F-aspiration is another topic for which the chartulary can help provide more data. The town *Villa Foteiz* (#178, 1024) and the names of two gentlemen known as *Lifuarez* (#418, 1074) and *farrameliz* (#251, 1047) appear with *h*s in other documents from the same period: *Villa Hoteiz* (S. Millán #418, 1074), *Lihoarrez* (#402, 1072), *harramelli* (S. Millán #343, 1065).[8] A third family name *Fanniz* (#402, 1072) occurs earlier as *Hannez* (#273, 1050). These tokens, along with other evidence (see Blake 1989a and 1989b) suggest that F-aspiration was at least an allophonic if not phonemic property of Old Spanish, despite rarely being signaled by this conservative orthographic system. Although this type of evidence confirms F-aspiration (or loss) as part of the linguistic reality of the day, it naturally fails to provide a sociolinguistic profile of usage — one takes what is available from the Latinate texts.

Similar and more extensive examinations of Latinate texts will, undoubtedly, help reshape our present ideas concerning the phonological development of Old Spanish.[9] The same will be true for lexical dating.

---

[8] See Blake (1989a, 1989b) for a more thorough discussion of a chronology for F-aspiration.

[9] Walsh (1991) reaches a similar conclusion for the dating of dental-stop voicing ([t > d]), although he doesn't seem to accept the basic thesis defended here that Latinate texts were read aloud as Old Spanish.

For instance, in a minor 11th-century donation, reproduced below (#297, 1057), the words *lino* 'flax', *marfega* 'sack', and *plumazo* 'large cushion' appear in Romance form a century or two before all other previous accounts.[10]

> ... Et duas in Seccero, duos ortos, duas cupas maiores et duas minores, duos scannos, uno *plumazo*, una pluma, una *marfega* de *lino*, uno tapete, uno lizar, uno carro, duas ruetas, tres forteras, tres cuencas, una caldera, cum suas lares, duas azatas, et illa casa cum una vice de molino.   [my emphasis]

Actually, both *lino* and *plumazos* first occur in this chartulary in a mid 9th-century document (#7, 864). These and other lexical occurrences have not been noticed because the Latinate veneer has kept linguists from looking for lexical data in this type of texts.

Other lexical issues are not so transparent. For example, why does a moribund VOLERE (Classical VELLE) dominate in the chartulary to the virtual exclusion of *querer* < QUAERERE (only one token *kisieret*, #260, 1049, was found in the entire chartulary), although the latter will replace VOLERE as the sole Old Spanish expression of volition? That *querer* was preferred to VOLERE in the Early Middle Ages seems irrefutable from its frequent appearance in the *Glosas silenses* (*uoluerit* = *kisieret* #287; *negat* = *non quisieret dare* #105; *consensient* = *qui quisieret* #354). Propriety, once again, rears its head. The tokens of VOLERE most commonly occur in the closing ceremonial curses aimed at potential violators of the document's provisos. The use of VOLERE helps create a ceremonial 'punch' on the page and, maybe, in speech as well. Either way, it would not be inconceivable for scribes to replace the now archaic VOLERE with *querer* while reading aloud or leave it in, thereby adding to the legal hocus-pocus of the event — a question beyond resolution from our vantage point.

With respect to syntax, the benefits of examining Latinate texts as Romance are potentially greater than phonology; word order can be studied effectively in spite of phonological or orthographic disputes. For instance, consider the development of clitics in Hispano-Romance.

---

[10] Corominas and Pascual give the following dating for first appearance: *lino* 1112 (*DCECH* III:663; also see Oeschläger 1940), *marfega* 1266 (*DCECH* III:851), *plumazo* 1214 (*DCECH* IV:383).

Wanner (in press) has proposed a linearization rule for 13th-, 14th, and 15th-century Castilian, which states, in greatly simplified terms, that proclisis (the norm) is blocked if the clitic pronoun becomes stranded as the leftmost phonetic element of the clause.[11] In that case, enclisis is required. The 9th-, 10th-, and 11th-century examples given below follow Wanner's description to the letter: proclisis in examples (a), (b), and parts of (c); enclisis in one case from (c), and in (d) through (f) as well. In (f), the example *unde ego mitto illam* demonstrates an optional rule of subject-induced enclisis which Wanner also posits for the data he examined. In other words, the data from Latinate texts, written down four centuries earlier, parallel Wanner's syntactic description of Old Spanish clitics.

> (a) ... ego Paulus abba et Iohannes presbiter et Nunno clerico nos *ella* tradimus ad patrono nostro sancti Martini ... (#11, 872?)

> (b) ... illo die quando *me* saccaron de captivitate ... (#99, 986).

> (c) Et accepi de te in precio caballo castaneo, valente D solidos, Persigna nominato, illo qui fuit que *tibi dedit* comite Fredinando Munnioz, et *abeo illum* aput me, et nichil contra *te remansit* precium. (#217, 1040)

> (d) Placuit *nobis* et vendimus ad vos germanos Oveco Belascoz et Citi Belascoz ... (#197, 1032).

> (e) Placuit *mihi* pro salute anime mee ... (#54, 949)

> (f) et tenebant *me* pro illo homicidio ... et solvit *me* de isto pecto ... Unde ego mitto *illam* et corroboro ... et confirmo *illud* sibi et filiis suis. (#198, 1033)

With these types of parallelisms, it becomes even more untenable to suggest that the language of Latinate texts represented a code maintained apart from the vernacular (i.e., diglossia) for over six centuries (but doomed to suffer an instantaneous literary death by the 1200s).

---

[11] The conjunction *et* is outside of the clause (i.e., CP) and does not count as a phonetic element to the left of the clitic (Wanner, in press).

Latinate syntax also suffers from certain rigid medieval notions of propriety, as did some of the phonetic and lexical features examined above. For instance, the retention of the synthetic passive forms appears to aggravate a smooth oral performance of these texts, since Old Spanish has no phonetic derivative for the synthetic passive. Green (1991) has shown, however, that the replacement of the synthetic passive by the analytic passive was slowed or disguised by the existence of other strategies: reflexive passives or third person plural impersonal expressions.[12] He conjectures that the encroachment of reflexive passives into the vernacular might still not have felt 'right' for more formal registers. So scribes continued to reproduce the *consciously learned* synthetic forms in writing.[13]

Evidence from the *Glosas emilianenses* bolsters his supposition because the synthetic forms were frequently glossed by reflexive passives or impersonal constructions (Green 1991:90-91). But whether scribes substituted these archaic synthetic forms when reading aloud or expected them to be understood as lexical formulae is difficult to determine. The synthetic forms do not seem very productive in the San Millán chartulary; they are confined to the single type, *dicitur* (with an occasional *vocitatur*), which is repeated endlessly in the cliché *in loco qui dicitur* ... 'in a place that is called ...' But a 9th-century text offers a possible clue of how *dicitur* might have been pronounced: the phrase *in loco qui dicitur* is followed a few lines later by *in loco que dicent*.[14] So it would seem that *dicent* [didzen ~ ditsen] — or its popular contraction *diz* (Green 1991:96-97) — was the favored vernacular form. At first blush, then, the synthetic passives cast doubt on the feasibility of performing a smooth Romance reading, but Green's study should dispel any worry on that account.

What has preceded represents only a small distillation of the linguistic information that can be extracted from Latinate texts. I have

---

[12] See Bastardas y Parera (1953:127-37) for a chronology of the analytic passive forms; the complete paradigm doesn't appear until the 13th century.

[13] Green (1991) also incorporates Politzer's (1961) novel suggestion that scribes in the Early Middle Ages spelled the synthetic passive forms correctly precisely because the forms were by then dead in the vernacular.

[14] Other phrases with VOCARE/VOCITARE encountered in the chartulary follow the DICERE pattern, which equates the synthetic passive with an impersonal expression: *in flumen que vocitant Tirone* (#16, 873), *in valle cui vocitatur Salinas* (#20, 932), and *in flumen Cantabrie que vocantur Barbarana et Barbaraniella* (#42, 946).

argued not to let the conservative scribal practices of the Early Middle Ages and the conceptual limitations of the diglossia model obscure the value of this largely unexplored body of data. There is much work to be done in Hispanic philology, even after the efforts of the master Ramón Menéndez Pidal (1950), who first systematically studied these Latinate texts but stopped short of treating them as Old Spanish. Building on his legacy, let us now give the press another turn.

References

Bastardas y Parera, Juan. 1953. *Particularidades sintácticas del latín medieval*. Barcelona: Escuela de Filología (CSIC).

Blake, Robert. 1987. New linguistic sources for Old Spanish. *Hispanic Review* 55.1-12.

_____. 1989a. Radiografía de un cambio lingüístico. *Revista de filología española* 69.39-59.

_____. 1989b. Sound change and linguistic residue: The case of f > h > Ø. In *GURT '88: Synchronic and diachronic approaches to linguistic variation and change*, ed. Thomas J. Walsh, 53-62. Washington, D.C: Georgetown University Press.

_____. 1991. Syntactic aspects of Latinate texts of the Early Middle Ages. In Wright 1991.219-32.

Corominas, Joan and José Antonio Pascual. 1980-. *Diccionario crítico etimológico castellano e hispánico*, 5 vols. to date. Madrid: Gredos.

Craddock, Jerry. 1970. On Old Spanish municipal charters as primary sources for linguistic history. *Romance Philology* 24.119-28.

Cravens, Thomas D. 1991. Phonology, phonetics, and orthography in Late Latin and Romance: The evidence for early intervocalic sonorization. In Wright 1991.52-68.

Green, John N. 1991. The collapse and replacement of verbal inflection in Late Latin/Early Romance: How would one know? In Wright 1991.83-99.

Hoenigswald, Henry M. 1960. *Language change and linguistic reconstruction*. Chicago: University of Chicago Press.

Marcos Marín, Francisco. 1984. Review of Wright 1982. *Revista de filología española* 64.129-45.

Menéndez Pidal, Ramón. 1950. *Orígenes del español.* 3rd ed. Madrid: Espasa-Calpe.

Oeschläger, V.R.B. 1940. *A medieval Spanish word-list.* Madison: University of Wisconsin Press.

Penny, Ralph. 1984. Review of Wright 1982. *Bulletin of Hispanic Studies* 61.43-45.

Politzer, Robert L. 1961. The interpretation of correctness in Late Latin texts. *Language* 37.209-14.

Pulgram, Ernst. 1987. The role of redundancies in the history of Latin-Romance morphology. In *Latin vulgaire - latin tardif: Actes du 1er colloque international sur le latin vulgaire et tardif (Pécs 2-6 Sept. 1985),* ed. Jószef Herman, 189-97. Tübingen: Niemeyer.

Stengaard, Birte. 1991. The combination of glosses in Códice Emilianense 60 (Glosas emilianenses). In Wright 1991.177-89.

Ubieto Arteta, A. 1976. *Cartulario de San Millán de la Cogolla.* Valencia: Anubar Ediciones.

Walsh, Thomas J. 1986. Latin and Romance in the Early Middle Ages. *Romance Philology* 40.199-214.

_____. 1991. Spelling lapses in early medieval Latin documents and the reconstruction of primitive Romance phonology. In Wright 1991.205-18.

Wanner, Dieter. in press. Subjects in Old Spanish: Conflicts between typology, syntax and dynamics. In *Papers from the XX Linguistic Symposium on Romance Languages, University of Ottawa April 1990,* ed. Paul Hirschbuhler et al. Amsterdam: Benjamins.

Wright, Roger. 1982. *Late Latin and Early Romance in Spain and Carolingian France.* Liverpool: Cairns.

_____ (ed.) 1991. *Latin and the Romance languages in the Early Middle Ages.* London: Routledge.

_____. in press. Complex monolingualism in Early Romance. In *Papers from the XXI Linguistic Symposium on Romance Languages, University of California at Santa Barbara, March 1991,* ed. William Ashby et al. Amsterdam: Benjamins.

Homonymy and Polysemy in Diachronic Perspective: The Genesis in Spanish of *macho* 'male', *macho* 'mule', and *macho* 'blacksmith's hammer'

Steven N. Dworkin

University of Michigan

Although the pioneering work of Jules Gilliéron († 1926) and his students in the first quarter of this century brought to the attention of Romanists the important role of homonymy in lexical change (especially word loss), many relevant issues with important theoretical and methodological implications remain to be explored. One such question is the distinction between homonymy and polysemy. Do speakers view formally identical lexical items of the same grammatical class as separate words (homonyms) or as one word with a host of, at times apparently irreconcilable, meanings? From the historical perspective, what appears to be synchronically an example of polysemy often turns out to be in reality a homonymic clash. Conceivably, the real or perceived relationship between the meanings of a given item may here play a major role in how speakers (and linguists) treat individual cases.[1] In what follows, I wish to illustrate the reverse situation in which a set of words, analyzed as homonyms by many lexicologists, may indeed go back (directly or indirectly) to a common base.

The genesis of the triad *macho* 'male', *macho* 'mule', and *macho* 'blacksmith's hammer' poses a series of complex problems involving difficult questions of sound change, phonosymbolism, lexical borrowings, as well as homonymy and polysemy. Do the three nouns at issue descend from a common ancestor, or do they represent the outcomes of different bases which have converged in Hispano-Romance (through local developments and/or borrowings) as *macho*?

---

[1] A fine general introduction to these problems appears in Lyons (1977:550-69). Baldinger (1984:19-20) briefly touches on this matter and offers bibliography oriented towards Romance.

macho 'male'

I shall first examine the history of *macho* 'male'. Convinced that
-*ch*- could not represent the Spanish outcome of -SC'L-, Diez rejected the
connection between *macho* and MASCULUS 'male', originally a diminutive
of MAS (gen. MARIS) 'male'. In all five editions of his *Etymologisches
Wörterbuch der romanischen Sprachen*, Diez derived *macho* from
MARCULUS 'small hammer', which, in his opinion, also was the source of
macho 'hammer'. Despite the alleged phonological difficulty, Monlau
(1881:834, s.v. *macho*), usually a faithful adherent to Diez's etymological
dicta, could not bring himself to disassociate *macho* from MASCULUS. In
the three versions of his *Lateinisch-romanisches Wörterbuch* Körting
continued to advocate MARCULUS over its rival MASCULUS which was
favored by Michaëlis de Vasconcelos (1886:135)[2] and Gröber (1886:527-
28).[3] As semantic justification, Körting suggested that MARCULUS had
become an obscene designation for the male sexual organ. To the best of
my knowledge Baist (1906:903) was the first to claim that *macho* can
represent only the regular Portuguese reflex of MASCULUS and that
Spanish *macho* is a Lusism. Meyer-Lübke endorsed the Western origin
of *macho* in both editions of his *Romanisches etymologisches Wörterbuch*.[4] This analysis was rejected by various scholars who had no
difficulty in accepting the shift MASCULUS > *macho* as native to Hispano-
Romance e.g., Menéndez Pidal (1941: par. 61$_2$), García de Diego (1954),
Corominas (1956: s.v. *macho$_i$*), Corominas and Pascual (1980-:s.v.
macho$_i$), Lloyd (1987:255), Meier (1988:63-68).

While not denying a genetic connection between *macho* and
MASCULUS, Hartman (1984) adduces new arguments in favor of the
Portuguese origin of *macho* and challenges the view that the Spanish
form represents an authentic native reflex of the Latin base. In his view,

---

[2] Michaëlis (1876:269) implicitly derived both *macho* and OSp. *maslo* 'male' from
MASCULUS.

[3] Gröber regarded -*ch*- as the regular product of -SC'L-, with loss of the *s* due to the
unacceptability in Spanish and Portuguese of the sequence -*sch*-. He classed *muslo* 'thigh'
< MUSCULUS as a learned word and suggested that *maslo* represented the adaptation to
Hispano-Romance of OFr. *masle* (mod. *mâle*) < MASCULUS.

[4] Meyer-Lübke (1890: par. 488 and 1921:232 n.3) employs without qualification the
equation MASCULUS > *macho*.

OSp. *maslo*, abundantly attested until the fifteenth century,[5] is the sole orally-transmitted local reflex of MASCULUS. Corominas and Pascual cite *Calila e Digna* as the first source documenting *macho*. Hartman points out that although this work was written in 1251, the two extant manuscripts of the *Calila e Digna* date from the late fourteenth and the second half of the fifteenth centuries respectively. He makes here the crucial distinction between the original production date of a given work and the specific production date of the manuscript(s) in which it has survived. Three other thirteenth-century works in which Hartman has found *macho* (*Libro de los engaños*, *Historia de la Donzella Teodor*, and the Second Part of the Alfonsine *General estoria*) are also preserved only in much later manuscripts. He claims that in the aforecited works *macho* is a late medieval scribal substitute for original *maslo* which by that time had possibly acquired taboo or obscene associations.[6] Particularly compelling for Hartman is the absence of *macho* in the Alfonsine manuscripts traceable to that king's Royal Scriptorium and in the writings of don Juan Manuel.

Following in the footsteps of Diez, Körting, Baist, and Meyer-Lübke, Hartman rejects the possibility that *macho* represents a native phonological development of MASCULUS. Citing such examples as AMPLUS > *ancho* 'wide, broad', MARC'LUS > *macho* 'blacksmith's hammer' (see below), MA(N)C'LA > *mancha* 'stain', INFLARE > *hinchar* 'to swell, inflate',[7] he states that the change of consonant + (primary or secondary) -PL-, -CL-, -FL- to the affricate -*ch*- (a process which he labels *Cheísmo*) is regular only after a voiced consonant and that 'the data suggesting that *Cheísmo* in Castilian is equally active after a voiceless consonant are quite scarce' (1984:103). In contrast, the change -SC'L- > -*ch*- is regular in Portuguese. In addition to the equation *macho* < MASCULUS, Hartman adduces the derivation of Ptg. *bucho* 'animal's

---

[5] The orthographic variant *masclo* probably reflects the model of MASCULUS; in Aragonese texts, where *masclo* is particularly frequent, Cat. *mascle* may have played a role.

[6] Cf. OProv. *mascle* 'membre viril' (cited in *FEW*, s.v. MASCULUS).

[7] Lloyd (1987:255) cites the following examples of postconsonantal C'L: CONCHULA > *concha* 'sea-shell', TRUNCULU > *troncho* 'stalk', MA(N)CULA > *mancha* 'stain', CICERCULA > *cizercha* 'blue vetch', SARCULARE > *sachar* 'to weed'. Lloyd includes in his list the equation MASCULUS > *macho*.

stomach; gizzard' from MUSCULUS. In his view, only *maslo* and *muslo*
represent the authentic Castilian reflexes of MASCULUS and MUSCULUS.
Thus, for Hartman, the chronological and phonological evidence indicate
that *macho* is a late medieval Lusism.[8]

Both the philological and the phonological sides of Hartman's
hypothesis call for re-examination. No advocate of the borrowing
hypothesis has explained why speakers of Spanish would have felt
compelled to turn to a Lusism to replace *maslo* (whatever the underlying
defect which led to its semantic narrowing and obsolescence). I have
found no instances of *macho* in Galician-Portuguese compositions preserved in the *Cancionero de Baena* or in Spanish texts which are known
to be based on Portuguese or Leonese originals. The few Lusisms found
in Medieval Spanish refer to human emotions and may have entered
Castile with the vogue of Galician-Portuguese lyric poetry (e.g., *echar
[de] menos* 'to miss', *ledo* 'happy, joyful').[9] In addition, the medieval
record does provide examples of *macho* which contradict Hartman's
assertion 'there is as yet no direct evidence that *macho* for "male" was
ever so spelled by a scribe in Castilian before the 15th century'
(1984:102). An inventory from Carrizos (León) of the year 1268 records
*duas bestias asnales con sos fiyos, el uno **maxo**, el otro femna* (Casado
Lobato 1983:61); a document from Huesca of the year 1284 refers to a
García Macho.[10] This adjective turns up in a passage from the *Siete
partidas* as preserved in the mid-fourteenth-century BN Madrid MS
12793.[11] The abundant use of *macho* in the version of the Bible

---

[8] Lorenzo (1977:785a) provides examples of *macho* 'male' extracted from Old
Galician-Portuguese documents and literary texts.

[9] On the fate of *ledo*, see Malkiel (1981) and Dworkin (1990).

[10] I wish to take this opportunity to thank Professor Bodo Müller for making available
to me these and other instances of *macho* from the files of his *Diccionario del español
medieval* (see Dworkin forthcoming).

[11] *deue dezir esta oracion tan bien sobre las fembras commo sobre los **machos*** (fol.
21v); the parallel passage in other mss offers the readings *mas(c)los*. Yet at fol. 22r of
MS 12793 one reads *et despues que esta oracion oujere dicha a de dezir otra sobre los
maslos*. In this passage two mss offer the variant reading *varones*. The parallel passages
in the *Setenario* offer *masculos* and *maslos* respectively (ed. Vanderford 1945:139.29,
140.13. I am grateful to Jerry R. Craddock for verifying the readings in the MSS of the
Siete partidas and for bringing to my attention the relevant portions of the *Setenario*.

preserved in Escorial MS i-j-4 and in fifteenth-century medical treatises renders unlikely the hypothesis that this adjective is a Lusism first employed in Spanish in the fifteenth century. The set phrase *(por arte de) macho y fembra* occurs five times in Spanish compositions found in the *Cancionero de Baena* (compiled ca. 1445). This technical term refers to a rhyming pattern which 'consists in the alternation of masculine and feminine rhymes which are derived from each other' (Lang 1927:516). The use of *macho* in a fixed binomial phrase with a technical meaning in a mid-fifteenth-century text would bespeak its earlier presence in the language. It seems reasonable to conclude that *macho* was employed (alongside *maslo*) in the thirteenth-century originals of such works as *Calila e Digna, Libro de los engaños*, and the *Donzella Teodora*.

Hartman provides no cogent phonetic evidence to show why in Castilian a voiceless consonant would mitigate against the formation in this environment of the voiceless affricate. The early and possibly rapid reduction of **mascho*[12] to *macho* poses no serious problem. He is unaware of Granadine Mozarabic *mulch* 'fleshy part of the upper arm' < MUSCULUS and *pilch(e)* < PESCULUM (cf. Cl. PESSULUS) both recorded in Pedro de Alcalá's *Vocabulario* of 1505 (Galmés de Fuentes 1983:242-43) and ignores the problem posed for his analysis by Sp. *buche* 'maw, gizzard', clearly a cognate of Ptg. *bucho* < MUSCULUS.[13] The two parallel examples he cites to illustrate the alleged regular development in Castilian of -S'CL- are the sets MUSCULUS > *muslo* and USTULARE 'to scorch' > OSp. *uslar* 'to cause grief', a rare word documented only in two consecutive stanzas (110 & 111) of Berceo's *Duelo de la Virgen*.[14] Also relevant to the history of the cluster -SC'L- in Hispano-Romance are

---

[12] Great care must be exercised in determining the phonetic reality behind the form *mascho* 'male' found in the Aragonese version of the *Libro de Marco Polo* (ed. Nitti 1980) and in the Aragonese translation, preserved in Stockholm Royal Library MS 1272a (ed. Geijerstam and Wasick 1988: fol. 10r21) of Lucas de Tuy's *Chronicon Mundi*. This form may well represent *macho* influenced only on the orthographic level by Lat. MASCULUS, OArag. *masclo* or by Cat. *mascle*.

[13] Lusists have accepted the equation *bucho* < MUSCULUS proposed by Leite de Vasconcellos (1890-92:272). Corominas and Pascual (1980-: s.v. *buche*) consider the Spanish and Portuguese forms as well as It. *buzzo*, Balearic *butza*, *betza*, Menorquin *bitza* to be of expressive origin.

[14] According to Lapesa (1931:119), *uslar* 'doler' has survived in some rural dialects spoken to the north of Palencia.

the equations ACISCULUS 'little adze' > *aciche* 'paver's hammer' (whose
-*e* may betray a non-Castilian origin), and *FASCULA (Cl. FACULA 'little
torch' < FAX) > OSp. *facha*.[15] Hartman is right in rejecting the
explanation (voiced as a mere possibility by Gröber 1886:528) that *maslo*
and *muslo* are so-called 'semi-learned' formations. The analyst perhaps
should not dismiss with undue haste Gröber's alternative hypothesis,
namely that *maslo* and *uslar* represent adaptations to Hispano-Romance
of OFr. *masle* and OProv. *usclar* (the Gallo-Romance reflexes of
MASCULUS and USTULARE). However, it is not inconceivable that within
the complex of dialects that constitutes Castilian, both *maslo* and *macho*
can represent (socially-differentiated) regional vernacular products of
MASCULUS (a possibility already suggested by Brüch 1922:50).

In the early stages of its history in Spanish *macho* may have been
considered a coarse, rural word, deemed unworthy of inclusion in highly-
refined scholarly or didactic writing such as the works prepared in the
Alfonsine Royal Scriptorium or by don Juan Manuel. The data contained
in Kasten & Nitti (1978) indicate a complete absence of non-participial
attributive adjectives of the shape *(C)VchV* in the Alfonsine corpus. Both
Alfonso and don Juan Manuel were known for taking care with the style
and lexical choices in the works prepared under their supervision.[16] The
suffixes of such derivatives as *machiego* (cf. the obsolete apicultural term
abeja machiega 'queen bee') *machorro* 'sterile' and *machuno* may
bespeak both the antiquity and the original rural flavor in Hispano-
Romance of *macho*. Also indicative of the early status of *macho* is its use
alongside colloquial *perro* 'dog' in the *refrán Una vez burlan al perro*
macho, set down in the fifteenth-century *Refranes que dizen las viejas*
tras el huego, attributed to the Marqués de Santillana (O'Kane 1959:67).
The analyst must exercise great care when dealing with phonosymbolism
or tendential iconic associations between form and meaning; however,
there is independent evidence that speakers may have tendentially linked

---

[15] Still awaiting satisfactory explanation is the behavior of -SC'L- in the equation
MISCULARE 'to mix' > OSp. *mesclar* (mod. *mez-*).

[16] All instances of OSp. *macho* that I have uncovered occur in prose texts;
conceivably, this adjective was considered inappropriate for poetic usage. In like fashion
macho seems to be absent from medieval Galician-Portuguese poetry; to judge by the
available glossaries, *macho* does not turn up in the Alfonsine *Cantigas de Santa Maria*,
in the *Cantigas d'escarnho e de mal dizer*, in the *Cancioneiro de Ajuda*, or in the
Cancioneiro Colocci-Brancutti.

the sequence *VchV* in disyllabic nonparticipial adjectives with rustic speech. Unless they represent later internal creations, such adjectives (of obscure origin) as *chocho* 'senile, doddering', *mocho* 'shorn, blunt' *tocho* 'boorish, stupid', must have existed in the colloquial language of the Middle Ages, although they are not documented in medieval literary sources.

The obsolescence of *maslo* merits comment here. The textual evidence shows a notable reduction in instances of *maslo* in the second half of the fifteenth century. Pero Guillén de Segovia recorded *maslo* in his rhyme dictionary (1475). Although the 1493 *Exemplario contra los engaños y peligros del mundo* (ed. Gago Jover 1989) still offers eight examples of *masclo* alongside three of *macho*, Nebrija's 1492 *Diccionario latino-español* (ed. Colón and Soberanas 1979) glosses Lat. MAS (gen. MARIS) as 'el macho en cada especie' and MASCULUS as 'cosa machorra'; *maslo* does not appear as an entry in either the 1495 (?) (ed. Real Academia Española) or 1516 (ed. Macdonald) version of his *Vocabulario de romance en latín*. By the end of the thirteenth century *maslo*, used substantively, had acquired narrower technical meanings: 'root of the tail', recorded in the *Fuero de Sepúlveda* (ed. Sáez et al. 1953: par. 96), 'root of an animal's nail', found with reference to horses in the late thirteenth-century *Libro de los caballos* (ed. Sachs 1936:40, 41, 44) and to falcons in Pero López de Ayala's *Libro de la caça de las aves*,[17] and 'root of the beak' also found in López de Ayala's treatise (ed. Cummins 1986:99). Baist, Corominas, and Hartman all observed that this semantic development presupposed an intermediate stage *'penis'; according to Hartman (1984:105), the association of *maslo* with the membrum virile was the decisive factor in its replacement by *macho*. Throughout the Middle Ages *maslo* also faced competition from *varón*. The loss of *maslo* may have allowed the long-submerged *macho* to enter the mainstream of respectable usage and the literary language.

macho 'mule'

Scholars remain divided as to whether *macho* 'mule' represents a semantic specialization (accompanied by substantivization) of *macho*

---

[17] OPtg. *macho* is used identically in Mestre Giraldo's *Livro de alveitaria*; see Michaëlis de Vasconcelos (1910:340).

'male' or a genetically-distinct homonym. Michaëlis (1886:135) proposed
the latter analysis, claiming that Ptg. *macho* 'mule' resulted from
reduction of the diphthong in the OPtg. derivative *muacho* (< *mu* ~ *mua*);
she implied that the corresponding Spanish noun is a Lusism.[18]
Specialists such as Coelho and Figuereido disagreed so sharply that
Michaëlis chose not to include the equation *macho* < *muacho* among
examples of the reduction in popular speech of the diphthong *ua* because
'esta etymologia não teve o assentimento dos entendidos' (1893-94:185).
A few years later (1898-1900:344) she hesitatingly suggested the
possibility of a blend involving MULUS and MASC(U)LUS. This approach
to the problem merits further consideration. It seems quite reasonable to
hypothesize that in Old Portuguese *macho* 'male' may have exerted
formal influence on the almost phonetically identical *muacho*. Nascentes
(1932:479a) surveyed earlier opinions on the origin of Ptg. *macho* 'mule',
but refrained from stating his own views. Other supporters of the
derivation of *macho* from the family of MASCULUS include Megacles
(cited by Nascentes) and Machado (1967:1456). Michaëlis de Vasconcelos's analysis of Spanish *macho* 'mule' as a Lusism gained acceptance
from such notables as Meyer-Lübke in both editions of his *REW* (no.
5742), Menéndez Pidal (1941: par. 4$_6$), and Corominas.

   Michaëlis presented no independent supporting evidence for the
Western origin of *macho* 'mule'. Although Old Portuguese texts
document *muacho*, I have come across no medieval attestations of *macho*
'mule'. Michaëlis does not attempt to provide historical or cultural
justification for the alleged adaptation of a Lusism to designate the mule,
for which Old Spanish regularly used *mulo/mula*.[19] The rustic term
macho 'mule' first appears in Juan de Mena's composition *Qual diablo
me topó* (ed. de Nigris 1988:421-31). In Medieval Spanish *macho* 'male'
was frequently employed adjectivally alongside an animal designation to
denote the male of the species; among such combinations on record is
mulo macho. It appears reasonable to see in Sp. *macho* a reduction of the
phrase *mulo macho* (although I cannot explain why this syntagm and not

---

[18] With regard to the proposed reduction of *muacho* to *macho*, she stated 'A für *ua*
gehört dem westlichen Sprachgebiet an' (1886:136).

[19] Revealing in this context is the statement in Juan Manuel, *Libro del caballero y del
escudero*: 'llaman mulo a los maslos e mulas a las fembras' (ed. Ayerbe-Chaux
1986:16r11-12).

others involving *macho* were shortened in this way). Perhaps the frequent coupling by speakers of *macho* with *mulo* further demonstrates the original rustic and humble character of *macho* 'male'. This explanation of the origin of *macho* 'mule' could also account for its late appearance in the written language.

macho 'blacksmith's hammer'

Etymologists have paid little attention to *macho* 'blacksmith's hammer'. Since 1853 most scholars have routinely accepted Diez's derivation of this noun from MARCULUS. Two dissenting opinions merit consideration. Sachs (1936:136, s.v. *machucar*) considers *macho* 'blacksmith's hammer' to be a semantic outgrowth of *macho* 'male'. In both versions of his Spanish etymological dictionary Corominas argues on formal and semantic grounds against any link between MARCULUS and *macho*.[20] For Corominas, the genesis of this noun is linked with that of well-documented OSp. *maço* 'wooden hammer, mallet'. Specifically, he asserts that on phonological grounds *macho* can be analyzed as the Mozarabic cognate of *maço*, itself derived from *maça* 'mallet' < *MATTEA. Rather than viewing *macho* as a residual Mozarabism, I wish to propose (albeit tentatively) an alternative analysis. Given the expressivity that speakers associated with -*ch*-, *macho* might represent a phonosymbolically-motivated colloquial alteration of *maço*.[21] Fear of homonymic clash with *macho* 'male' obviously did not prevent speakers from coining *macho* 'sledgehammer'. The chances of referential confusion in the context of discourse between these two nouns was minimal. Indeed, the formal similarity between *maço* and *macho* 'male' may have led speakers to forge a semantic association between these two items. The use of a blacksmith's hammer was linked to a strong man; in addition, *maço* may well have acquired secondary meanings which brought it into the semantic realm of *macho* (cf. OPtg. *maço* 'testicle').

Macho, so used, is rarely found in medieval texts. It occurs with reference to the hammer of Vulcan four times in one passage of the

---

[20] Specifically he was troubled by the lack of any trace of **marcho* and by the semantic incompatibility between *macho* and MARCULUS.

[21] On the tendential phonosymbolic substitution of -*ch*- for 'expected' -*ç*- see Malkiel (1990:9-42).

General estoria, I (ed. Solalinde 1930:92), and in MS P of the *Alexandre*, 1725c (in rhyme with *estajo, trabajo, ajo*). The corresponding passage in MS O offers *majo* (cf. *majar* 'to strike a blow'), the reading chosen by Nelson (1979) in his 'critical reconstruction' of the poem. *Macho* 'hammer' is not recorded in Nebrija's dictionaries; the *Diccionario latino-español* glosses MARCULUS with 'por el martillo de hierro'. The vitality displayed by the verb *machucar* (the forerunner of *machacar*) in Old Spanish may well indicate that *macho* 'hammer' enjoyed greater currency in the medieval language than is indicated by the extant documentation. In contrast there is no evidence for the existence of *macho* so used in Portuguese, which may strengthen the hypothesis that the Spanish noun represents a secondary internal creation.

A summary of this paper's conclusions is in order. Sp. *macho* 'male' can be cogently explained as a native development of MASCULUS which, for sociolinguistic reasons, failed to gain currency in the early medieval literary language. Sp. *macho* 'mule' represents a semantic outgrowth of *macho* 'male' which came into being through reduction of the syntagm *mulo macho*. In contrast, phonosymbolic considerations, near-homonymy and a possible secondary figurative semantic overlap with *macho* 'male' led to the transmutation of *maço* into *macho* 'black-smith's hammer'. In the case of the genesis of the three words under study here, polysemy has played a more important role than homonymic convergence. On the synchronic level, the question of homonymy and polysemy may be moot for many speakers, whose repertoire includes neither *macho* 'mule' nor *macho* 'blacksmith's hammer'.[22]

---

[22] My colleague John Lipski informs me that *macho* is the common term for 'mule' in many varieties of Central American Spanish. My own informal survey of several native speakers from Spain revealed complete unfamiliarity with *macho* 'mule' and *macho* 'blacksmith's hammer'.

References

Ayerbe-Chaux, Reinaldo (ed.) 1986. *Texto y concordancias de la obra completa de Juan Manuel.* Microfiches. Madison: Hispanic Seminary of Medieval Studies.

Baist, Gottfried. 1906. Gibt es ein Suffix SCL? *Zeitschrift für romanische Philologie* 30.464-67.

Baldinger, Kurt. 1984. *Vers une sémantique moderne.* Paris: Klincksieck.

Brüch, Joseph. 1922. Zu Spitzers kat.-sp. Etymologien in der Bibliotheca archivi romanici III. *Miscellanea linguistica dedicata a Hugo Schuchardt per il suo 80.° anniversario.* Biblioteca dell' «Archivum Romanicum», Series 2, Vol. 3, 26-74. Genève: Olschki.

Casado Lobato, María Concepción (ed.) 1983. *Colección diplomática del monasterio de Carrizo.* Vol. 2. León: Centro de Estudios e Investigación 'San Isidoro' (CSIC).

Casas Homs, José María (ed.) 1962. *'La Gaya ciencia' de P. Guillén de Segovia. Transcripción de O. J. Tuulio. Introducción, vocabulario e índices.* Madrid: CSIC.

Colón, Germán and Amadeu-J. Soberanas (eds.) 1979. *El Diccionario latino-español de Elio Antonio de Nebrija.* Barcelona: Puvill.

Corominas, Joan. 1956. *Diccionario crítico etimológico de la lengua castellana.* Vol. III. Madrid: Gredos.

_____ and José A. Pascual. 1980-. *Diccionario crítico etimológico castellano e hispánico.* 5 vols. to date. Madrid: Gredos.

Cummins, John G. (ed.) 1986. *Pero López de Ayala. Libro de la caça de las aves.* London: Tamesis.

de Nigris, Carla (ed.) 1988. *Juan de Mena. Poesie minori.* Napoli: Liguori.

Diez, Friedrich. 1853. *Etymologisches Wörterbuch der romanischen Sprachen.* Bonn: Marcus.

Dworkin, Steven N. 1990. The role of near-homonymy in lexical loss: The demise of OSp. *laido* 'ugly, repugnant'. *La Corónica* 19.32-48.

_____. forthcoming. Progress in medieval Spanish lexicography. To appear in *Romance Philology.*

Gago Jover, Francisco. 1989. *Texto y concordancias del 'Exemplario contra los engaños y peligros del mundo' (1493) [of] Juan de*

Capua. I-1994, Biblioteca Nacional, Madrid. Madison: Hispanic Seminary of Medieval Studies.

Galmés de Fuentes, Álvaro. 1983. *Dialectología mozárabe*. Madrid: Gredos.

García de Diego, Vicente. 1954. *Diccionario etimológico español e hispánico*. Madrid: SAETA. 2nd ed. Madrid: Espasa-Calpe, 1985.

Geijerstam, Regina af and Cynthia M. Wasick (eds.) 1988. *Text and Concordance of Kungliga Bibliotekt Stockholm MS D 1272a: 'Lucas de Tuy, Obra sacada de las crónicas de Sant Isidoro, arcebispo de Sevilla'*. Microfiches. Madison: Hispanic Seminary of Medieval Studies.

Gröber, Gustav. 1886. Vulgärlateinische Substrate romanischer Wörter. *Archiv für Lateinische Lexikographie und Grammatik* 3.507-31.

Hartman, Steven Lee. 1984. On the history of Spanish *macho*. *Hispanic Linguistics* 1.97-114.

Kasten, Lloyd and John Nitti. 1978. *Concordance and texts of the Royal Scriptorium Manuscripts of Alfonso X el Sabio*. Microfiches. Madison: Hispanic Seminary of Medieval Studies.

Körting, Gustav. 1891. *Lateinisch-romanisches Wörterbuch*. Paderborn: F. Schoningh. 2nd ed. 1901; 3rd ed. 1907.

Lang, Henry R. 1927. Las formas estróficas y términos métricos del *Cancionero de Baena*. *Estudios eruditos in memoriam de Adolfo Bonilla y San Martín*, 1.485-523. Madrid: Jaime Ratés.

Lapesa, Rafael. 1931. Notas para el léxico del siglo XIII. *Revista de filología española* 18.113-19.

Leite de Vasconcellos, José. 1890-92. Etymologias portuguesas. *Revista lusitana* 2.267-72.

Lloyd, Paul. 1987. *From Latin to Spanish*. Philadelphia: American Philosophical Society.

Lorenzo, Ramón. 1977. *La traducción gallega de la 'Cronica general' y de la 'Crónica de Castilla'*. Vol. 2: *Glosario*. Orense: Instituto de Estudios Orensanos Padre Feijoo.

Lyons, John. 1977. *Semantics*. 2 vols. Cambridge: Cambridge University Press.

Macdonald, Gerald J. (ed.) 1973. *Antonio de Nebrija. Vocabulario de romance en latín*. Philadelphia: Temple University Press.

Machado, José Pedro. 1967. *Dicionário etimológico da lingua portuguesa*. Lisbon: Confluência.

Malkiel, Yakov. 1981. The Old Spanish and Old Galician-Portuguese adjective *ledo*, Archaic Spanish *liedo*. *La Corónica* 9.95-106.

_____. 1990. *Diachronic problems in phonosymbolism. Edita and inedita, 1979-1988*, I. Amsterdam: Benjamins.

Meier, Harri. 1988. *Etymologische Aufzeichnungen. Anstöße und Anstößiges*. Romanistische Versuche und Vorarbeiten, 54. Bonn: Romanisches Seminar der Universität Bonn.

Menéndez Pidal, Ramón. 1941. *Manual de gramática histórica española*. 6th ed. Madrid: Espasa-Calpe.

Meyer-Lübke, Wilhelm. 1890. *Grammatik der romanischen Sprachen, I: Lautlehre*. Leipzig: Fues.

_____. 1911-20. *Romanisches etymologisches Wörterbuch*. Heidelberg: Carl Winter. 3rd ed. 1930-35.

_____. 1921. La evolución de la C latina delante de E e I en la Península Ibérica. *Revista de filología española* 8.225-51.

Michaëlis [de Vasconcelos], Carolina. 1876. *Studien zur romanischen Wortschöpfung*. Leipzig: Brockhaus.

_____. 1886. Studien zur hispanischen Wortdeutung. In *Memoria di Napoleone Caix e Ugo Angelo Canello: Miscellanea di filologia e linguistica*, 113-66. Firenze: Successori Le Monnier.

_____. 1893-94. Fragmentos etymologicos. *Revista lusitana* 2:129-90.

_____. 1898-1900. Portugiesische Sprache 1891-94. *Kritischer Jahresbericht über die Fortschritte der romanischen Philologie* 4.321-47.

_____. 1910. Mestre Giraldo e os seus tratados de alveitaria e cetreria. Estudos etimológicos. *Revista lusitana* 13.222-432.

Nascentes, Antenor. 1932. *Dicionário etimológico da língua portuguesa*. Rio de Janeiro.

Monlau, Pedro Felipe. 1881. *Diccionario etimológico de la lengua castellana*. Reprint ed. Buenos Aires: J. Gil.

Nelson, Dana A. (ed.) 1979. *Gonzalo de Berceo. El Libro de Alixandre*. Madrid: Gredos.

Nitti, John J. (ed.) 1980. *Juan Fernández de Heredia's Aragonese Version of the 'Libro de Marco Polo'*. Madison: Hispanic Seminary of Medieval Studies.

O'Kane, Eleanor S. 1959. *Refranes y frases proverbiales españolas de la Edad Media*. Boletin de la Real Academia Española, Anejo 2.

Real Academia Española (ed.) 1951. *Vocabulario español-latino de Elio Antonio de Nebrija, de su edición príncipe (Salamanca ¿1495?).* Madrid: RAE.

Sachs, Georg (ed.) 1936. *El libro de los caballos: Tratado de albeitería del siglo XIII. Revista de filología española*, Anejo 23.

Sáez, Emilio, et al. (eds.) 1953. *Los fueros de Sepúlveda. Estudio lingüístico y vocabulario.* Segovia: Diputación Provincial.

Solalinde, Antonio G. (ed.) 1930. *General estoria.* Madrid: Centro de Estudios Históricos.

Vanderford, Kenneth H. (ed.) 1945. *Setenario.* Buenos Aires: Instituto de Filología.

Apocope in Alfonsine Texts: A Case Study

Ray Harris-Northall

University of Wisconsin—Madison

Since the publication of Rafael Lapesa's fundamental studies on the phenomenon of apocope in Old Spanish (Lapesa 1951, 1975), very little investigation has been carried out into the alternation of apocopated and unapocopated forms in Medieval Spanish texts. Further research has been done into the question of the origins and development of the phenomenon (e.g., Montgomery 1975), but the study of individual texts generally only produces marginal comments on the existence or otherwise of apocopated forms within that text. It appears that the only attempt to discuss apocope from a general phonetic perspective has been Allen's article (1976), which concentrates principally on the influence of stress patterns on the loss of the vowel. Lapesa himself voiced the impression that at least in part, the demise of 'extreme' apocope (for the term, see Lapesa 1951: passim, 1982:172) was one aspect of the emerging consciousness of Castilian as a language in its own right, ready to be freed of foreign influence in a parallel manner to the lessening dependence on foreign assistance taking place in the Castilian nation in the second half of the thirteenth century: 'es bien extraño el hecho de que la apócope ... notablemente violenta en el siglo XII y primera mitad del XIII, decaiga a continuación con gran rapidez' (1951:185).[1]

Lapesa did not, however, support this claim in his articles published in 1951 and 1975 with any firm documentary evidence. The widely-held belief that the standardization of Castilian was strongly impelled by Alfonso X, and that this standardization involved, among

---

[1] An important part of Lapesa's analysis of apocope was, of course, that it was at least abetted in its 'extreme' manifestations by strong ultra-Pyrenean cultural influences, and also the physical presence of French and Occitan speakers in the upper cultural echelons of Castilian society. The sociolinguistic prestige accorded these politically powerful groups would naturally have declined along with the wane of that political power. See especially Lapesa (1951).

other aspects, the elimination of 'extreme' apocope, would lead us to believe that in the works produced under the king's aegis in the Royal Scriptorium, we should find extreme apocope at least in decline, if not in absolute retreat.[2]

In a later article, however, Lapesa (1982) analyzed the Alfonsine texts paying closer attention to the appearance of apocopated and unapocopated forms. He found that there was no absolutely clear pattern of decrease in the use of apocopated forms when the frequency of those variants was laid alongside the chronological composition of the texts. In fact, his conclusion was no longer that usage of apocopated forms decreased in the Royal Scriptorium (the activity of which, under Alfonso X, corresponds to most of the second half of the 13th century), but rather that 'la oposición no debió ser únicamente entre las generaciones viejas y la de don Alfonso y sucesivas; hubo de consistir además en el conflicto entre dos tradiciones que tenían en su respectivo apoyo distintos motivos de prestigio' (1982:188). Another, perhaps less contrived, possibility was that the later historical works were in all likelihood particularly susceptible to the influence of the considerably earlier texts containing larger doses of apocopated forms from which they were in part composed (1982:189). Part of Lapesa's difficulty here in matching his findings with his earlier impression conceivably lies in the fact that, with the exception of a few marginal comments, he pays little attention to the phonetic environment of the tokens he calculates, while in fact it seems eminently plausible that the phonological structure of Medieval Spanish had a part to play in the alternation.[3]

---

[2] Thus Lapesa says that extreme apocope 'recibió un golpe definitivo cuando los esfuerzos de Alfonso X para combatirla obtuvieron como resultado póstumo excluir del modelo de buen lenguaje los finales consonánticos duros' (1975:14), i.e., those left by extreme apocope. Lapesa goes so far in according personal intervention to the king that he says 'Alfonso X vertía sobre la apócope extrema su irritación contra la política intervencionista de Felipe III el Atrevido' (1951:220), referring to the war of the Navarrería in 1276. 'Alfonso X el Sabio decide la contienda [between apocopated and unapocopated forms] al escoger como tipo de lenguaje literario el «castellano drecho», sin apócope extrema' (1951:226).

[3] Thus throughout the article, Lapesa speaks of numbers of tokens or percentages of totals, but does not break the figures down; only occasionally do comments such as the following surface: 'es muy intensa la apócope de los pronombres átonos ... apoyados en cualquier palabra que termine en vocal' or 'quedan casos de elisión ante vocal' (1982: 184).

Access to the enormous corpus of Alfonsine prose has been facilitated considerably by the transcriptions and concordances produced by Kasten and Nitti (1978), which make it relatively easy to approach the question of frequency of variants in these medieval texts, and thereby elucidate the linguistic circumstances of particular alternations.

As a first step towards an analysis of this variation, this brief study takes a look at the alternation of apocopated and unapocopated variants of the form *(a)delant(e)*. This form was chosen for several reasons: first, and most obviously, its ending in *-ante* was one of those subject to 'extreme' apocope; that is, while *(a)delant*, alongside many other forms such as *andant, calient, ardient*, were relatively frequent in medieval texts, only their full forms ending in *-nte* would survive the passage of Medieval Spanish to the modern language.

More importantly, however, it is a form belonging to the patrimonial stock of Spanish, inherited directly from Hispanic Latin, its ultimate etymon being a prefixed form of ANTE, presumably DE-INANTE, with dissimilation of the nasal consonants (Corominas and Pascual 1980-, s.v.). The significance of this is the fact that many of the forms in *-ante* (and *-(i)ente*) so abundantly represented in the Alfonsine corpus are clearly borrowings, either from Latin (i.e., *cultismos* in the traditional sense) or from Gallo-Romance, often based on Latin present participles. This makes them more easily suspect of non-Castilian influence, and therefore of proportionately less use in analyzing the extent of the effects of apocope in Castilian.[4] In the third place, its dual syntactic function as preposition and adverb allowed it to appear in a variety of positions in the sentence, including phrase-final.[5] A few examples may serve to illustrate this:

---

[4] Lapesa criticizes Catalán for presenting as examples of Castilian apocope forms which were 'carentes ya de vocal final en la forma con que penetraron en el castellano de los siglos XI al XIII' (1975:18). He cites as borrowings from Catalan, Occitan or French such relevant examples as *ardiment, argent, aveniment, aymant, convent, estrument, talant* (1975:19).

[5] The obligatory appearance of *de* following *delante* in its prepositional function was not yet the case in Medieval Spanish, as may be appreciated from the examples. Prepositional *delante* was not therefore restricted to occurring before only one consonant.

si algun obispo ha pleyto **dela\<n>te** su arçobispo

LEY 19r55-56[6]

dalli **adelante** nol ualdrie nada la orden q\<ue> recibiera

LEY 6r36-37

cuemo si las touiesse **delante**.

LEY 107r33

e\<n> muchas cosas segund dize **adelante**;

LEY 19r38-39

estando los senadores **delante**. dixol herodes aq\<ue>llo

EE1 73v5-6

mando q\<ue>l troxiessen **delant** a Paulo

EE1 181v50-51

salieron ellos **delant** sus azes paradas

EE1 17v54-55

pusolo **delante** aq\<ue>llos angeles

GE1 56r89

nu\<n>ca te me pares **delant** otra uez.

GE1 155r68

q\<ue>les fuessen **delant** & los guiassen

GE1 213v66-67

In the fourth place, *(a)delante* was relatively untouched by the analogical spread of [r] in the ending, a circumstance which makes the analysis of adverbs (or adverbial phrases) in *-m(i)ent(e)*, *-m(i)entre* much more difficult: are forms in *-m(i)ent* to be seen as apocopations of *m(i)ente* or more reduced forms of *-mientre*? It is true that the Alfonsine corpus does contain tokens of *(a)delantre*; indeed, in *AST*, there are seven tokens of *delantre,* and only one each of *delant* and *delante*. But this is unusual; in the larger works the number of occurrences of *adelantre* is so small as to be insignificant.

---

[6] The abbreviations used are: LEY: *Libro de las leyes*
                                     EE1: *Estoria de España*, part 1
                                     EE2: *Estoria de España*, part 2
                                     GE1: *General estoria I*
                                     GE4: *General estoria IV*
                                     AST: *Libros del saber de astronomía*
                                     JUZ: *Judizios de las estrellas*
                                     CRZ: *Libro de las cruces*
The editions are those of Kasten and Nitti (1978).

Special attention has been paid here to the longer works in the Alfonsine corpus, particularly *LEY* (which is perhaps a special case, as will be discussed below), the two parts of the *Estoria de España*, and the two parts of the *General estoria*, since their considerable length contains a number of occurrences high enough to have statistical significance. It is also important that portions of the *Estoria de España* were written rather later than the other works, indeed, after the death of Alfonso, and if it is true that apocope was on the decline, we should expect to find a proportional diminution in the number of apocopated forms in these later texts.

The texts, however, demonstrate that this is not so. Practically all of them show usage of both apocopated and unapocopated variants, with more or less complex patterns of distribution. The one exceptional text in this sense is *LEY*: *delant(e)* occurs 42 times in the text, only twice in its apocopated form. In much the same way, there are 52 cases of *adelante*, and none of *adelant*. Even in the shorter texts such consistency is not generally apparent; thus in the *Judizios*, only four tokens of *delant(e)* appear,[7] but we have both

dela<n>t o detras *JUZ* 16v70-71

and

delante o detras *JUZ* 186r60;

and in *CRZ* we find

si la quadradura fuere detras. & **delant**. Judgale muerte sin dubda
ninguna *CRZ* 183v23-25

and

& la quadradura fuere **delante**. Judga q<ue>l accaeceran
emfermedades *CRZ* 196v4-6

A possible explanation for the surprising lack of alternation in *LEY* is suggested in studies accompanying an earlier edition of the British Library manuscript. Arias Bonet concludes that it is 'un códice que por su ornamentación y contextura paleográfica, podría quizás situarse en las postrimerías del reinado de Alfonso X, como datación más temprana'

---

[7] There are no occurrences of *adelant* in the text; *adelante* and *adelantre* appear once each.

(1975:cii), while Ruiz Asencio believes that 'se trata de una obra del scriptorium real castellano copiada en tiempos de Sancho IV o de Fernando IV entre 1285 y 1312, ó más concretamente en torno al año 1300' (1975:xliv-xlv).

Whatever the specific case of the *LEY* manuscript may be, the situation of inconsistency seems to be confirmed in the lengthier texts, though a closer look reveals a certain pattern. When both apocopated and unapocopated variants appear in a text, it is natural to search for a clue to the alternation within the phonetic context; thus apocope would seem more reasonable in a context where the form was followed immediately (i.e., without a pause) by another form with a vowel in initial position. Such a context would enable resyllabification to take place, with consequent loss of the word-final consonant group typical of extreme apocope; for example, *delant o detras* would be syllabified $de^slan^st\ o^sde^stras$, while *delant. Judgale* could only be syllabified as $de^slant^sjud^sga^sle$, with the cluster appearing inevitably in syllable-final position.[8] Bearing this in mind, the occurrences of *(a)delant(e)* were considered in the light of the phonetic segment immediately following.

At this point, certain clarifications are in order. First the ampersand (&) is taken conventionally as a representation of the vowel /e/, the normal pronunciation in Medieval Spanish of the conjunction (Penny 1991:198). Second, the period (.) is not to be taken necessarily as a mark of the end of an intonational group in these manuscripts; it is also used conventionally to mark, for example, numerals, and even the ampersand itself; thus it is justifiable to believe that in cases like

estando se el **delant**. & ueyendo lo.   *GE4* 70v64

or

fi\<n>caron los ynoios **delant**. & abaxaro\<n>se antel
                                                    GE1 105v63-64

---

[8] In such circumstances, it is questionable from the phonetic point of view whether apocope had actually taken place; we might just as accurately speak of coalescence of vowels, a common enough occurrence in the history of Spanish, and, of course, in the modern spoken language, though not normally reflected in the standard orthography (Navarro Tomás 1977:147-60). However, since so little work has been done on sandhi phenomena in Spanish historical phonology, I shall for the moment maintain what is perhaps no more than a convenient fiction, labeling these forms as instances of apocope. In the final analysis, of course, the question is merely terminological.

the period does not necessarily mark a pause. Nevertheless, since in many instances the period does seem to mark the end of an intonational curve, all those contexts in which *(a)delant(e)* is followed by any mark of punctuation, whether a period, a *calderón*, or any other, have been eliminated from the calculation of tokens in context in order to preserve absolute consistency.

In *GE1*, the tokens of *(a)delant* followed by a vowel or & total 125, those of *(a)delante* in the same context, only 51; before a consonant *(a)delant* appears 173 times, *adelante* 114. There is, therefore, a clear preference for the apocopated form, even when a consonant immediately follows. In *GE4*, the preference for the apocopated form persists even more clearly: *delant* appears 25 times before a vowel or &, *delante* only once; *delant* 26 times before a consonant, *delante* only nine. *Adelante* is found only three times in the whole text, while there are over 200 tokens of *adelant ~ adeland*.[9] Generally speaking, then, it would be inaccurate to say that in the two parts of the *General estoria* we find the use of apocope declining; it would be true, however, to say that there is a certain preference for the apocopated form, restricted on occasions by the presence of a following consonant.

The tendency towards unapocopated forms begins to show itself in the *Estoria de España*. In *EE1*, *(a)delant* appears 27 times before a vowel or & and also 42 times before a consonant; *(a)delante* 88 times before a consonant, but 31 times before a vowel or &: it is therefore more frequent in both types of context. In *EE2* the preference for *(a)delante* becomes overwhelming: 121 tokens before a consonant and 52 before a vowel or &; *(a)delant* shows up only 38 times before a consonant and 31 before a vowel or &.

The fundamental question we are faced with at this point is whether this shift corresponds with what we know of the chronology of the texts. Certainly the most outstanding shift, that of the *EE2* in comparison with the other texts, does: we know that its composition continued well into the fourteenth century. *EE1* was not finished until 1284 either, though its date does not separate it so markedly from the others: *GE1* is dated 1272-75 and *GE4* 1280. It is unlikely that such a short time lapse would reflect major linguistic changes; but all these texts

---

[9] The variant *adeland* is presumably hypercorrected on the analogy of forms in which devoicing had taken place subsequent to apocope, such as *grande ~ grant*.

fall into the later years of Alfonsine production. Certainly the manuscript of *LEY* does not fit in with any interpretation of chronological decline in apocopated forms, and taken together these texts provide no evidence for a gradual decline in the use of apocopated forms traceable along the time axis.

If the usage of *(a)delant(e)* is a valid indicator, the decline in the use of apocopated forms does not seem to have been so drastic or clear-cut as previously suggested. The exceptional case of *LEY* would support the findings reported above that the text was not completed until at least the end of the thirteenth century; a careful editorial revision (perhaps on account of its status as a legal text), may also have contributed to the elimination of apocopated forms. In more normal (i.e., less arbitrary) circumstances, it appears that no particular 'standard' was imposed in the Alfonsine texts; rather there was a natural phonetic tendency toward the reinstatement of full forms in preconsonantal position. The gradual disappearance of apocopated forms was therefore not an immediate concern of standardization, but probably the result of analogical levelling of the preconsonantal form to all positions. Such a tendency is explicable in purely linguistic terms, without recourse to prescriptive accounts. This is not to deny that some editorial intervention may have taken place; the case of *LEY* is to some extent in favor of such a view. But at most we must interpret it as a stimulus for a tendency which was already establishing itself: a restoration of the vowel in final, preconsonantal position, with subsequent resyllabification of the consonant cluster. Given what we know of syllable structure in the history of Spanish, a string such as

$de^{s}lant^{s}su^{s}s\ a^{s}zes$ *EE1* 17v54

must have been in a precarious situation (Harris-Northall 1990:38-47); the replacement of *delant* by *delante* restores a more acceptable pattern.

This fits in more reasonably with what we know of apocope in other forms, such as *much(o)* ~ *muy(t)*. Though in this case, excep-tionally, both apocopated and unapocopated forms have been maintained in Modern Spanish (albeit in different syntactic functions, since *muy* is only used adverbially), the Medieval alternation of *muy* + consonant, *muyt* / *much* + vowel has been lost, and precisely in favor of the pre-consonantal form.

Despite the unquestionable contemporary prestige of a figure like Alfonso X, it is difficult to accept the degree of influence attributed to him by Lapesa. He may indeed have overseen or edited some of the texts produced under his patronage, but the scribes were, in the final analysis, reflecting contemporary speech patterns (albeit perhaps with a certain sociolinguistic bias), whose historical development tends to be oblivious to individual taste, however regal, unless supported by the social prestige of some group.

References

Allen, J. H. D. Jr. 1976. Apocope in Old Spanish. In *Estudios ofrecidos a Emilio Alarcos Llorach*, 1.15-30. Oviedo: Universidad de Oviedo.

Arias Bonet, Juan Antonio (ed.) 1975. *Primera partida, según el manuscrito ADD.20.787 del British Museum*. Valladolid: Universidad de Valladolid.

Corominas, Joan and José A. Pascual. 1980-. *Diccionario crítico etimológico castellano e hispánico*. 5 vols. to date. Madrid: Gredos.

Harris-Northall, Ray. 1990. *Weakening processes in the history of Spanish consonants*. London: Routledge.

Kasten Lloyd and John Nitti (eds.) 1978. *Concordances and texts of the Royal Scriptorium manuscripts of Alfonso X, el Sabio*. Madison: Hispanic Seminary of Medieval Studies.

Lapesa, Rafael. 1951. La apócope de la vocal en castellano antiguo. Intento de explicación histórica. *Estudios dedicados a Menéndez Pidal*, 2.185-226. Madrid: CSIC.

_____. 1975. De nuevo sobre la apócope vocálica en castellano medieval. *Nueva revista de filología hispánica*. 24.13-23.

_____. 1982. Contienda de normas lingüísticas en el castellano alfonsí. *Actas del coloquio hispano-alemán Ramón Menéndez Pidal*, ed. Wido Hempel and Dietrich Briesemeister, 172-90. Tübingen: Niemeyer.

Montgomery, Thomas. 1975. La apócope en español antiguo y la «ī» final latina. *Studia hispanica in honorem R. Lapesa*, 3.351-61. Madrid: Gredos.

Navarro Tomás, T. 1977. *Manual de pronunciación española.* 19th ed.
    Madrid: CSIC.
Penny, Ralph. 1991. *A history of the Spanish language.* Cambridge:
    Cambridge University Press.
Ruiz Asencio, José Manuel. 1975. El manuscrito del British Museum
    ADD.20.787: Estudio paleográfico. In Arias Bonet 1975.xxxv-
    xlv.

On the Emergence of *(a)mi* as Subject in Afro-Iberian Pidgins and Creoles

John M. Lipski

University of Florida

0. Medieval Spanish had not yet become a worldwide language, but by the end of the medieval period, Spanish had been enriched and diversified through a wide variety of language contacts. Some contact events contributed to the general Spanish stock, while others, at times involving speakers for whom Spanish was not a native language, resulted in the creation of parallel varieties, both fleeting and long-lived. In the case of Spanish exploration and settlement of the Americas, the results of extra-Hispanic linguistic influences have been widely discussed, if only imperfectly comprehended. With the exception of Mozarabic, the use of medieval and early post-medieval Spanish as a second language in and around Spain has received less attention. Nor has there been extensive study of the rich inter-Romance linguistic contacts encompassing the Mediterranean region and, beginning with the 15th century, West Africa. Spain enjoyed a strategic location vis-à-vis the countries which exercised the greatest influence on Mediterranean and Atlantic trade and exploration, namely Portugal and the major Italian city-states, and multilateral linguistic contacts involving Spanish merit more attention than they have received to date. In particular, the early use of Spanish as a contact vernacular, trade language and maritime jargon deserves further inquiry, since some of these same transformed varieties were undoubtedly instrumental in the eventual spread of Spanish as a language of discovery and conquest. The present study, while dealing with a specific problem (the formation of subject pronouns in pidginized varieties of Spanish and Portuguese and the medieval roots thereof), can be taken as a demonstration of the range of interactions which involved the Spanish language as it emerged as a world language, carried to every continent.

1. The existence of significant morphological and syntactic parallels among many Spanish- and Portuguese-based creoles in Africa, Asia, Latin

America and Oceania has led to well-known claims of a single common source.[1] This is usually presumed to have been a Portuguese-based pidgin, carried via maritime routes around the coast of Africa and into Asia beginning in the second half of the 15th century (Naro 1978, Taylor 1971, Thompson 1961, Whinnom 1956). Some of the earliest-formed creoles descended from this 'reconnaissance language' (Naro 1978) are spoken in Cape Verde, São Tomé, and Annobón, with later offshoots possibly including Papiamento (formed on Curaçao) and Palenquero (formed in the Colombian village of Palenque de San Basilio) in Latin America, Papiá Kristang in Malacca (Malaysia), as well as earlier creoles in South Africa (Valkhoff 1966, 1973). Even more far-reaching claims implicate the medieval *Lingua Franca* or *Sabir*, which was used in the Mediterranean region for several centuries (Coates 1971, Collier 1976, Fronzaroli 1955, Hadel 1969, Whinnom 1956, 1977). Although mono-genetic accounts are based on similarity or identity of lexical items, the strongest proposals involve convergent syntactic patterns. These theories are counterpoised with research on universal aspects of creolization, which has targeted many of the same patterns as minimally marked alternatives which might arise spontaneously, providing that requisite conditions for radical creolization are met. It is therefore of interest to scrutinize the development of a single form in a related group of creoles, in search of test cases of universal processes vs. language-specific events. The present study will direct attention at one such cluster of forms, the use of *(a)mi* as subject pronoun in Afro-Iberian pidgins and creoles.

2. Afro-Iberian creoles share with French- and English-based creoles the use of subject pronouns apparently based on disjunctive object pronouns, such as are used after prepositions. This is most evident in the first person singular, where instead of Spanish *yo* or Portuguese *eu*, Afro-Iberian creoles have converged on *(a)mi* (cf. Sp. *mí*, Ptg. *mim*). The *a* which often accompanies *mi* is identical to the dative preposition *a*. Analogical extension of *a* to other subject pronouns is found *abo* (< *vos*) in Papiamento and Cape Verdean/Guinea-Bissau *crioulo* (Almada 1961:95; Wilson 1962:17), *anos* (< *nos*) in Guinea-Bissau creole and the occasional *anos, aboso, anan* in Papiamento (Holm 1988:203, Wilson 1962:17). Annobonese is the only Afro-Iberian creole to have retained a reflex of

---

[1] But cf. Ivens Ferraz (1987) for rejection of a single origin for Afro- and Asian-Portuguese dialects.

the second person singular disjunctive pronoun *ti*, having *achí* < *a ti* as a variant of *bo* (Barrena 1957:37).

All Afro-Iberian creoles, including Papiamento and the creoles of Cape Verde, Guinea-Bissau, Annobón, São Tomé and Príncipe, have forms based on *mi(m)*. The longer variant *ami* occurs, at least occasionally, in all these languages; *ami* is always the more emphatic form, and the one to be used alone. Colombian Palenquero has *í*, also derived from *mí*; the latter form is used as direct object (Friedemann and Patiño Rosselli 1983:156). That *mi* was not necessarily present in all Iberian-based pidgins is evidenced by current and recently disappeared Asian Spanish and Portuguese creoles, including those of India, Sri Lanka, Macao, Indonesia and Malacca, together with Philippine Creole Spanish (Chabacano), all of which have retained *eu/yo* as subject pronoun (cf. the comparative data in Lipski 1988).

3. It has become received opinion in creole studies that disjunctive object pronouns are adopted during creolization because of their more 'emphatic' status; this fits in with other pan-creole traits such as the use of *too much* for *very*, as well as elements derived from imperatives, insults, derogatory words, and the like. Exactly what is to be construed as 'emphatic' is seldom specified, and in the case of Ibero-Romance pronouns, this attribution must be challenged.

Spanish/Portuguese subject pronouns have always been semi-optional companions of a fully inflected verb. Unlike French, Ibero-Romance subject pronouns have not evolved to phonological clitics. They may stand alone, with contrastive stress, although due to their redundant status in the face of a rich verbal inflection, they do not ordinarily receive strong tonic stress.[2] In any situation where emphasis is required, or when a free-standing subject pronoun is called for (e.g., in response to a question), it is invariably the *subject* pronoun which is used. Disjunctive object pronouns can only be used in isolation if accompanied by an

---

[2] In syntactic terms, overt subject pronouns in Ibero-Romance behave somewhat differently than their null counterparts, generally acquiring a contrastive function which excludes them from certain configurations. The overt-null distinction is not unlike the emphatic/non-emphatic pronominal distinction in such languages as Yoruba (cf. Pulleyblank 1986).

appropriate preposition.[3] Overt subject pronouns are never replaced by disjunctive object pronouns for emphasis, to answer questions, etc.[4] There is no a priori reason for Ibero-Romance-based pidgins or creoles to have abandoned a viable set of already emphatic subject pronouns. Ibero-Romance subject pronouns, although optional, do occur frequently in received speech (particularly of the 'emphatic' or imperative varieties typical of proto-pidgin encounters), and could easily have been used with and among Africans during survival-level communication.

Despite the fact that Ibero-Romance subject pronouns can be as 'emphatic' as needed by any contact language or pidgin, it is derivatives of *mi(m)*, rather than *yo/eu*, which appear in the earliest Afro-Iberian texts; unquestioning acceptance of the derivation of *(a)mi* from object pronouns has been the result.[5] In the present study, a possible alternative to the 'emphatic pronoun' theory is explored. It will be suggested that *(a)mí* spearheaded the creation of a new subject pronoun system in developing Afro-Lusitanian speech, aided by the fact that several other pronouns are identical in the subject and disjunctive object forms. Two other factors contributed substantially to the choice of *mi(m)* rather than *yo/eu* in Afro-Iberian contact languages. The first is the collateral use of *mi* in the Mediterranean Lingua Franca. This is in turn linked to regional dialects of medieval Italy, particularly Venetian and Genoese, which shortly before had begun to employ *mi* and *ti* as subject pronouns. These dialects influenced the development of the Lingua Franca and, via the latter, Afro-Lusitanian pidgin. The second contributing factor is the fortuitous parallel between *(a)mi* and first person singular subject

---

[3] This is acknowledged, e.g., by Holm (1988:203): 'the use of the subject pronoun in Portuguese implies emphasis ... the emphasis of an object pronoun requires an additional prepositional phrase ...'

[4] This contrasts sharply with French, where subject pronouns became phonological clitics early in the development of the language, and where the disjunctive object pronouns *moi, toi*, etc. are used as free-standing pronouns or for emphasis. This is reflected in all French-based creoles. Colloquial English also uses *me* as an alternative to *I* in answer to questions, or (together with the subject pronoun), for emphasis: *Me, what I think is* ... English-based creoles have adopted *mi* as the generic first person singular pronoun, but in some areas this may also have been influenced by English speakers' stereotypes of foreigner-talk or early pidgin English.

[5] For example, Schuchardt (1909) stated that the use of *mi* and *ti* in the medieval Lingua Franca come from Spanish/Portuguese 'accusative' *mi/mim, ti*. The same etymology was offered for Afro-Portuguese creoles in general. Naro (1978:328) declares that 'in standard Portuguese, subjects are normally indicated both by verbal inflections and by weakly-stressed pronouns ... in normal usage, fully-stressed pronouns follow prepositions ...' Wilson (1962:18) asserts that disjunctive pronouns beginning with *a* 'are probably derived from the Ptg formula: the preposition *a*+pronoun, to convey emphasis, and have final stress ...'

pronouns in a large subset of the first West African languages encountered by the Portuguese in their 15th-century explorations, and whose speakers were protagonists in the formation of Afro-Lusitanian pidgin.

4. The earliest known Afro-Lusitanian text is found in the *Cancioneiro geral* of Garcia de Resende, published in 1516. The item in question, by the court official Fernam da Silveira, bears the date 1455. If this dating is accurate (cf. Teyssier 1959:228-29), it means that an Afro-Lusitanian pidgin was already in use only a few decades after Portugal had begun exploration of the sub-Saharan African coast. The text, a poem, imitates the speech of a tribal king from 'Sierra Leone', and contains examples of *a mim* as subject:

(1)

    a. *a min rrey de negro estar Serra Lyoa, lonje muyto terra onde viver nos* 'I am the king of the blacks in Sierra Leone, far from the land where we live';

    b. *querer a mym logo ver vos como vay* 'I wanted to see you right away, to see how you were';

    c. *se logo vos quer mandar a mym venha* 'if you want to order me right away to come'

Nos in (1a) and *vos* in (1b) could be subject or disjunctive object pronouns, since the forms are identical; it is noteworthy, however, that the 'preposition' *a* accompanies no subject pronoun other than *mym/min*.

    The *Cancioneiro Geral* contains another specimen of Afro-Lusitanian pidgin, in a text by Henrique da Mota written perhaps half a century after Silveira's poem (Leite de Vasconcellos 1933). Da Mota's poem makes reference to the Kingdom of the Congo (*Manicongo*), an area first explored by the Portuguese in the late 15th century. This text uses *(a)mym* as subject, and shows other morphological and syntactic similarities with Silveira's text:

(2)

    a. *mym andar augoá jardim, a mym nunca ssar rroym* 'I was watering the garden, I am not bad'

    b. *Vós a mym querê pinguar, mym morrer* 'You want to beat me, I [will] die'

    c. *a mym logo vay tê laa, mym também falar mourinho* 'I will get some wool soon, I also speak Moorish'

In analyzing the language of this poem, Leite de Vasconcellos (1933:243-44) stated without further comment that in Afro-Portuguese pidgins and creoles, 'dative' pronouns are used as subjects. He also noted that it is common in modern Portuguese to imitate the halting speech of foreigners (especially English speakers) by phrases such as *mim falar portugués* 'Me speak Portuguese'.

Gil Vicente incorporated Afro-Lusitanian pidgin into plays written in the 1520's and 1530's. *(A)mí* is used as subject; as in all modern Afro-Portuguese creoles, there is no indication of the vowel nasalization which characterizes Portuguese *mim*. *Eu* also occurs in apparent free variation with *(a)mí*, and *boso* makes its first appearance as an Afro-Lusitanian second person plural:

(3)

 a. *Ja a mi forro, Ø nam sa cativo. Boso conhece Maracote?* 'I am already free, [I] am not a captive. Do you know Maracote?' [*O clérigo da Beira* (Vicente 1907:353)]
 b. *A mi abre oio e Ø ve* 'I open my eyes and see' [*O clérigo da Beira* (Vicente 1907:355)]
 c. *Eu chamar elle minha vira, e elle chama-mo cão. A mi dá elle romao doze, que a mi comprae ... se a mi vai elle fallae* ... 'I call her my love and she calls me a dog. I give her sweet rosemary that I buy ... if I leave, she will say ... [*Nao d'amores* (Vicente 1834:312)].

The last well-known writer to make use of Afro-Lusitanian pidgin was Antônio Ribeiro Chiado, in the short plays *Pratica d'oyto figuras* (OF; Chiado 1961) and *Auto das regateiras* (AR; Chiado 1968: 103-81), written in the middle of the 16th century. In these works, use of 'object' pronouns as subject predominates, both with and without *a*:

(4)

 a. *A mim frugá, boso matá* '[If] I rest, you kill [me]' {AR p. 106}
 b. *A boso sempre sá graia* 'You are always [talking like a] crow' {AR p. 107}
 c. *Mim não quebrar bosso porta* 'I did not break your pitcher' {AR p. 135}
 d. *Boso nunca tendê bem* 'You never understand well' {AR p. 135}
 e. *a mim traze turo junto* 'I bring everything together' {OF}
 f. *Quando mi bay confesa dize padere confessoro que oficio que boso que tem* 'When I go to confess, the father confessor says "what work do you do?"' {OF}

The African characters use only *boso* for the second person singular. However, a Portuguese character in AR addresses the African woman in

his own approximation to Afro-Portuguese pidgin, and alternates between *vós* and *boso*:[6]
(5)

> a. *Quantos filhos vós parir?* 'How many children have you borne?' {AR p. 149}
> b. *A boso tem inda dente?* 'Do you still have teeth?' {AR p.150}

From the 17th century to the beginning of the 19th century, 'Africanized' pidgin Portuguese continued to appear in pamphlet literature and plays published in Portugal (Leite de Vasconcellos 1901:46-47), but these were burlesque stereotypes based on the first Afro-Lusitanian contacts, and nothing suggests the continued existence and evolution of a genuine Afro-Lusitanian pidgin in Portugal past the late 16th century.

5. In Spain, the first known use of Africanized pidgin Spanish is found in two *coplas* by Rodrigo de Reinosa, probably written around 1520 (Russell 1973). The poems, allegedly addressed to Africans living in Seville, portray Afro-Hispanic pidgin used by a 'Negro de Gelofe Mandinga' [Wolof/Mandinga Negro] and a 'Negra de Guinea' [Guinea Negress]. In this context, the designation 'Guinea' refers to the coastal region from Senegal to roughly Sierra Leone.

The language of Reinosa's poems is nominally Spanish, but both pidgin and standard Portuguese features are also present. This would suggest that an Afro-Lusitanian pidgin was in use among the earliest black residents of Seville, or at least that a stereotype thereof existed among white Spaniards (Russell 1973). The first of the poems contains several examples of *(a)mí* used as subject, alternating with *yo*; the second person is *tú/vos* (Cossío 1950:111-15):
(6)

> a. *A mí llamar Comba de terra Guinea* 'My name is Comba from the land of Guinea'
> b. *A mí llamar Jorge, Mandinga es mi terra ... yo te juro a vos* ... 'My name is Jorge, Mandinga is my land ... I swear to you ...'
> c. *A mí tener yo un otro guardián ...* 'I have another provider'

---

[6] Regardless of the origin of *a* in Afro-Iberian subject pronouns, *boso* appears to have derived from *você*, via an African-inspired process of vowel harmony, which has played such an important role, e.g., in the development of the Gulf of Guinea creoles (cf. Ivens Ferraz 1979). Vowel harmony involving rounding is not found in Cape Verde/Guinea-Bissau *crioulo*, nor in nearby West African languages. In Afro-Iberian texts, *boso* does not appear until well into the 16th century, i.e., after Portuguese contact with Congo Basin languages had been commonplace for several decades.

d. *Estar yo buen negro de obispo criado ... a mí andar en Corte*
'I am a good Negro, raised by a bishop, I have been to
the Court'

(The second poem, although embodying some pidgin features, uses only *yo* as subject pronoun.)

In the 1530s and 1540s, Diego Sánchez de Badajoz wrote some *farsas* which embody Afro-Hispanic pidgin (Barrantes 1882, 1886). The 'Farsa teologal' avoids the use of first person singular pronouns altogether, while using *vos/tú* for the second person. The 'Farsa del Moysen' uses both *yo* and *vos*. The 'Farsa de la hechicera' similarly uses *tú/vos*, while the 'Farsa de la ventera' uses *vos* and *yo*. Feliciano de Silva's *Segunda Celestina*, written about 1530, contains what is asserted to be Afro-Hispanic speech, but which shows characteristics of 'Moorish' or Arabic-influenced pronunciation (especially the writing of syllable-final /s/ as *x*, which represented the sound [š]). Most of the features are not typical of the sub-Saharan African speech found in earlier works, but given that black Africans in southern Europe had often arrived overland through Arabic-speaking North Africa, the text may not be totally irrelevant (cf. Sloman 1949). Silva's 'black' characters use *(a)mí* and *vos/tú* as subject:

(7)

a. *Gentil homber, ¿qué querer vox, voxa merxé ...* 'Dear sir, what do you, your grace, want....' (Silva 1988:128).
b. *a mí no extar tan bovo como tú penxar, ¿tú penxar que no entender a mí ruindadex?* 'I am not as stupid as you think. Do you think that I don't understand about evil things?' (Silva 1988:128)

Only a few years later, Gaspar Gómez de Toledo wrote his *Tercera Celestina*, in which 'black' characters with Moorish speech characteristics also appear. These characters similarly use *mi/yo* as subject:

(8)

a. *a mi cayar y xeruir extax merxedes* 'I will be silent and will serve these people' (Gómez de Toledo 1973:117).
b. *Para yo dexemulaxones no extar a mí taibo* 'As for deception, I am no good' (Gómez de Toledo 1973:117).

Lope de Rueda used Afro-Hispanic pidgin, in plays written in the 1530s and 1540s. In the plays making greatest use of Afro-Hispanic pidgin, *Eufemia* and *Los engañados* (Lope de Rueda 1908), the African characters use *vos* and *tú*, but almost invariably use *yo* for the first person singular pronoun.

The last significant Spanish author to include use of *(a)mí* as a subject pronoun was Jaime de Guete, in his comedy *Tesorina* (ca. 1550).

In this play, which also exemplifies 'Moorish' phonetic stereotypes, the occasional *mí* alternates with the more common *yo* (Guete 1913:153-55):
(9)
    a. **Box** *mentir! no xaber* **tu** *qui digir* 'You are lying. You don't know what you are saying'
    b. *Yo me la quere xtar qui* 'I want him to be here'
    c. *Ti xolo, don puto vejo* 'just you, you old fool'
    d. *En toro oy* **mi** *no comer* 'I haven't eaten all day'

Example (9c) is unique among literary examples of Afro-Iberian pidgin in the apparent use of *ti* as subject pronoun.

Afro-Hispanic pidgin made its ways into many 17th-century Spanish plays and poems, beginning with Simón de Aguado's *Entremés de los negros* (1602), and including works by Lope de Vega, Góngora, Sor Juana Inés de la Cruz and Quiñones de Benavente. Although these works contain a variety of deformations of Spanish syntax, morphology and pronunciation, all use *yo* as subject.

6. Use of *(a)mí* as subject in Afro-Iberian pidgin was confined to the 15th and early 16th centuries. This represents the first century of linguistic and cultural contacts between Ibero-Romance and sub-Saharan Africa, and towards the end of this period the creoles of Cape Verde, São Tomé, Annobón and Palenque de San Basilio were formed. Subsequent contacts between speakers of Spanish or Portuguese and other language families, giving rise to pidgins and creoles in southern and southeastern Asia, the Philippines and Latin America exclusively adopted Ibero- Romance subject pronouns, as befits the stressed/emphatic status of the latter. Some factor must have differentiated the first group of creoles from the second; unique to the first group is the combination of African language contacts and the potential, both chronological and geographical, for a direct influence of the Mediterranean Lingua Franca.

7. Much has been written about the contact language known as the Lingua Franca or Sabir, but only the most fragmentary evidence survives upon which to base any conclusions. This language had a high proportion of Italian elements, together with Arabic, and in certain areas Turkish, Berber, Persian and French (cf. Kahane and Kahane 1958). Most reasonably, each community of users added elements of their native language, while retaining the basic core lexicon and grammar. The Lingua

Franca may have arisen as early as the Crusades, and it survived in full form until at least the beginning of the 19th century.[7]

Only a handful of attestations of Lingua Franca antedate the 19th century, making reconstruction speculative and venturesome. Surviving texts are suspect as true specimens of a pan-Mediterranean Lingua Franca, rather than local attempts at mimicking broken Romance spoken by foreigners, or derogatory stereotypes of 'infidel' Arabs and Turks. The earliest extant text, dating from 1353, contains a language obviously based on Italian (Grion 1891). The 'object' pronoun *ti* is already used as subject. The first person singular, however, is sometimes null, sometimes *io*:

(10)

    a. *come **ti** voler parlare?* 'how do you want to speak?'

    b. *Ø non aver di te paura* '[I] am not afraid of you'

    c. *se per li capelli Ø prendoto, come Ø ti voler conciare!* 'If I grabbed you by the hair, how I would like to beat you!'

    d. *Ch'**io** ti farò pigliare* 'I will have you caught'

It is not impossible to rule out the interpretation of *ti* as *object* pronoun, even in (10a), given the existence of sentences like (10c). This would suggest that the original strategy was to eliminate first and second person singular pronouns in direct conversation, the reference being clear from the context.

The next glimpse comes in a mid 16th- century Italian farce, *La cingana* (Ascoli 1865:124), representing the speech of a Gypsy who mixes Lingua Franca with Arabic (Schuchardt 1909); *mi* and *ti* are used as subject:

(11)

    a. ***mi** no saber certa* 'I am not sure'

    b. ***mi** andar co'l to dinari, **ti** restar ...* 'I will go off with your money, you will stay ...'

As in the earlier text, the infinitive is used as the unmarked verb form. Since the text frequency of the Romance infinitive is considerably less than, e.g., the third person singular, Schuchardt (1909) and Fronzaroli (1955:210) have suggested that Europeans themselves provided the model of using the 'dictionary' form when speaking to foreigners. Collier (1976:292-93) cites a mid 16th-century Italian song which appears to

---

[7] Schuchardt (1909) indicated that Lingua Franca was still in use by Berbers at the turn of the 20th century, and had only recently disappeared from the Levant; this may, however, have been a more recent contact language, with a higher proportion of Arabic elements. On the other hand, Hancock (1984) was still able to elicit oral specimens of Lingua Franca nearly a century after Schuchardt's observations.

contain Lingua Franca material, and in which *mi* is invariably used as subject, e.g., **mi non esser poltron, mi ficar tutta notte** 'I will not be lazy, I will stay all night'.

An important text for evaluating the possible impact of Lingua Franca on the development of Afro-Iberian pidgins comes in a *villancico* by Juan del Encina, written in the 1520s (Harvey et al. 1967). This poem, composed during the time when Afro-Hispanic pidgin first came into its own, should provide a collateral probe of the sort of Lingua Franca that might have been available to Spaniards, when speaking to or writing about newly arrived African *bozales*. As in the earlier texts, Encina largely uses null first and second person subject pronouns (cf. Harvey et al. 1967:574):

(12)

    a. *Por ala Ø te recomenda ...* 'By Allah [I] recommend to you...'

    b. *Per benda Ø dar dos o tres* 'For a *benda* [I will] give [you] two or three [eggs]'

    c. *Peregrin taybo cristian si Ø querer andar Jordan ...* 'Pilgrim, good Christian, if [you] want to go to Jordan ...'

The last known Spanish text containing Lingua Franca materials, written ca. 1612, comes from Diego de Haedo, and represents late 14th-century Algiers.[8] Like the earlier cases, Haedo's examples contain more null first and second person pronouns, although subject *mi* does appear:

(13)

    a. *mirar como mi estar barbero bono y saber curar, si Ø estar malato y ahora Ø correr bono* 'Look what a good doctor I am and how I know how to cure [him], if [he] is sick, and now [he] runs well' (Haedo 1927: v. II, 106)

    b. *mi saber como curar a fe de Dio ... Ø trabajar, Ø no parlar que Ø estar malato* 'I know how to cure him, by God ... [he will] work, [he] will not say that [he] is sick' (Haedo 1927: v. II, 106)

    c. *mi parlar patron donar bona bastonada, mucho, mucho* 'I will tell the master to give [you] a good beating' (Haedo 1927: v. III, 235)

Examples of Lingua Franca are conspicuously absent from extant Portuguese texts of the same time period, but given active Portuguese

---

[8] It is possible that Spanish *aljamiado* or 'Moorish' texts, purporting to represent the broken Spanish used by Arabic speakers or to communicate with them, also represent some form of Lingua Franca of the period (as suggested by Schuchardt 1909). However, the linguistic characteristics of available *aljamiado* texts do not coincide with independently verified Lingua Franca texts.

participation in Mediterranean trade and exploration, it is reasonable to assume that language similar to that of the preceding examples was also known in Portugal. After Haedo, no more Lingua Franca texts from the Iberian Peninsula are known, but several are found in France (cf. Schuchardt 1909, Fronzaroli 1955). The most famous comes in Molière's *Le bourgeois gentilhomme* of 1670 (cf. Wood 1971), where a 'Turkish' character speaks an Italian-based Lingua Franca, making abundant use of *mi* and *ti* as subject (Molière 1882:130):

(14)

    a. *Se ti sabir, ti respondir, se Ø no sabir, Ø tazir* 'If you know, you answer, if you don't know, you be quiet'
    b. *Mi star Mufti; ti qui sar si?* 'I am Mufti; who are you?'

A number of 19th-century French texts also reproduced the Lingua Franca, the best known being an anonymous dictionary written in 1830, which gave a lexicon, dialogues and a descriptive 'grammar' of Lingua Franca (Anon. 1830). As with Molière, *mi* and *ti* are used as subject:

(15)

    Comme ti star? Mi star bonou, et ti? Mi star contento mirar per ti. 'How are you? I am fine, and you? I am glad to see you.'

8. Lingua Franca texts from the period in which Afro-Iberian linguistic contacts were being solidified show incipient use of *mi/ti* as subject, a development which does not stabilize in Lingua Franca until considerably later. More frequent in early documents are null subjects, with reference being determined contextually. This is not surprising given that the two languages on which early Lingua Franca was based, Italian and Arabic, are both 'pro-drop' languages in which null subjects are preferred. Although pidgins, like the Lingua Franca, have no verbal inflection which would obviate the use of overt subject pronouns, most pidgin speech acts involve face-to-face exchanges in which the reference of null pronominals can be effected through physical gestures, or pragmatic rules of conversational turn-taking.

    The gradual emergence of *mi* as subject in Lingua Franca suggests that disjunctive object pronouns were not the natural and inevitable choice from the outset. Nonetheless, at the same time that *mi* as subject was developing in the Mediterranean Lingua Franca, *(a)mí* as subject appears in Afro-Iberian pidgin. It is not unlikely that a solution to one issue will bear immediately on the other. Beginning at the end of the 15th century and continuing for nearly two centuries, Afro-Iberian speech forms were widely used in Spanish and Portuguese literature, suggesting that they were relatively well known to the same elements of society (merchants in coastal areas, sailors and traders, etc.) who used

Lingua Franca. A cross-fertilization of Afro-Iberian pidgin and Lingua Franca forms could well have occurred, since the former would have also occupied a prominent place in the popular imagination as the appropriate way of addressing 'Africans', whether Arabic-speaking or from sub-Saharan regions. Two originally unrelated events converged to boost *(a)mi* as the preferred first person subject in Afro-Iberian pidgin: the first linguistic encounters between Portugal and West Africa, and a morpho-syntactic change in the dialects of northern Italy.

9. Geographical and ethnolinguistic knowledge of sub-Saharan Africa was limited in 15th-century Spain and Portugal (cf. Silva 1959), and terms like *Guinea* were used indiscriminately to refer to coastal areas stretching from modern-day Senegal all the way to Angola. The term *Congo* received almost as broad a set of referents, and even geographically limited ethnic names like *Mandinga* cannot be taken at face value. In reconstructing early Afro-Iberian pidgin, it is necessary to compare the probable dates of writing with the facts of Portuguese exploration along the coast of West Africa.

In the 15th century text by Fernão de Silveira, reference is made to Sierra Leone, a region which had already been visited by the Portuguese in the first half of the 15th century. Assuming that the 1455 date assigned to the poem is approximately correct, Portuguese exploration of West Africa had not proceeded much beyond Sierra Leone, so the language families to be scanned include Wolof, Mandinga, Vai, Mende, Temne and related languages. The Henrique da Mota poem mentions the *Manicongo*. Portuguese contacts with the Kingdom of the Congo commenced towards the end of the 15th century, making the suggested date of 1510 (Teyssier 1959:229) consistent with the facts of Portuguese exploration. A larger pool of African languages enters the picture, including Yoruba, Igbo, Efik, Ewe, Gã, Akan and KiKongo.

Portuguese contact with Africa had begun in the 1420s, with voyages commissioned by Prince Henry the Navigator. The first permanent contacts with sub-Saharan Africa were established in 1445, when the Portuguese built a trading station on Arguim Island, off the coast of present-day Mauritania. Direct contact with the Senegambia region had been made the previous year, but permanent mainland settlements were not established until a few years later. The Arguim station was important for the African slave trade from the very beginning, despite lying to the north of black Africa. Slaving caravans brought slaves from the Senegambia to Arguim, whence they were shipped to Portugal. By 1455, more than 1000 slaves per year were passing through Arguim (Vogt 1979:5), so that the presence of Wolof- and Mandinga-speaking slaves in Portugal did not have to wait until permanent Portuguese settlements in Senegambia. In addition to the Euro-African contacts occasioned by the slave trade, by the late 1450s Portugal was buying considerable quantities of gold from the Gambian region (Barry 1988:73).

By the early 1460s Portuguese explorers had reached Sierra Leone, and a decade later the Ivory Coast and the Gold Coast (Ghana) were the subject of intense Portuguese interest. Shortly thereafter the fortress of Elmina was constructed, consolidating Portuguese control in a zone which was increasingly contested by Spain. Portuguese explorers first arrived in the Kongo Kingdom in 1483, and speakers of Congo Basin languages were taken to Portugal in the following years (Hilton 1985: chap. 3). The Portuguese established diplomatic relations with the *Mani Congo*, leader of this kingdom, and by the beginning of the 16th century, when Henrique da Mota's text was written, considerable Kongo nomenclature was in circulation among participants in the African trade. All these contacts engendered greater awareness of the specifics of 'African' linguistic interference in Portuguese. Portugal was also acquiring greater familiarity with African geographical and ethnological terminology, albeit with considerable inaccuracy.

Spain began encroaching upon Portugal's African trade interests early in the 1470s, and in 1475 direct Spanish commerce with El Mina was initiated. From this time onward, Spain was able to import African slaves and free laborers directly, without relying on transshipment from Portugal. This provides a plausible mechanism for the spontaneous emergence of Afro-Hispanic pidgin in southern Spain, without filtering through Afro-Lusitanian pidgin. The chronology of the earliest Afro-Hispanic texts, and the rapid decline of pidgin Portuguese features, support this reconstruction.

10. All the ethnic designations in the early Afro-Portuguese texts are consistent with dates of Portuguese exploration. Whereas it is unlikely that 15th- and early 16th-century residents of Portugal had the linguistic sophistication to distinguish pidgin features attributable to diverse African language families, one can postulate a pool of African foreigner-talk characteristics that might have collectively influenced Europeans' perceptions of Africanized speech. In this connection, a comparative survey of the pronominal systems of major coastal West African languages reveals not only internal parallels, which may simply be due to historical interrelatedness, but also a startling coincidence with Ibero-Romance.

The majority of West African languages divide pronouns not only by grammatical function (subject, object, etc.), but also by stressed vs. clitic status. Stressed forms are frequently two syllables long and behave as free nouns, while unstressed variants are clitics consisting of a single consonant or syllable. Second and third person singular pronouns are represented primarily by vocalic nuclei, and in many cases the second and third person forms are identical except for tonal differences. The plural series is more often bisyllabic, but cross-linguistic consistency is minimal.

Similarity between West African and Ibero-Romance pronouns is nonexistent, with one striking exception. In a broad West African cross-section, first person singular pronouns begin with /m-/, and the accompanying vowel is often /i/ (cf. Migeod 1911:98-99). First person singular pronouns similar or identical to *mi* (sometimes with a non-labial nasal) occur in the majority of language families which are identified by name in early Afro-Iberian texts. Fula and most of the coastal languages of the Gold and Slave coasts (including Twi, Ashanti, Fanti, Gã, Ewe, and numerous smaller groups) have *mi* or *me*. Temne has *i*, with *mi* as the objective form. Wolof, Bambara, Vai, Mende and Malinke have forms beginning in /n-/ or /ng-/, most often followed by /i/ in at least some variants. Coastal languages of Benin, Nigeria and the Bight of Biafra cluster around *mi* as first person singular, with strong forms including *emi* and *ami*: this includes Nupe, Gbari, Yoruba, Efik and Igbo. A number of western Bantu languages, including those spoken in the Congo Basin and coastal Angola, also have first person singular pronouns which converge on *(a)mi*.[9]

11. The fortuitous similarity between the first person singular pronoun in many West African languages and a member of the Ibero-Romance pronominal paradigm would surely have been noticed by Europeans attempting to make sense of Africans' speech, a comfortably familiar item in the midst of otherwise unintelligible speech. A Portuguese or Spanish speaker hearing a combination like *(a)mi*, especially when accompanied by a clear deictic reference to the speaker such as a self-pointing gesture, would immediately seize upon the similarity with Spanish/Portuguese *(a)mi(m)*. In West African languages these pronouns may only be occasional stressed variants, but Europeans would not recognize other members of the African pronominal paradigm and would assume that the familiar-sounding strong forms were the only pronouns. To describe or imitate Afro-Iberian pidgin, a Spanish or Portuguese speaker would naturally overgeneralize use of *(a)mi*. In speaking to Africans, this pronoun might also be used instead of the correct subject pronouns, with the goal of facilitating the first halting attempts at communication through recourse to what was regarded as a mutually identifiable word. This is not a version of the 'baby talk' model of pidgin formation, since there is no

---

[9] Schuchardt (1882:905-7) also suggested the possibility that the subject pronoun *(a)mi* in São Tomé and Principe creoles mimics the use of similar forms in, e.g., Twi, Efik, Yoruba and 'Angolan' languages. Although these languages undoubtedly figured in the pool of African languages that influenced Afro-Iberian pidgin, it is unlikely that these creoles were formed in situ, given the undeniable similarities with Cape Verde creoles.

a priori reason why a speaker of Spanish or Portuguese should feel that
(a)mí would be inherently more comprehensible than *yo/eu* to an African.
If genuine, albeit misguided, attempts at facilitated communication were
at work, Africans in turn might seize upon the word being proffered to
them, especially if it resembled a pronoun in their native language. A
mutual misinterpretation at the early stages of pidgin formation would
potentially have long-lasting consequences among both Africans and
Europeans, propagating the view that 'African' versions of the first person
singular all involved *mi*.

12. A Lingua Franca contribution to the development of *(a)mi* in Afro-
Iberian pidgin is also consistent with the chronology of both languages.
The emergence of *mi/ti* as subject in Lingua Franca coincides with the
first Afro-Iberian attestations, and there is no doubt that Spanish and
Portuguese sailors and merchants had knowledge of Mediterranean Lingua
Franca. There is an additional piece in the puzzle which draws Afro-
Iberian pidgins and Lingua Franca closer together, stemming from the
Italian basis for the latter language. It is misleading to judge the Italian
contribution to Lingua Franca through comparison with modern standard
Italian, a codified and artificially restricted derivative of educated Florentine patterns. Nothing suggests that medieval Lingua Franca was ever
inspired by erudite speech patterns. To the contrary, this contact vernacular was the linguistic vehicle of choice among sailors, merchants and
nomadic traders. The search for 'Italian' sources of Lingua Franca must
concentrate on regional and social dialects likely to have been used by
Italian sailors and merchants in key trading regions. Genoa and Venice
were particularly important commercial and mercantile centers during the
14th-17th centuries. Significantly, the regional dialects of Genoa and
Venice use first person singular subject pronouns derived from Latin
MIHI, rather than EGO, including *me*, *mi* and *min*. The same dialects have
largely adopted *ti* for the second person singular, although in some cases
this may have resulted from the unrounding of [ü].[10] In a number of

---

[10] This was already present in medieval Italian texts from Milan, Genoa and other
northern cities (Rohlfs 1968:131). Vanelli (1987) contains a helpful collection of examples
from the 13th century onward. The 'Sermone' of the Lombard Pietro da Barsegapè,
probably written at the very end of the 13th century, already gives occasional examples
of *mi* as subject pronoun: *sempre staremo mi e le* ... 'he and I will always be ...' (Salvioni
1891:476). Bonelli and Contini (1935) give many texts from early 15th-century Brescia
in which *mi* and *ti* are used as subject pronouns: *Mi sot tut innocent denanz da vo e da
la zent de la mort de quest iust hom* 'I am innocent before you and before the people of
the death of this just man'; *Christ, se ti é fïol de De* 'Christ, if you are the son of God'
(p. 130). In these texts, *mi* alternates with *e* < EGO, and it is possibly this severe phonetic
erosion, together with the ensuing homophony with the conjunction *e* < ET which was
instrumental in the choice of objective pronouns for subject positions. An early Genoese

northern Italian dialects, second-person plural *voi* has evolved to *vo/bo*, which could have reinforced the Afro-Iberian development of *(a)bo* from *vos*.

Northern Italian dialects originally had only a single series of subject pronouns, derived from Latin and cognate with those of modern Italian. The adoption of *mi* as subject in northern Italian dialects, arose during the 14th-15th centuries (Vanelli 1984, 1987). This shift apparently occurred when the original subject pronouns eroded to stressless clitics, bound to the verb and lacking their earlier contrastive meaning. To fill the gap formerly occupied by free-standing subject pronouns, disjunctive object pronouns were pressed into service, thereby giving the northern Italian dialects their characteristic 'dual' subject pronouns: an optional stressed pronoun and (for most forms) an obligatory preverbal clitic. Thus in a very real sense, but only in these dialects, use of *mi* as subject represents a 'stressed disjunctive' element replacing what had become a stressless subject pronoun.

13. The chronology of the development of *mi* as subject in Genoese and Venetian corresponds closely to the choice of subject pronouns in Lingua Franca. The earliest texts use null subjects, alternating with etymologically correct overt subject pronouns. At this stage, subject pronouns had not fully evolved to clitic status in northern Italy and could still be dropped, and disjunctive object pronouns were not yet being widely used as subjects. By the early 16th century, *mi* as subject pronoun was in use both in Lingua Franca and in northern Italian dialects, as well as in Afro-Lusitanian pidgin.[11] Under the very natural assumption that regional dialects of Italian prevailed over a literary 'national language' in medieval and Renaissance times, and given the increasing prevalence of the lower classes in the Venetian/Genoese maritime trade (e.g., Folena 1968-70, McNeill 1974:51), the most influential dialects would provide a model for

---

text has, for example, *mi e me fijo* 'I and my son' (Parodi 1901:19). By the early 16th century, Genoese shows combinations which are strikingly similar to the Afro-Iberian texts under consideration (Donaver 1910:24): *Mi son Zeneize, e Zena ho sempre amaou* 'I am Genoese, and I have always loved Genoa'. Although in contemporary Italian dialects use of *mi/ti* as subject pronouns is restricted to northern dialects, these pronouns once had a wider distribution. For example, a series of Salentino texts from the late 14th century show *my/mi* as subject pronoun, e.g., *my Sabatyno Russo judio de Leze vy saluto* 'I, Sabatino Russo, a Jew from Leze, greet you' (Stussi 1965).

[11] For example, Machiavelli, in his *Discorso intorno alla nostra lingua*, commented without surprise that some Italians used *mi* instead of *io*, and *ti* instead of *tu* (Machiavelli 1971:925).

the incorporation of overt subject pronouns into Lingua Franca.[12] The
dialects of the major trading cities Genoa, Venice and Pisa, enjoyed
special prominence, together with Sicilian (Fronzaroli 1955, Folena 1968-
70). The existence of Venetian, Pisan and Genoese lexical items in the
Lingua Franca, e.g., as recorded by Haedo (Fronzaroli 1955:224f.)
demonstrates that these regional languages were indeed instrumental in
the formation and development of the Lingua Franca, and may well have
contributed their pronouns.[13]

First person subject pronouns derived from Latin EGO vary widely
among Italian dialects, while disjoint object pronouns exhibit only slight
variation between *mi* and *me*. In the true sense of a 'lingua franca', a set
of common denominators recognizable to the widest possible group, the
use of *mi* and by extension *ti* as subject pronouns would be further
enhanced, once backed by the economic and political force of the
Northern Italian city-states. If to these factors was added a popular
perception, among speakers of other Italian dialects, that use of *mi* and
ti represented either infantile or 'foreign' (e.g., French) interference in
Italian, the conscious adoption of these elements in a trade vernacular
would be a natural outcome.[14] Finally, it is not irrelevant that Venetians
and Genoese were central to the establishment of the sugar/slave
plantation systems, first in the Mediterranean and later in the Azores,
Madeira, Cape Verde and São Tomé (Duncan 1972, Granda 1976,
Washabaugh and Greenfield 1981). In the first two island groups,
Portuguese settlers soon outnumbered speakers of other languages, and
only regional forms of Portuguese developed. In Cape Verde and São
Tomé, the majority of the population was drawn from the African

---

[12] Cortelazzo (1977:535) has observed that the use of *mi* and *ti* as subject in the
earliest Lingua Franca text is decidedly Northern Italian in flavor, but does not directly
include these pronouns among Genoese and Venetian contributions to the medieval
Lingua Franca. Schuchardt (1909:449) speculated that *mi/ti* in Lingua Franca could be of
Venetian origin, but ultimately rejects this possibility, since Lingua Franca is found far
from Venice. Given the importance of Venetian and Genoese colonies and the trading
empire that developed around these city-states, Schuchardt's objection loses force.
Interestingly, Haedo (1927: v.I) observed that there were many Venetian *renegados* living
in Algiers during the 15th and 16th centuries when the Lingua Franca was developing
there, and at least one Venetian ruled the city for a while (Haedo 1927: v.I, 374-75, 396-
97).

[13] Indeed, Bartoli (1906:263-66) went so far as to speculate that Lingua Franca may
have been at bottom a simplified form of Venetian.

[14] This is demonstrated in the *greghesco* literary stereotypes of the 16th and 17th
centuries, in which Greek merchants were portrayed as speaking a broken Italian which
some have confused with the Lingua Franca, and in which *mi* and *ti* were used as subject
pronouns. See for example Cortelazzo (1972, 1977) for sample texts and Coutelle (1977)
for additional discussion.

mainland, with creolization resulting from the consequent linguistic heterogeneity. Fortuitous similarity of Portuguese *(a)mim* and first person singular forms in local African languages could aid the adoption of disjunctive object pronouns in the developing Afro-Lusitanian pidgin. The regional Italian dialects of Genoese and Venetian sailors and merchants add to the list of contributing factors. This chain of events constitutes an indirect connection between medieval Lingua Franca and Afro-Lusitanian pidgin: in both contact languages, first and second person subject pronouns could have been influenced by regional Italian dialects.[15]

13. According to the solution proposed above, what has been described as a 'typically creole' adoption of disjunctive object pronouns as subjects in Afro-Iberian pidgin results from a complex series of overlapping events, all of which targeted a single member of the pronominal paradigm. The notion that 'emphatic' pronouns are necessarily drawn from the ranks of disjunctive object pronouns has been challenged, since both the possibility and the feasibility of alternative developments have been sketched out. Further investigation may eventually shed light on the development of first person subject pronouns like *mi* in other creoles, where similarly complex routes of developments might have occurred. Afro-Iberian pronouns represent a radical break with the lexifier languages, a fact which has motivated the present analysis. The preceding proposal, while not discrediting the notion that pidgins and creoles generally adopt stressed, emphatic and exaggerated forms whenever possible, has questioned the facile assumption that all creole replacements can be attributed to a general pidiginizing strategy. More work remains in the reconstruction of a plausible model of early Afro-Hispanic language, and the preceding remarks have been offered as a tentative contribution to the ongoing enterprise.

---

[15] Beginning in the 13th century, there was a large Genoese mercantile community in Portugal, and Granda (1976) has suggested this group as a possible source of widespread knowledge of Lingua Franca in late medieval and Renaissance Portugal and insular Portuguese colonies.

References

Almada, Maria Dulce de Oliveira. 1961. *Cabo Verde: contribuição para o estudo do dialecto falado no seu arquipélago.* Lisboa: Junta de Investigações do Ultramar.

Anonymous. 1830. *Dictionnaire de la langue franque ou petit mauresque, suivi de quelques dialogues familiers et d'un vocabulaire de mots arabes les plus usuels à l'usage des français en Afrique.* Marseille: Feissar Ainé et Demonchy.

Ascoli, Graziadio I. 1865. *Zigeunerisches.* Halle: Niemeyer.

Barrantes, D. V. (ed.) 1882. *Recopilación en metro del bachiller Diego Sánchez de Badajoz,* I. Madrid: Librería de los Bibliófilos.

_____. 1886. *Recopilación en metro del bachiller Diego Sánchez de Badajoz,* II. Madrid: Librería de los Bibliófilos.

Barrena, Natalio. 1957. *Gramática annobonesa.* Madrid: Instituto de Estudios Africanos.

Barry, Boubacar. 1988. *La Sénégambie du XV⁰ au XIX⁰ siècle.* Paris: L'Harmattan.

Bartoli, Matteo. 1906. *Das Dalmatische, altromanische Sprachreste von Veglia bis Ragusa und ihre Stellung in der Apennino-balkanischen Romania.* Wien: Kaiserlichen Akademie der Wissenschaften zu Wien.

Bonelli, Giuseppe and Gianfranco Contini. 1935. Antichi testi bresciani. *L'Italia dialettale* 11.115-51.

Chiado, Antônio Ribeiro. 1968. *Autos.* Vol. I. Lisboa: Instituto Nacional do Livro.

Coates, William. 1971. The Lingua Franca. In *Papers from the fifth annual Kansas Linguistics Conference,* ed. Frances Ingemann, 25-34. Lawrence: University of Kansas, Linguistics Department.

Collier, Barbara. 1976. On the origins of Lingua Franca. *Journal of Creole Studies* 1.281-98.

Cortelazzo, Manlio. 1972. Nuovi contributi alla conoscenza del grechesco. *L'Italia dialettale* 35.50-64.

_____. 1977. Il contributo del veneziano e del greco alla lingua franca. In *Venezia, centro di mediazione tra Oriente e Occidente (secoli XV-XVI),* ed. H.-G. Beck, M. Manoussacas, A. Pertusi, 2.523-35. Firenze: Olschki.

Cossío, José M. de (ed.) 1950. *Rodrigo de Reinosa.* Santander: Antología de Escritores y Artistas Montañeses XVI. Imp. y Enc. de la Librería Moderna.

Coutelle, Louis. 1977. Grec, greghesco, lingua franca. In *Venezia, centro di mediazione tra Oriente e Occidente (secoli XV-XVI),* ed. H.-G. Beck, M. Manoussacas, A. Pertusi, 2.537-44. Firenze: Olschki.

Donaver, Federico. 1910. *Antologia della poesia dialettale genovese.* Genova: Editrice Moderna.

Duncan, T. Bentley. 1972. *Atlantic islands: Madeira, the Azores and the Cape Verdes in seventeenth-century commerce and navigation.* Chicago: University of Chicago Press.

Folena, Gianfranco. 1968-70. Introduzione al veneziano 'de là da mar'. *Bollettino dell'Atlante linguistico mediterraneo* 10-12.331-76.

Friedemann, Nina and Carlos Patiño Rosselli. 1983. *Lengua y sociedad en el Palenque de San Basilio.* Bogotá: Instituto Caro y Cuervo.

Fronzaroli, Pelio. 1955. Nota sulla formazione della lingua franca. *Atti e memorie dell'Accademia Toscana di Scienze e Lettere* 'la Colombaria' 20.211-52.

Gómez de Toledo, Gaspar. 1973. *Tercera parte de la tragicomedia de Celestina,* ed. Mac Barrick. Philadelphia: University of Pennsylvania Press.

Granda, Germán de. 1976. A sociohistorical approach to the problem of Portuguese creole in West Africa. *Linguistics* 173.11-22.

Grion, G. 1891. Farmacopea e lingua franca del dugento. *Archivio glottologico italiano* 12.181-86.

Guete, Jaime de. 1913. *Comedia intitulada Tesorina. Teatro español del siglo XVI, tomo primero,* 81-170. Madrid: Sociedad de Bibliófilos.

Haedo, Diego de. 1927. *Topografía e historia general de Argel.* Madrid: Sociedad de Bibliófilos Españoles.

Hadel, Richard. 1969. Modern creoles and Sabir. *Folklore annual of the University Folklore Association* 1.35-43.

Hancock, Ian. 1984. Shelta and Polari. In *Language in the British Isles,* ed. Peter Trudgill, 384-403. Cambridge: Cambridge University Press.

Harvey, L. P., R. O. Jones and Keith Whinnom. 1967. Lingua franca in a Villancico by Encina. *Revue de littérature comparée* 41.572-79.

Hilton, Anne. 1985. *The kingdom of Kongo.* Oxford: Clarendon Press.

Holm, John. 1988. *Pidgins and creoles, volume I: Theory and structure.* Cambridge: Cambridge University Press.

Ivens Ferraz, Luis. 1979. *The creole of São Tomé.* Johannesburg: Witwatersrand University Press.

_____. 1987. Portuguese creoles of West Africa and Asia. In *Pidgins and creole languages: Essays in memory of John E. Reinecke,* ed. Glenn Gilbert, 337-60. Honolulu: University of Hawaii Press.

Kahane, Henry and Renée Kahane. 1958. *The Lingua Franca in the Levant: Turkish nautical terms of Italian and Greek origin.* Urbana: University of Illinois Press.

Leite de Vasconcellos, José. 1901. *Esquisse d'une dialectologie portugaise.* Paris: Aillaud.

_____. 1933. Língua de preto num texto de Henrique da Mota. *Revue hispanique* 81.241-46.

Lipski, John. 1988. Philippine creole Spanish: Reassessing the Portuguese element. *Zeitschrift für romanische Philologie* 104.25-45.

Machiavelli, Niccolò. 1971. *Tutte le opere*, ed. Mario Martelli. Firenze: Sansoni.

McNeill, William. 1974. *Venice, the hinge of Europe 1081-1797*. Chicago: University of Chicago Press.

Migeod, Frederick. 1911. *The languages of West Africa*, vol. II. London: Kegan, Paul, Trench, Trubner.

Molière, Jean-Baptiste. 1882. *Oeuvres complètes de Molière*, vol. 16. Paris: L. Hébert.

Naro, Anthony. 1978. A study on the origins of pidginization. *Language* 54.314-49.

Parodi, E. G. 1901. Studi liguri. *Archivio glottologico italiano* 15.1-82.

Pulleyblank, Douglas. 1986. Clitics in Yoruba. In *Syntax and semantics vol. 19: The syntax of pronominal clitics*, ed. Hagit Borer, 43-64. Orlando: Academic Press.

Rohlfs, Gerhard. 1968. *Grammatica storica della lingua italiana e dei suoi dialetti, vol. II: Morfologia*. 2nd ed. Torino: Einaudi.

Rueda, Lope de. 1908. *Obras de Lope de Rueda, tomo I*. Madrid: Real Academia Española.

Russell, P. E. 1973. Towards an interpretation of Rodrigo de Reinosa's 'poesía negra'. In *Studies in Spanish literature of the Golden Age presented to Edward M. Wilson*, ed. R. O. Jones, 225-45. London: Tamesis.

Salvioni, C. 1891. Il 'Sermone' di Pietro da Barsegapè riveduto sul cod. e nuovamente edito. *Zeitschrift für romanische Philologie* 15.429-92.

Schuchardt, Hugo. 1882. Kreolische Studien I: ueber das Neger-portugiesische von S. Thomé (Westafrika). *Sitzungsberichte der kaiserlichen Akademie der Wissenschaften zu Wien* 101.889-917.

_____. 1909. Die Lingua Franca. *Zeitschrift für romanische Philologie* 33.441-61.

Silva, Artur Augusto da. 1959. Apontamentos sobre as populações oeste-africanas segundo os autores portugueses dos séculos XVI e XVII. *Boletim Cultural da Guiné Portuguesa* 14 (55).373-406.

Silva, Feliciano de. 1988. *Segunda Celestina, ed. by Consolación Baranda*. Madrid: Cátedra.

Sloman, Albert. 1949. The phonology of Moorish jargon in the works of early Spanish dramatists and Lope de Vega. *Modern Language Review* 44.207-17.

Stussi, Alfredo. 1965. Antichi testi salentini in volgare. *Studi di filologia italiana* 23.191-224.

Taylor, Douglas. 1971. Grammatical and lexical affinities of creoles. In *Pidginization and creolization of languages*, ed. Dell Hymes, 293-96. Cambridge: Cambridge University Press.

Teyssier, Paul. 1959. *La langue de Gil Vicente*. Paris: Klincksieck.

Thompson, Robert. 1961. A note on some possible affinities between the creole dialects of the Old World and those of the new. In *Creole Language Studies* 2.107-13. (*Proceedings of the Conference of Creole Language Studies*, ed. Robert Le Page. London: Macmillan).

Valkhoff, Marius. 1966. *Studies in Portuguese and creole*. Johannesburg: Witwatersrand University Press.

_____. 1973. *New light on Afrikaans and 'Malayo-Portuguese'*. Louvain: Peeters.

Vanelli, Laura. 1984. Pronomi e fenomeni di prostesi vocalica nei dialetti italiani settentrionali. *Revue de linguistique romane* 48.281-95.

_____. 1987. I pronomi soggetto nei dialetti italiani settentrionali dal Medio Evo a oggi. *Medioevo romanzo* 12.173-211.

Vicente, Gil. 1834. *Obras de Gil Vicente*. Vol. II. Hamburg: Langhoff.

_____. 1907. *Obras de Gil Vicente*. Vol. I. Coimbra: França Amado.

Vogt, John. 1979. *Portuguese rule on the Gold Coast 1469-1682*. Athens: University of Georgia Press.

Washabaugh, William and Sidney Greenfield. 1981. The Portuguese expansion and the development of Atlantic creole languages. *Luso-Brazilian Review* 18.225-38.

Whinnom, Keith. 1956. *Spanish contact vernaculars in the Philippines*. Hong Kong: Hong Kong University Press.

_____. 1977. The context and origins of Lingua Franca. In *Langues en contact — pidgins-creoles — languages in contact*, ed. Jürgen Meisel, 3-18. Tübingen: Gunter Narr.

Wilson, W. A. A. 1962. *Crioulo of Guiné*. Johannesburg: Witwatersrand University Press.

Wood, Richard. 1971. The Lingua Franca in Molière's *Le bourgeois gentilhomme*. *USF Language Quarterly* 10.2-6.

Un reanálisis de la '*l* leonesa'[1]

Carmen Pensado

Universidad de Salamanca

Uno de los rasgos más característicos del dialecto astur-leonés es la llamada '*l* leonesa' (vid. Tabla 1 para un inventario de ejemplos).[2]

Tabla 1. Ejemplos de '*l* leonesa'

b-d (< P-T, B-T, V-T, P-D)

> *ACCAPITARE > ast. *acaldáse* 'ataviarse, componerse'; CAPITALE > ast. *caldar* 'ubre de la vaca', CUBITU > ant. leon. *coldo* Alexandre O 1204, ast. *coldu, culdera* 'codera', *reculdáse* 'acodarse'; CUPIDITIA > ast. *coldicia;* BIBITU > *enbeldar* Alexandre O 2399d, DEBITA > ant. leon. *delda, deldor* Alexandre 1323, Fuero Juzgo; DUBITA >. ant. leon. *duldar* Alexandre O 1221b, *dulda* Alexandre O 458d, 1826a, ant. ast. *dolda* Potes 1282; INSAPIDU > ast. *xaldu;* *LEVITU > salm. *yeldo*, ast. y sant. *dieldu, dieldar,* ast. *tsieldu, tseldadura, tseldar*; MOVITA > ant. leon. *muelda* Alexandre O 524c; NEPETA > ast. *nielda* 'cierta hierba medicinal' (Rodríguez Castellano 1952 piensa en MEDICA); RECAPITARE > ant. leon. *recaldar* Alexandre O 1049b, 1572d, 2333c, *recaldo* Alexandre O 1837d, 2195b, ast. *rrecaldái*; TRIPEDES > ast. *estrelde* (Besullo), sayag. *trelvis, treldes*

---

[1] Quiero manifestar mi agradecimiento a E. F. Tuttle, quien generosamente me ha facilitado un trabajo suyo inédito y ha hecho incontables sugerencias y mejoras a una versión manuscrita de este trabajo.

[2] Datos de Corominas *DCECH,* García Arias (1988:140), Menéndez García (1963), Pattison (1973), Rodríguez Castellano (1952, 1954), Sas (1976), Seward (1976), Staaff (1907). La *-l* puede alterarse secundariamente en *-r*.

v-ts (< V-Ḱ)

*AVICE > ant. leon. *alze* Alexandre O 573a (o < A.B.C., cf. Malkiel 1966)

b-t DUBITARE > ant. leon. *dulta* Alexandre O 753b, 1568c, *dultança* 1723c

d-g (< T-K, D-K)

-ATICU, -A: *AFFLATICA > ast. *ayalga, chalga* 'tesoro escondido'; top. ast. *Entralgo*; ant. leon. *montalgo;* ant. leon. *padronalgo;* ant. leon. *portalgo;* ant. leon. *prioralgo;* ast. *tsamarga, tsamuerga* 'terreno húmedo'; ant. leon. *viñalgo;* NATICA > *nalga* 1400 Glos. Esc.; JUDICARE > ant. ast. *julgar* Fuero de Avilés, Oviedo 1311; ant. leon. *julgar* Alf. XI, 339 y Alexandre O 59a, 470a, 917c, 1694c; top. ast. *Olgo,* aldea de Cangas del Narcea < med. *Odgo;* PEDICA > ast. *pielga* 'pieza de madera cerrada con una clavija que se pone en la mano del vacuno para que no pueda saltar', ast. *pielgu* 'tetas de la cerda' (Casomera), ast. occ. *empilgar* 'detenerse el agua', ant. sant. *pelgar* 1252, salm. *pielga* 'madero para formar la corraliza', *pielgo* 'trozo de piel que cubre el pie o mano de un animal; colgadero, tendón'[3]

d-dz (< D-Ḱ)

DUODECIM > ant. leon. *dolze*; TREDECIM > ant. leon. *trelze*

v-d, d-v (< D-V)

VIDUA > ant. leon. *bilda* ms. S de J. Ruiz, *vilda* F. Salamanca, *vilva*

t-n (< NT-N, PT-M)

ANTENATU > *alnado* Partidas, Gr. Conqu. Ultr. SEPTIMANA > ant. leon. y ast. *selmana*, Alexandre O 1177a, *sermana* (Casomera)

d-n (< T-N)

CATENATU > ant. leon. *calnado* Alexandre 110a

---

[3] En berc. *revelgao* 'torcido en espiral' (García Rey 1934) de *VERSICU una *-s* etimológica ha entrado también en el juego de la '*l* leonesa'.

A veces, en documentos con ortografía aún latina, la '*l* leonesa' resulta de una consonante geminada, especialmente una -ss- (cf. García Arias 1988:109, 140): CESSU > *celsum* (San Pelayo, Oviedo, 1043), *celsum* (Carrizo, 1113), EX CESSU > *exelso* (Carrizo, 1126, 1127), ABYSSU > *abilsos* (San Bartolomé de Nava, 1354). El asturiano *yelso* < GYPSU puede ser un resto de formas de este tipo y lo es sin duda la forma *sielso* < SESSU, localizada por García de Diego (1916) en las provincias de Santander, Palencia, Ávila y Soria, junto a *sieso* (prov. de Ávila y Burgos). La '*l* leonesa' procede de una geminada árabe *qq* en *enxelco* (Lucas Fernández) < ár. *šiqq*, cf. cast. *enjeco* (*DCECH*, s.v. y Seward 1976:164, n. 4).

En cuanto a su extensión geográfica, el fenómeno parece rebasar el dominio leonés. García de Diego (1916) encontró casos de '*l* leonesa' en toda Castilla: *pielgo* en las provincias de Ávila, Burgos, Segovia, Logroño y Soria; *dieldo, lieldo* en Burgos, Ávila, *acaldar* en Santander, Burgos y Palencia, *yelso* en Santander, Burgos, Soria y Segovia, *bilma* < EPITHEMA en Burgos, Ávila, Soria, Segovia, *alnado* en Soria. El ejemplo más claro sería el resultado *nalga* < NATICA, para la que no se documenta ningún correlato castellano.[4] Según el mismo autor, (1916:313), 'el número de casos suscita un problema fundamental en la biología de nuestra lengua; pues demostrar que este fenómeno es un leonesismo valdría tanto como reconocer la participación sustancial del leonés en la formación del castellano'.

Formas con '*l* leonesa' aparecen también esporádicamente en gallego-portugués: *julgar*, junto a *juigar, judgar, juzgar; nalga,* junto a *nádega.* Otro ejemplo posible es el gall. *pelgo,* en los diccionarios gallegos con el sentido de 'brazo de cepa o vid' desde Valladares (1884), con el de 'parche que se pone a los odres o pellejos para tapar herméticamente las aberturas', desde Rodríguez González (1958/61). La palabra fue empleada ya por Sobreira (cf. J. L. Pensado 1979): '*anchear:* hablando del fruto es ensancharse o dilatarse su *pelgo*'. También *pelgueira* 'vara con que se ata el haz de paja para transportarlo' (La Mezquita); *pelgacho* (Novefontes), *pelgato* (Val do Suarna), *peldracho* (Gudiña, Vilardevós), *peldregacha* (Guntín) 'ubre seca' (en García 1985), que parecen proceder de PEDICU. Pero existen motivos para pensar que

---

[4] Corominas (*DCECH*, s.vv) y Galmés (1967:312) consideran estas formas simples leonesismos.

todas estas formas pudieran ser simples préstamos.[5] En gallego-portugués
el tratamiento estrictamente popular parece haber sido la conservación de
la postónica y de la intertónica, con pérdida de la -D- intervocálica
cuando la había (Williams 1938: §§51, 54): *CAVITARE > *cavidar-se*,
CUPIDITIA > *cobiça*, DEBITA > *dívida*, DUBITA > *dúvida*, GABATA > gall.
gábado 'pipa, tonel', NEPETA > gall. *nébeda*, *néboda*; por lo tanto la
propia presencia de la síncopa resulta sospechosa. Además, en casos de
síncopa, existen otros tratamientos para las consonantes finales de sílaba
en competencia con el paso a -*l*. El grupo *b-t* se asimila: SUB(I)TANEU >
ant. *sotanho*, CUBITU > *côto* junto a *côvado*, REPUTARE > *retar* junto a
reptar (probable galicismo). En *b-d* hay asimilación o vocalización como
en castellano: APOTHECA > ant. *abdega* 1147, port *adega*, CAPITALE >
caudal, cabedal, CAPITELLU > *coudel, cabedel*, RECAPITARE > *recadar,
arrecadar, acadar*. Así Machado (1967, s.vv) defiende el carácter leonés
de *julgar*, aunque duda para *nalga*.

1. Estado de la cuestión

A primera vista se diría que todos los autores coinciden en la
interpretación del fenómeno: la primera de las consonantes agrupadas se
ha transformado en *l*. Desde los primeros trabajos sobre el tema en la
segunda mitad del siglo pasado hasta nuestros días, se observa un paso

---

[5] Hay que descartar *melga* (< MELICA, no de MEDICA, cf. Corominas *DCECH*, s.v.
mielga). *Embeldar, embeudar* 'embriagar', mencionadas por Cuveiro (1876) como gallego
antiguo, parecen ser simplemente las formas del *Alexandre*. Algunas formas leonesas
fueron introducidas en los diccionarios gallegos por los primeros lexicógrafos. Antonio
de la Iglesia (1886: III, 78-79), por ejemplo, considera la lengua del *Libro de Alexandre*
muy similar al gallego (J. L. Pensado, comunicación personal). El gallego *celme*
'sustancia, jugo' es relacionado por Corominas (*DCECH*, s.v. *sentar*) con *SEDIMEN*, pero
esta etimología presenta un grave inconveniente: las formas mencionadas por Meyer-
Lübke (*REW*, s.v.) como procedentes de *SEDIMEN (ant. it. *sedime* 'Untergrund', Canavese
sim 'Hof' y *simp* 'Bauernhof', friul. *sedim*) proceden todas de una ī larga. El resultado
prol < *prod* < PRODE también se relacionaría con la '*l* leonesa' según Corominas
(*DCECH*, s.v. *pro*), pero existen varias hipótesis alternativas (cf. R. Lorenzo 1977: II s.v.
prol): una refección analógica a partir del pl. *proes* sobre el modelo de s. *frol* / pl. *froes*
(C. Michaëlis), un cambio *prode* > *prole* en posición intervocálica (Cornu, C. Cunha) o
un cruce con *prole* (cf. infra para otros ejemplos de -*l* final no etimológico).

gradual de la mera formulación de unas correspondencias diacrónicas[6] a la formulación de una verdadera ley fonética.[7] Con todo, bajo la aparente unanimidad se oculta una impresión generalizada de que la transformación de las implosivas en *l* es, en palabras de Millardet (1923:18), 'une transformation étrange'; cf. también Seward (1976). Los cambios que en una descripción superficial parecen muy simples, son en realidad bastante complejos. Esto queda bien patente si se consideran las descripciones pormenorizadas del fenómeno. Según la interpretación de Millardet (1923:18),

> [las formas procedentes de P-T, B-T, T-K, D-K] attestent une différenciation ancienne: occlusive + occlusive > continue + occlusive. Dans *-at(i)cu, jud(i)co*, le remplacement du *d*, devenu plus ou moins spirante, par *l* est tout naturel et comparable au traitement castillan *-azgo, juzgo*. Dans le cas de labiale + occlusive, *capitale* > *caldal*, il est vraisemblable que la différenciation a entraîné tout d'abord la substitution de ɫ vélaire à une bilabiovélaire spirante *cabdal*. Les cas de *dolce* < **dodecim, trelce* < *tredecim* se ramènent au cas de *–aticum*, car *c* devant *e* a eu primitivement, en léonais comme en castillan, la valeur d'une mi-occlusive *ts*. *Muelda* < **movitam*, qui est *muebda* en castillan, est sur le même plan que *caldal* < *capitale*. Il est à peu près de même, bien

---

[6] Gessner (1867:10) y Morel Fatio (1875:31) simplemente describen el fenómeno como cambio de *p, b* en *l* ante *d*. Lo mismo hace Meyer-Lübke (1890: I §538) 'quand la posttonique est précédée d'une consonne devenue spirante avant la syncope [celle ci] devient l < d, ɫ < v'. Más tarde Menéndez Pidal 1906 (= 1962:82-84) se limita a afirmar: 'en los grupos de dos explosivas formados por la pérdida de una vocal latina la primera de las consonantes se hace *l*'. La misma formulación se conserva en Zamora (1967:152-53) y es general en las monografías dialectales.

[7] Toda la discusión del aspecto fonético del cambio se centró exclusivamente en el problema de si habría que partir de consonantes fricativas, como sugería Meyer-Lübke (1890: I §538), u oclusivas, de acuerdo con la contrapropuesta de Staaff (1907: §39, p. 243). Según este autor, si la consonante implosiva fuera fricativa se esperaría más bien una asimilación (**sedze* > ***seze* como PLACITU > *plazo*, cf. infra). Esta hipótesis fue criticada por Krüger (1914:229), quien prefiere partir de una fricativa basándose en su propia experiencia de las hablas actuales y apoyándose en la autoridad de Josselyn. Es preciso darle la razón a Krüger en cuanto al valor de la consonante final de sílaba en la actualidad — aunque eso no implica nada para la plausibilidad mayor o menor de [d] > [l] frente a [ð] > [l] — pero indirectamente su autoridad como fonetista no sale muy bien parada de este párrafo. Krüger no percibió que, salvo en el grupo homorgánico [ld], la segunda de las dos consonantes también es fricativa y así siempre la transcribe como oclusiva. Para este detalle fonético del español hubo que esperar a los estudios de Navarro Tomás. En cuanto a la consonante final de sílaba, después de Krüger todos los autores (Millardet, Grammont) parten de una fricativa.

qu'ici l'ordre des éléments soit renversé, pour *vilva*, lire *biℓba* de *bidba* < *viduam*, mot dans lequel le castillan a résolu la difficulté par une méthatèse: *viuda*. Enfin *selmana* est sorti de **sebmana* < *septimanam:* le groupe *-lm-*, favorisé par l'existence de *-ld-*, *-lg-*, *-lb-*, a permis à la langue d'éviter l'assimilation menaçante de *bm* à *-mm-*, *-m-*. Il y a donc là toute une série de substitutions de phonèmes destinées à parer au danger de l'assimilation.

Una vez que se consideran los ejemplos caso por caso, en lugar de un único cambio aparecen al menos dos: -ð > -l y -ß > ł > l, y un conjunto de contextos dispar: ante *g, d* (o las fricativas correspondientes), *ts, dz, b, m.* Si completamos los casos estudiados por Millardet con los datos de la Tabla 1 habría que añadir también un contexto *t*, y un origen geminado para el que habría que formular una nueva hipótesis: ¿un fenómeno de disimilación?, ¿una epéntesis de *-l*?

No parece que existan fenómenos estrictamente comparables a los supuestos cambios del leonés en otras lenguas. Para *d > l* se citan como paralelos el dialectalismo sabino del latín, por el que alternan LINGUA y DINGUA, OLEO y OLFACIO frente a ODOR, solium y SEDERE (cf. Lindsay 1963: §87, Leumann 1963:155-56) o también CICADA junto a CICALA.[8] En Italia se da la misma evolución en Ischia y Procida *(pélə* 'piede', *vəlitə* 'vedete') y Córcega *(nulu* 'nudo', *rálica* 'radice'; cf. Rohlfs 1966: § 216). En castellano existen varios ejemplos: CODA > *cola,* ant. y vulg. *melecina* (desde Berceo), ant. *lexar > dexar,* con el cambio inverso; en asturiano occidental *lanzare* 'danzar' (cf. Rodríguez Castellano 1952:115; quien observa que la *l-* inicial debe de ser tardía ya que no pasa a *ts-* como en el fondo patrimonial). Pero tanto el fenómeno latino como el italiano y el español son cambios esporádicos y atribuibles a contaminaciones léxicas (cf. Dworkin 1980, Corominas *DCECH,* s.v. *cola*). En otras familias lingüísticas, como en las lenguas del grupo niger-congo, existen alternancias [t] o [d]/[l] que parecen presuponer un paso regular *d > l.* En bandi, loko, loma y mende hay una alternancia grado fuerte [t] grado débil [l]. En nzema [d]/[l] y en serer [t], [d]/[r]/[l] (datos de Ultan 1970).[9] El factor común de estos posibles paralelos es que, a diferencia

---

[8] El paralelo entre el fenómeno leonés y el latino fue establecido ya por Lamano (1915:50).

[9] No se puede deducir claramente en ninguno de estos casos si la lateral se remonta a una fricativa o a una oclusiva (como suponía Staaff 1907, vid. supra nota 7). El cambio va siempre asociado a fenómenos de lenición [d] > [ð] o [d] > [r], pero no se puede descartar que [d] > [l] sea una alternativa a la fricativización. No es posible dejar zanjada

de la '*l* leonesa', se dan en posición intervocálica o inicial de palabra, esto es, en posición inicial de sílaba. No parecen, sin embargo, existir paralelos exactos con un proceso [d] o [ð] > [l] en posición pre-consonántica. Para un cambio fonético [ß] > [ł] no parece existir ningún paralelo. Por otra parte, la supuesta [ł] procedente de [ß] tendría luego que perder su velaridad.[10] En los grupos labial + obstruyente, las lenguas romances presentan sistemáticamente, bien asimilación a la consonante siguiente como en francés (cf. CUBITU > fr. *coude,* TEPIDU > *tiède,* CIVITATE > *cité*), bien vocalización en [u̯] como en provenzal y catalán (CIVITATE > prov., cat. *ciutat,* DEBITA > cat. *deute*). Así, en castellano alternan *beodo, caudillo, ciudad, deuda, duda, recaudar, viuda, raudo* (< RAPIDU o *RAPITU), arag. *treudes* con *codicia, recado* (también port. CUBITU > *côto*), sin vocalización.

Las anormalidades en el conjunto de cambios que habrían dado lugar a la '*l* leonesa' condujeron a algunos autores a intentar matizar su naturaleza. Dicho en términos actuales, no se trataría de cambios fonéticos en el sentido estricto de tendencias articulatorias comunes al conjunto de las lenguas, sino fenómenos condicionados por algún aspecto de la fonología del leonés. Según Staaff (1907:243), el cambio *-dg-* (con [d] oclusiva) > *-lg-* se explicaría como una remodelación de un grupo insólito inspirada en los grupos de *l* + consonante. Más que de un cambio fonético se trataría de una adaptación basada en una regla fonotáctica. Esta interpretación, seguida por Seward (1976), fue criticada explícitamente por Krüger (1914:229), quien no consideraba probable el influjo de otros grupos.

Tampoco Grammont (1939:204-5) consideró el fenómeno como un cambio fonético auténtico:

> Ceux de ces phonèmes qui n'étaient pas sonores et spirantes le sont devenus, puis, la voyelle continuant à agir sur eux, en a fait des *h* sonores, point

---

la cuestión, aunque, como veremos, si nuestra interpretación es correcta, todo esto resulta irrelevante para el leonés.

[10] La fase con [ł] procedente de *-b* había sido postulada ya por Meyer-Lübke (1890: I §538). Staaff (1907) observó que sería de esperar una diferencia entre dos tipos de *-l* en la actualidad y que tal diferencia no había sido notada por Munthe (1887). De hecho tal diferencia no existe (cf. Rodríguez Castellano 1954:172). Para este caso, como para las evoluciones de -L latina la reconstrucción de diferentes tipos de *l* es totalmente ad hoc.

d'articulation vague sur la moitié antérieure du palais, du sommet de la voûte
aux dents. L'*h* est un phonème à glissement, l'*l* est un autre phonème à
glissement articulé dans la même région. La confusion acoustique entre les deux
est facile.

La fase intermedia [ɦ] — extrañamente descrita — debe de ser
un intento de reflejar la erosión del gesto oral. El origen de la '*l* leonesa'
no se encontraría en un cambio lineal, sino que sería el fruto de una
identificación del producto del debilitamiento con el sonido que estaba
fonéticamente más próximo. Esta vez la adaptación estaría condicionada
por el inventario fonético superficial.[11]

A pesar de que ni la interpretación de Staaff ni la de Grammont
resulten satisfactorias, sí parece correcta su intuición de que '*l* leonesa'
no es el resultado de una simple evolución fonética.

2. Existencia de otros resultados

Un aspecto importante de la cuestión que no ha sido observado
más que por Staaff (1907:242), es que la '*l* leonesa' no parece ser la
única solución de los grupos romances. Coexiste con ella la conservación
del grupo, idéntica al resultado del castellano medieval (CUBITU > *copdos*
1140 Eslonza p-43; *prioradgo* 1254, 1260 Leon Staaff 1907, docs. 52, 55;
APOTHECA > *abdega* Sant. 1104 1157; JUDICARE > *jutgar* Fuero de
Avilés; PEDICARE > *apedgar* 1212, *pedgador* Vall. 1260, Staaff 1907 doc.
56.34) y — lo que es más problemático — la vocalización y la
asimilación de la consonante final de sílaba a la siguiente: *LEVITU >
salm. *lludo*, sanabr. *lloudo;* top. ast. *Entragu* (Teverga, junto a *Entralgo*),
SEDECIM > ant. leon. *seze* Staaff 1907, doc. 62.42; SEPTIMANICA o
*SEPPOMANTICA > *Simancas*. No se atestigua nunca la '*l* leonesa' para los
resultados de v-g procedente de –IFICARE como sería esperable por el
paralelo de d-g. Al igual que el portugués, el leonés puede presentar
pérdida de -D- en lugar de síncopa: CUPIDITIA > ant. leon. *cubiçia*,
cobiçiar, cobizante Alexandre O 1704d, *cobizar, cobiciar* Fuero Juzgo,
ast. *cubiciar, cubicia* Sistema; TRITICU > ant. leon. *trigo* 964 León,
Sahagún, Eslonza, *tridigo* 1003 León. De este conjunto de fenómenos se
llega fácilmente a la conclusión de que la '*l* leonesa' no era sino uno de

---

[11] La interpretación de Grammont no ha tenido ningún eco. Rodríguez Castellano
(1952, 1954) es el único en mencionarla sin más comentarios.

entre varios recursos para adaptar los grupos romances: así como el castellano presenta tres resultados, la vocalización o asimilación para las labiales y el paso regular *-d* > *-z* (–ATICU > *-adgo* > *-azgo*) — que no sabemos muy bien qué encubre —, el leonés presenta, además de la '*l* leonesa', una asimilación y una vocalización idénticas a la del castellano, aunque con menor frecuencia. Esto indica que el paso a *-l* no era un cambio fonético regular.

Además, la aparición frecuente de formas con los grupos resultantes de la síncopa todavía intactos indica que la vocalización, la asimilación y el cambio en *-l* eran aún fenómenos en marcha durante los siglos XIII y XIV. Al igual que en castellano, la acomodación de los grupos romances en leonés tiene lugar en el período literario. Por lo tanto, es necesario considerar los resultados de otras [b], [d] o [ß], [ð] finales de sílaba que ya se habían introducido en el romance de la época a través de los latinismos o préstamos romances y de los arabismos.

Los latinismos del español medieval presentan una gran variedad de grafías. Las variantes del ms. O del Alexandre indican que el antiguo leonés presentaba el mismo conjunto de variantes que los otros dialectos: pérdida total, asimilación en una geminada y vocalización.

Tabla 2. Resultados de los grupos con una obstruyente final en cultismos medievales

-bs- > -s-, -us-: *asencio* Poridad de Poridades 74.24, APSICTOS > *isynçio* Alexandre P. 1484a, *osoluçion* Apolonio 21d

-pt- > -t-, -bt-, -ut-: *babtisterio* Fazienda de Ultramar 103.24; *batismo* Razón de Amor 255, *baptismo* Fuero de Soria 113.11, Berceo San Lor. 91c, *vautysmo* Fernán González, *cativaronle* Bonium 114.11; *captiverio* Fazienda de Ultramar 135.2, *cativerio* 135.8, *cautiverio* 198.6; *cativo* Sta. María Egipcíaca 470, Alexandre O 954d, *corrubtas* Poridat de Poridades 52.11, *Egibto* Alexandre P 10a, *rresçebtor* Bonium 163.15, *setiembre* DL 273, 1215, *setentrion* Bonium 164.14, *setenario* Alexandre O 651c

auct- > auct-, aut-, at-, ot-: AUCTORICARE > *auctorjgare* Carrizo 3, *auctorgare* Otero 54, *autorigare* Otero 48, 50, Bravo 5, 9, *autorgare* Bravo 18, *atorgamiento* 1234 DL 226, *atorgar* Cid 198, *otorgar* DL 1184, 305

La conservación hasta nuestros días de resultados geminados o vocalización indica bien a las claras que las obstruyentes finales de sílaba no siempre se perdían sin dejar huella (como se deduciría de Alvar y Mariner 1967: §18). Además, las grafías ultracorrectas permiten reconstruir los procesos a los que se sometían las formas escritas: *abténtico; abtoridat* Nobleza y Lealtad X, Alexandre P 1561d (*octoridat O*); *rrectorico* Alexandre O 1614c, *rrectorica* Alexandre O 261a, 361a. Estas ultracorrecciones son especialmente frecuentes en los documentos más antiguos, de grafía latina, tanto en la zona leonesa como en la portuguesa:[12] *acmentare* 'augmentare' 895 Floriano, *admorem* 1086 S.Vic.Oviedo, *abdominare* 'addominare' 1136 S.Vic.Oviedo, *obprobium* 1145 S.Vic.Oviedo, *zeptionis* 'cessionis' Vega Cartul. 4, AUCTORICARE > *obturgare* 1123 Carrizo, *obtuicare* 1118 Carrizo, *obturcare* 1123 Carrizo; *adput* 'apud' 1097 Bravo; *Sancta Oblalia* 1103 Docs. Med. Port., *ocrasa* 'abrasa' 1107 Docs. Med. Port., *satlutem* 1073, 1103 Liber Fidei. También se puede reconstruir el tratamiento de las obstruyentes en sandhi: *af fundamina* 938 Sahg., *sub Cchristi* 938 Sahg.

Las grafías del español medieval dejan entrever una situación idéntica a la del español estándar y sus variedades regionales: pérdida total (*séptimo* > vulg. *sétimo*), asimilación en una geminada (*étnico* > vulg. [énniko]) y debilitamiento en una fricativa (vulg. [éθniko] en Castilla la Vieja). La vocalización es especialmente característica del asturiano (cf. Rodríguez Castellano 1954:158-59): *leición, faición, faicioso, aición; difeuto, pruyeutu, trayéutu, pirfeutu, Pirfeuta, efeutu, dialeutu, direutu, autu, oución, cunceutu, Cunceición*. Tanto es así que el rasgo ha sido adoptado por el estándar bable de la Academia de la Llingua Asturiana: *inaceutable, aceiciones, carauter despeutivu*. El gallego y el portugués se caracterizan también por preferir la vocalización ya desde época medieval: RAPSARE > ant. port. *roussar*, MAGDALENA > ant. port. *Moudalena, Moudanella*, que actualmente compite con la introducción de una vocal epentética (cf. Câmara 1968).

En la mayor parte de los casos los cultismos contienen una consonante sorda tras la implosiva (*-bs-, -pt-, -kt-, -ukt-*) de modo que no es esperable que se identificaran con los grupos romances, que presentan mayoritaria — aunque no exclusivamente — una sonora. A pesar de ello

---

[12] Los datos son míos. Las abreviaturas son las de Menéndez Pidal (1950). Además: Floriano = Floriano (1949/51), Carrizo = Fernández Catón (1982), Bravo = Fernández Catón (1973), Docs. Med. Port. = Azevedo (1940), Liber Fidei = Costa (l965/78).

se dan casos de '*l* leonesa'. En los dialectos hispánicos existe una total confusión en los resultados de la familia del latín vulgar ADAPTU 'apto'. Junto a *adapte* 'alto, noble' Alexandre O, 2142c, aparece una forma *altezas* (esto es, *apteza*) en el sentido de 'aptitudes, dotes, grandeza, riqueza' en el v. 394a del ms. O del Alexandre (en el v. 2142d, por el contrario, hay *alteza* en P y *apteza* en O).[13] También el provenzalismo *captener* (Berceo) aparece en asturiano y santanderino como *caltener, caltenencia*.

En el contexto AD + consonante sonora hay una coincidencia perfecta entre los cultismos y los grupos romances. A menudo, sobre todo en verbos que comienzan por *a-*, aparece *al-*, que parece el resultado de una confusión con el prefijo AD-. El resultado -*l* tampoco se limita aquí al dominio leonés: ADVERTERE > ast. *alvirtir* Vigón 1955, *alvertir* salm. y amer., ast. *alborrecer, albortar, alcontrar* 'encontrar', *alpenzar* 'empezar' Vigón 1955, *ADMORDIU > almuerzo*, port. *almoço*, junto a *aversario* Alexandre O 39c, en P *aduersario*.[14]

El paralelo con los grupos romances también es perfecto en los escasos arabismos que presentan los mismos grupos. Para ár. *rutba, nudba* existen soluciones con conservación, con metátesis del grupo o con pérdida de la implosiva: *ronda* J. Ruiz, *rodva* s.XIV, *rovda, roda, robda* 1274 'impuesto que se pagaba por los ganados'; *anutba, annubda, annutuba, annuteba* (tambien port. *anudiva, annuduva, anubda, anupda*). En el caso de *rubţ*, al lado de las formas *arobda* (Cid), *robda* y *ronda*, se registra una variante leonesa y portuguesa con -*l*: *rolda*, gall.port. *roldar* 'andar de ronda, à noite'. Corominas (*DCECH* s.vv *guisante, rebato*) recoge varios ejemplos de fluctuación de las obstruyentes finales de sílaba en palabras latinas transmitidas a través del árabe o del mozárabe. En ellas alternan la conservación de la obstruyente, su vocalización y su paso a -*l*, -*r*.[15] CAPICELLU > *alcaucil, alcarcil, alcancil;*

---

[13] No sería este el único caso de -*l* procedente de una obstruyente final de sílaba en aragonés: cf. ant. arag. *aladma, alalma* < ANATHEMA (cf. Malkiel 1946).

[14] Podría pensarse en una atracción por el artículo árabe (cf. infra) pero esta hipótesis tiene en su contra que no siempre existen sustantivos tipo ***alvierto*.

[15] Esta vacilación incluye también una nasal. Corominas relaciona con ella formas como gall. *engo* 'yezgo' (*DCECH*, s.v. *yezgo*) y (s.v. *rebato*) *epilensia, finso* — que se insertarán más bien en la vacilación de las nasales ante continuas — y, en posición final (s.v. *guisante*), ár. *al-ʕaqrab* > cat. *arreclåu, alacrán*. Un paso -*l* + consonante sorda

alcancil; CAPITELLU > *Caudiel, Qartíl;* CAPUT AQUAE > *Alqibdaq,
(Al)caudete, Alcardete, Alcandete;* MEDICA > *mielga, amenka;* PISU
SAPIDU > *bisalte, guisante.* La variación es idéntica a la que se da en
posición final: *rabâb > rabé, rabel; muhtasab > almotacén,* port. ant.
almotacel; alfeñique; alfil ant. *alfid, alfiler, alfinete,* que es inequívoca-
mente un fenómeno determinado por la acomodación a los finales
admisibles (cf. Steiger 1932:346, Wagner 1934:238-42; también Méndez
Dosuna y C. Pensado 1990:94-95, para la evolución inversa). Esto
demuestra que también en posición interior estas variantes se deben a
fenómenos de acomodación. En conclusión, si se comparan los resultados
de los grupos romances con los de grupos de otros orígenes, se deduce
que ni la '*l* leonesa' es exclusivamente leonesa, ni tan siquiera es regular
en territorio leonés.

3. Pérdida de -L final de sílaba

Falta añadir a este conjunto de vacilaciones un aspecto clave: la
pérdida de la -L final de sílaba, que recientemente se ha convertido en el
ejemplo típico de cambio esporádico en español (cf., p.ej., Hartman
1986), pero ya Schürr (1927:499) concluía: 'Gerade die Ergebnisse der
Entwicklung von $l^{Kons.}$ im Romanischen müssen ... davon überzeugen, daß
der Begriff des Lautgesetzes, so wie er früher gefaßt wurde, hinfällig ist:
es gibt nur Mischung'. Piel (1932:100) e incluso Menéndez Pidal
(1950:107) tienen opiniones muy parecidas.

En español y portugués existen casos de vacilación entre -*l* y $\emptyset$
en todos los contextos consonánticos: CULMINE > esp. *cumbre,* port.
cume, ULMU > esp., port. *olmo,* ULVA > esp. *ova,* PULVUS > esp. *polvo,*
SALTU > esp. *soto,* port. *souto,* ALTU > esp. port. *alto* (pero *otero,
outeiro*), incluso en grupo romance: *PULLITRU > esp. *potro,* frente a
SOLUTU > esp. *suelto, soltar* port. *solto, soltar* (para un estado de la
cuestión, cf. Malkiel 1975). Los datos castellanos y portugueses ni

---

n + consonante sorda, que no ha recibido hasta el momento una explicación fonética,
tiene paralelos en latín vulgar *cuntellum* (por CULTELLUM, App. Probi 197), en el Sur de
Italia (Rohlfs 1966: I §245) y en griego antiguo, en algunos dialectos del grupo dórico
y en arcadio (Buck 1955: §72). Sin embargo no existen paralelos de una sustitución
indiscriminada de sonidos orales finales de sílaba por nasales. Sería preferible considerar
los resultados nasales como un argumento a favor de la interpretación de esas consonantes
como reposiciones.

siquiera permiten reconstruir el patrón de difusión: es imposible saber si, como se defiende habitualmente para los dialectos italianos y para el franco-provenzal (cf. Schürr 1927, Rohlfs 1966), el cambio se inició ante las dentales o no.[16]

La vacilación no es un rasgo exclusivo del español y portugués, sino que aparece ya en latín vulgar y se da en todas las lenguas romances. Resultado de esta vacilación es la frecuente introducción de una -*l* no etimológica. Algunas de estas falsas regresiones tuvieron lugar ya en época latina (cf. Schuchardt 1866: II, 493-99), pero también han podido repetirse ya en época romance. Así, aparecen en Guittone di Arezzo *aldo* 'odo', *galdendo* 'godendo'. Estas falsas regresiones son frecuentes en el ladino de los Dolomitas (cf. Tuttle 1989:736, y en prensa) donde AL + dental > *au* > *o* y más tarde hay una introducción ultracorrecta de -*l*: AUDIRE > *oldir*, AUSARE > *olsar*, CAUSA > *colsa*. Un resultado de estas confusiones es it. *saldare* (< *sodo*, *soldo* < SOLIDU; cf. Corominas *DCECH*, s.v. *saldar*). Las regresiones son especialmente frecuentes en catalán (cf. Kuen 1929, Coromines 1971:302, *DECLLC*, s.v. *colze*). Los antiguos *gauta, deume, Palaudá* han pasado a *galta, delme, Palaldá*, y alternan ant. *adautar, aaltar, azautar* < ADAPTARE procedentes de -P. Algunos de estos ejemplos son idénticos a la '*l* leonesa': prerrom. **gauota* > *gauta, galta*, CUBITU > *colze, copde, code, cólser, coude*, MALE HABITU > *malaute, malalt*. El paralelismo entre los resultados del catalán y el leonés ha sido claramente percibido por Corominas (*DCECH*, s.v. *viuda*), a propósito de la forma *vilva* de R. Llull, 'forma que sólo indirecta y secundariamente viene a coincidir con el leonés antiguo *vilva*'. Corominas reconstruye el proceso leonés de la manera siguiente:

---

[16] Sería posible revisar esta generalización habitual entre los romanistas. Tal vez el fenómeno comenzara ante las consonantes continuas, donde el grupo constituido era menos aceptable (cf. la difusión de la pérdida de las nasales o la aspiración de *s*). Con la única excepción de *m* todas las continuas romances son dentales o alveolares. Precisamente dos de los casos con probable reposición ultracorrecta de -*l* en período latino (SAGMA > *salma*, καθμα > *calma*; cf. infra) se dan ante *m*. Los datos del latín vulgar no corresponden al presunto contexto: CAUCULUS, AUBIA en manuscritos y καυκουλατορι del Edicto de Diocleciano (cf. Schuchardt 1866: II, 493-99 para muchos más ejemplos de vocalización temprana en contextos no dentales). La restricción a un contexto dental pudo ser un fenómeno posterior. Es interesante que el contexto dental o alveolar de las alteraciones de -L en época romance parece apoyar una base [l]. La reconstrucción tradicional [ɫ] haría esperar un contexto velar o incluso labial, antes que dental — cf. infra el inglés americano.

Es evidente que el moderno *viuda* resulta de una transposición en la forma
etimológica, y se podría dudar de que la -*b*- interna de la forma *vibda (bibda)*
correspondiera realmente a la pronunciación, pues si *vidu̯a* pasó directamente
a *viu̯da*, mas bien podríamos creer que la -*b*- fuese una ultracorrección
meramente gráfica, según el caso de *cibdad, cabdillo, cabdal,* más tarde
pronunciados con *u̯*. Algo de esto pudo haber en algunos de los casos, pero en
otros la forma *vibda* correspondió a la pronunciación y hubo de ser muy
antigua, pues sólo partiendo de una consonante podemos llegar a la *l* de la
forma leonesa *vilda.*

El propio Corominas documenta casos de falsa regresión en
castellano, similares a los catalanes e idénticos a los que aparecen en
italiano y portugués: καῦμα > it. *calma* (> fr. *calme*), esp. y port. *calma,*
PEGMA o PEGMATIU > *pemaço, pelmaço* Alexandre, SMARAGDU >
esmaragde Alexandre O 1469a, *esmeraldo* P., *esmeralda* h.1295,
esmerada Canc. Baena, port. *esmeralda; Bagdad > Baldac (DCECH,* s.v.
esmeralda), SAGMA > *salma,* S. Isidoro > *enjalma, jalma,* it. *salma,* esp.
salma, port. *xalmas.*[17] Es difícil saber si las coincidencias entre las tres
lenguas han de explicarse por préstamo, por una regresión en romance
común (Vidos 1939:274-75) o por la reproducción del proceso en cada
lengua de manera independiente, como piensa Corominas para *esmeralda*
donde la *l* 'se explicaría por el paso de G a *u* y castellanización de esta
u según el modelo del sufijo -*aud* = -*aldo*'. Obviamente, las regresiones
específicas de cada lengua, como el ant. port. *algua < augua,* no admiten
más que esta última explicación. Todos estos fenómenos romances
representan un paralelo perfecto de la '*l* leonesa': después de todo, el
catalán *vilva* y el leonés *vilva* sí pueden proceder de evoluciones
idénticas.

3.1. Pérdida de -*l* sin vocalización

Podría objetarse que las regresiones del catalán y del castellano
difieren de la '*l* leonesa' en que, mientras que en ellas se reemplaza un
wau por *l*, en el dominio leonés son poco frecuentes las formas con
vocalización de obstruyentes finales de sílaba (aunque existe *lleudo*), que
serían necesarias para la confusión con -L. Esta dificultad nos lleva a
reconsiderar las fases intermedias en el proceso de pérdida de -L.

---

[17] Cf. Cornu (1888:728, n.4), Vidos (1939:274-76), Schürr (1927:496).

Pese a ser una opinión común entre los romanistas, no es en absoluto necesario que la pérdida de *-l* se produzca a través de una velarización y vocalización en wau. La pérdida de *-l* es un proceso gradual en que el gesto oral va debilitándose progresivamente, tal como lo intentó describir Grammont. El producto de ese debilitamiento no tiene ya oclusión oral (cf. Ladefoged y Maddieson 1986:106) y, aunque se conserve un vestigio de articulación, puede no tener sonido (cf. Nolan 1990 para la importancia de estos vestigios). Los distintos resultados de *–l* son producto de la reinterpretación de este residuo.

El segmento resultante del debilitamiento de [l] puede ser acústicamente muy parecido a una vocal. En el caso de una [ɫ] velar es parecido a una *u* laxa [ɷ], pero no tiene redondeamiento (cf. Ladefoged y Maddieson 1986:106, Wells 1982: I, 258-59). El paso a [o̞] o [u̞] es ya un proceso de acomodación al sistema fonológico. No es extraño que la asimilación a una yod en la sílaba siguiente pueda alterar el resultado en [i̯] como se ve en el asturiano actual: cf. *conceición* vs. *conceuto*.

Junto a la reinterpretación como una semivocal existen otras posibilidades de evolución. En primer lugar, ese residuo inaudible puede perderse por completo. Esto es posible incluso para [ɫ] velar. Wells (1982, III: 550-51) señala que, en el sur de los Estados Unidos, la *l* 'oscura' se pierde ante una labial o velar en palabras como *help, bulb, golf, shelve*. La posibilidad de una pérdida directa de *-l* es aún más clara en el caso de [l] alveolar.[18] También hay una pérdida total de *-l* final de palabra en francés y en rumano. El proceso comenzó en el francés medieval (cf. Pope 1934:155-56, 324, Straka 1968:288): *fil* [fi], *outil* [uti], *saoul* [su] y todavía se produce en francés moderno especialmente ante consonante o glide, con carácter variable, en el pronombre sujeto (*il, ils, elle, elles*) y también, con otra posición en la sílaba y con una frecuencia mucho menor, en los pronombres clíticos de tercera persona (*lui, la, les, leur*; cf. Ashby 1984). En rumano actual existe un proceso de pérdida de *-l* final de palabra, que afecta especialmente al artículo *-ul* (art. det. masc. sing.) > [u] — incluso reflejado en la grafía en los numerosos patronímicos en *-u* < *-ul*: *Popescu, Ionescu, Eminescu* — y a algunas palabras aisladas: *Mihai(l)* (cf. Nandriş 1963:141-42). Hay testimonios similares sin aparición de diptongo en Italia, tanto en el norte (Voghera *kad* 'caldo', *kadréi* 'caldarino', *vota* 'volta' *skǘpe* 'scalpello', *savja*

----

[18] No hay que olvidar que el carácter velar de la *-l* final de sílaba en período romance es una pura hipótesis.

'salvia'; Lombardía *tap* < TALPA) como en el sur (Castro dei Volsci: *atə* 'altro', *vota* 'volta' *pusə* 'polso'); cf. Schürr (1927:498), quien pretende explicar estos resultados por vocalización seguida de pérdida del wau.

Según Penny (1978:45), en Tudanca se aprecia un debilitamiento extremo, cuando no la pérdida total, de *-l* final de sílaba. Un debilitamiento análogo debe de ser el motivo de la frecuente aparición de una *-l* no etimológica en asturiano actual: *maltraca* 'matraca' (Casomera), *kilmera* 'quimera, riña' Casomera, *mostaldietsa* 'comadreja', *albierto* Casomera, Villar (en Rodríguez Castellano 1952:112, 115). La forma *rebilbar* 'reanimarse una persona muy débil' (Besullo) mencionada por Rodríguez Castellano (1954) parece proceder de *vivo*. Una secuencia más complicada de sustituciones (cf. n. 15 supra) es la que presuponen *estreldo* 'ruido, estrépito', *estreldar* 'hacer ruido', en Miño *estrueldo, estrueldar* (cf. Menéndez García 1963), que según Corominas (*DCECH* s.v. *atuendo*) procederán de *atruendo, estruendo* y no de STREPITARE como propuso García de Diego. Fenómenos semejantes se registran en otras zonas del dominio leonés. Así, Lamano (1915:54) menciona salm. *salvia* 'savia', aparte de otras formas que podrían tener otra explicación (cf. infra). Al menos una de estas formas se ha impuesto en la norma castellana: *esquilmar,* ant. y dial. *esquimar* < κῦμα (cf. Corominas *DCECH*, s.v.). La pérdida total es la reconstrucción comúnmente admitida en casos en que *-l* era el primer elemento de una coda compleja: SALICE > *salz* > *saz*, CALICE > *calz* > *caz* (cf. Corominas, *DCECH* s.vv).

Otra posibilidad es que *-l* se asimile por completo a la consonante siguiente. Esta es la solución que suelen adoptar las lenguas que disponen de una serie de consonantes geminadas. Dentro del romance se encuentra a menudo en dialectos del sur de Italia (Rohlfs 1966: I, 338-39: cal. merid. *caddu* 'caldo', *caddara* 'caldaia', Messina *sòddu* 'soldo', luc. merid. (Tursi) *sukk* 'solco', *upp* 'volpe', *kakkáñ* 'calcagno'). El resultado geminado es idéntico al de las obstruyentes finales de sílaba (cf. tosc. -AVIMUS > *-ammo*). La asimilación puede resultar incluso de una semi-consonante: tosc. FUIMUS > *fummo*. La asimilación es también una de las variantes en la evolución actual de *-l* en andaluz y en español de América: Santo Domingo *puppo* < *pulpo, amma* < *alma, aggo* < *algo* (Alonso 1953:301). E. F. Tuttle (per litteras) me señala una última posibilidad. Según Vignoli (1911 [non vidi]) en Castro dei Volsci, tras la pérdida de *-l*, se daría un alargamiento de la vocal precedente: *v[ō]ta* 'volta', *d[ū]ce* 'dolce'.

Son especialmente interesantes las evoluciones que se aprecian actualmente en sardo, porque coexisten tres posibilidades de evolución. En aquellas zonas que conservan o han adquirido una -*l* final de sílaba, esta — que es plenamente alveolar — sufre un proceso de debilitamiento (cf. Contini 1987: II, mapas 69-72). El debilitamiento tiene lugar ante consonantes de cualquier punto de articulación. La consonante resultante es siempre más larga, según la descripción de Contini, quien la transcribe como geminada en sílaba tónica. En el extremo noroeste de la isla y en el noroeste del Logudoro, ante labiales -*l* puede debilitarse en [i̪] o simplemente dar lugar a una geminada (Contini 1987: I, 370-73): Codrongianus CARBONE > *calbone* > [kai̪vóne], CORVU > *colvo* > [kói̪v(v)u] (informante M. N., 61 años); pero [kavvóne], [kóvvu] (informante A. R., 16 años). En la misma zona hay debilitamiento ante una velar sorda: [lk] > [ɬk] con una lateral fricativa. Los resultados de -*l* se pueden confundir entonces con los de -*s*, que también se debilita, reinterpretándose como [ʃç] palatal o [xx] velar: FALCE > [fáɬke, fáiɬke, fáiʃçe, fáxxe], pero también PASCHA > [páɬka] (Contini 1987: I, 303-4). Paralelamente [lg] > [fifi], con una fricativa postvelar sonora: ALGA > [áfifia] 'ordure', PURGARE > *pulgare* > [pufiáre] (Contini 1987: I, 308-13). En el noroeste del Logudoro, ante africadas alveolares [lts], [ldz] > [ls], [lz] > [ss], [zz] predorsales: HORDEU > [óldzu] > [ólzu], [ózzu] (Contini 1987: I, 279-84). También hay un resultado [tt] < [lt] en el Campidano de Oristano: ALTU > [átto].

Si realmente la -*l* se pudo perder sin vocalización habría una solución muy simple para un problema que siempre ha intrigado a los hispanistas.

En casos como port. *doce, ensôsso, enxôfre* (junto a ant. y pop. *enxúfre*), *potro, cume*, gall. ant. *mogir, mugir* < MULGERE, no se dan los diptongos *ou̯, oi̯* esperables (no hay **doice, etc). Además, tales diptongos ni siquiera están atestiguados. Nunes (1945:82, 137) inserta estos ejemplos en un conjunto de monoptongaciones explicables por la posición átona o por dialectalismo (hay monoptongación en Tras-os-Montes, en la Beira y en el sur), pero ninguna de estas explicaciones es convincente.[19] Lo más sencillo sería suponer que nunca hubo tal diptongo. Una fase intermedia sin vocalización explicaría igualmente la vacilación entre resultados *o, u* < ŬL del castellano y el portugués.

---

[19] Según Nunes (1945:83, n.2) *bôbo* < BALBU sería castellanismo.

Mientras que *u* es casi regular para ŬLT (MŬLTU > cast. *mucho*, port. *muito*), donde triunfó la vocalización en [i̯], en los restantes contextos hay gran vacilación. El ejemplo típico es cast. *soso* y port. *ensôsso*, con *o* y sin palatalización, frente a *empujar* < IMPULSARE con *u* y palatalización (cf. Malkiel 1975, Harris-Northall 1990:59-60).[20] También Ŭ seguida de labial en castellano plantea el mismo problema: *duda* vs. leon. *dolda, dulda*. Si nuestra hipótesis es correcta, la vacilación dependería de que hubiese o no vocalización. La yod o el wau procedentes de la vocalización de -L cerrarían la vocal — si es que no hay que partir de la conservación de Ŭ provocada por la contracción de [u̯u] cuando la vocalización era del período del latín vulgar. En cambio si la -L se perdía sin vocalización, habría el desarrollo regular Ŭ > *o*.[21]

3.2. Asimilación de -*l* en arabismos

Otro caso de pérdida de -*l* con asimilación total es la regla morfofonológica del árabe que asimila el artículo determinado '*al*- a las letras 'solares' (dentales y alveolares; cf. Smith 1953:64-65, Steiger 1932:374-76). A pesar de la asimilación, se mantiene en la grafía *l* (aunque acompañada de *tašdîd* para indicar la geminada resultante). En iberorromance a menudo los resultados no corresponden a la fonética árabe. Hay vacilación entre formas con y sin asimilación ante dentales y alveolares: *alnafe ~ anaf(r)e, altramuces ~ atramuces; alraual ~ arrabal; aldúcar ~ adúcar; aljarefe ~ ajarafe; arcidriche ~ axedrez* (con un paso -*l* > -*r*). O, por el contrario, aparece una asimilación inesperada ante labiales o velares: *auoroz ~ alborozo; aguacil ~ alguazil; abbuelbola ~ albuerbola; aiumada ~ aljumada*. También se ha añadido -*l* en *almirante*, donde la *a*- no era un artículo. La confusión de palabras patrimoniales con arabismos está en el origen de formas como *almorejo, almendra* (port. *a(l)mêndoa), almidón, almena, almeja, almorrana*. Para el

---

[20] Corominas (*DCECH*, s.vv *empujar, rebosar*) supone una evolución en *u* totalmente regular a base de descartar PULSU como base de *poso* (< PAUSARE), VULSARE para *rebosar* (< ant. *revessar*), INSULSU para *soso* (< INSALSU), y postulando *PUTTRU o *PUTRU (que no explicaría la -*l* de *poltro* [doc. leonés de 939, Menéndez Pidal 1950:323-24, 214 y port. y gallego *poldro*]) para *potro*. Esta solución obliga a separar el problema castellano del portugués, que es idéntico: *potro* (junto a *poldro), dôce, enxôfre*. El propio Corominas (*DCECH*, s.v. *soso*) admite las dificultades: INSALSU haría esperar un portugués **souso*.

[21] Ya Piel (1932:99) sugería para port. *dôce, ensôsso* 'o *l* ... se fundiu no *s* seguinte'.

salmantino, Lamano (1915) menciona *albarca, albondo, halbelidad*. Esta vacilación pudo ser otro de los factores que contribuyeron a la reposición tardía de *-l* en iberorromance y a la aparición de la *'l* leonesa'.

4. Interpretación de la '*-l* leonesa'

Sería, pues, posible que la -L en iberorromance se hubiese perdido sin vocalización, con o sin asimilación a la consonante siguiente. Esto es, los resultados de -L podrían haber sido idénticos a los de las obstruyentes de los latinismos y los arabismos, donde la vocalización es una posibilidad más junto a la pérdida o la asimilación. A partir de una situación con vacilación: [entráᵇɣo] / [entráˠɣo], [kóᵝðo] / [kóᵇðo], [sáldᶻe] / [sádᶻe] / [sáddᶻe] / [sáu̯dᶻe], pueden producirse confusiones entre las formas de una y otra serie. Una prueba de esto es la confusión en sentido inverso en la estrofa 778 de Juan Ruiz transmitida por el manuscrito S de Salamanca que hace rimar *sabçe-yaze-cabçe-plaçe* (líneas más arriba, en 776a escribía *sauzes*). El factor determinante de la confusión debieron de ser las variantes geminadas, que se daban en ambas series y, a diferencia de las formas con pérdida total, conservaban una huella de la consonante final de sílaba que podía provocar la ultracorrección. Esto proporciona una explicación para la *'l* leonesa' procedente de *-d-dz-* (*trelce*) o *-ss-* (*yelso, sielso*): una geminada conservada hasta época anormalmente tardía podía entrar en el juego de confusiones. La solución *-l* para las obstruyentes implosivas, posible también en castellano, se generalizó en leonés, aunque — es importante ponerlo de relieve — nunca llegó a ser totalmente regular. La *'l* leonesa' no es el resultado de una evolución fonética, ni siquiera una adaptación como proponían Staaff o Grammont, sino de una pura ultracorrección.

Tales fenómenos son relativamente frecuentes en romance. Junto a los señalados más arriba, existen ejemplos clásicos como el estudiado por Gilliéron: la sustitución de *fl* por *kl* en dialectos de oïl (Poitou *kya*, Saintonge *klị̂â*, Allier *xlo* 'fléau') a través de una fase común [hl']. En los dialectos meridionales del español y en español de América aparecen formas como *piesna, mislo* (también *arquitesto* 'arquitecto'), ultra-correcciones provocadas por la igualación de las consonantes finales de sílaba en [h] (cf. Alonso 1953:319-22). Casos de sorprendente parecido con la *'l* leonesa' se dan en el norte de Italia, especialmente en ladino de los Dolomitas (cf. Tuttle 1989:739 y en prensa). La igualación entre -L, AU y las obstruyentes labiales finales de sílaba se produce, según las zonas, en *-l, -u* o *-f, -v.* En Val Badia AUCA > [ālca], AUDIT > [ālda], LAUDAT > [lālda], PAUSAT > [pālsa] como ALTU > [ālt], CALIDU > [cālt]. En Val Gardena *áuda, láuda, páusa* siempre como *áut, tʃaut.* En cambio en las Giudicarie *kaft* 'caldo', como *aft* 'alto', *aftro* 'altro', *luvdar* < LAUDARE, *pufsar* < PAUSARE. También en Reggio Emilia, Piacenza y en romañolo hay *kavsa/kefsa* < CAUSA, *keft* < CALIDU, *levd* < LAUDO.

El fenómeno de la '*l* leonesa' matiza la caracterización habitual del leonés: el leonés no es simplemente un dialecto más arcaico que el castellano, sino deliberadamente arcaizante: elige de entre varias soluciones la más conservadora. Esta tendencia arcaizante puede llevar a ultracorrecciones. Un caso claro es la falta de diptongación, que va acompañada de diptongación excesiva. También los diptongos decrecientes ultracorrectos se dan desde los primeros documentos. La '*l* leonesa' es una manifestación más — aunque excesiva — de lo que Menéndez Pidal (1950:450) llamó la 'protesta culta' del reino astur-leonés.

Referencias

Alonso, Amado. 1953. *-r* y *-l* en España y América. *Estudios lingüísticos: temas hispanoamericanos.* 263-324. Madrid: Gredos.

Alvar, Manuel y Sebastián Mariner. 1967. Latinismos. *Enciclopedia lingüística hispánica.* 2.307-24. Madrid: CSIC.

Ashby, William J. 1984. The elision of /l/ in French clitic pronouns and articles. En *Romanitas: Studies in Romance linguistics* (Michigan Romance Studies, 4) ed. Ernst Pulgram, 1-16. Ann Arbor: Department of Romance Languages, University of Michigan.

Azevedo, Rui Pinto de (ed.) 1940. *Documentos medievais portugueses. Documentos particulares. Volume III. A.D. 1101-1115.* Lisboa: Academia Portuguesa da História.

Buck, Carl Darling. 1955. *The Greek dialects. Grammar, selected inscriptions. Glossary.* Chicago: University of Chicago Press.

Câmara, J. Mattoso. 1968. Muta cum muta in Portuguese. *Word* 24.286-89.

Contini, Michel. 1987. *Étude de géographie phonétique et de phonétique instrumentale du sarde.* 2 vols. Alessandria: Edizioni dell'Orso.

Cornu, Jules. 1888. Die portugiesische Sprache. *Grundriß der romanischen Philologie*, ed. G. Gröber, 1.715-803. Strassburg: Karl J. Trübner.

Coromines, Joan. 1971. Les vides de sants rosselloneses del manuscrit 44 de París. *Lleures i converses d'un filòleg*. Barcelona: Club Editor, 276-362 (originalmente en *Anales del Instituto de Lingüística* 1943, 3.126-211).

_____. *DECLLC* = 1980-. *Diccionari etimològic i complementari de la llengua catalana*. Barcelona: Curial y Caixa de Pensions 'La Caixa'.

_____, con la colaboración de José A. Pascual. *DCECH* = 1980-. *Diccionario crítico etimológico castellano e hispánico*. 5 vols. publicados. Madrid: Gredos.

Costa, P. Avelino de Jesus (ed.) 1965/78. *Liber fidei sanctae bracarensis ecclesiae*. 2 vols. Braga: Junta distrital de Braga.

Cuveiro Piñol, Juan. 1876. *Diccionario gallego*. Barcelona.

Dworkin, Steven N. 1980. Phonotactic awkwardness as a cause of lexical blends: The genesis of Sp. *cola* 'tail'. *Hispanic Review* 48.231-37.

Fernández Catón, José María. 1973. Documentos leoneses en escritura visigótica. Fondo M. Bravo del Archivo Histórico Diocesano de León. *León y su historia. Miscelánea histórica*. 2.203-95. León: Fuentes y estudios de historia leonesa.

_____. 1982. Documentos leoneses en escritura visigótica. Fondo del archivo del Monasterio de Carrizo. *Archivos Leoneses* 72.195-291.

Floriano Cumbreño, A. C. 1949/51. *Diplomática española del período astur*. Oviedo: Instituto de Estudios Asturianos.

Galmés de Fuentes, Álvaro. 1967. Dialectalismos. *Enciclopedia lingüística hispánica* 2.307-24. Madrid: CSIC.

García, Constantino. 1985. *Glosario de voces galegas de hoxe. Verba*, anexo 27. Santiago: Universidade de Santiago.

García Arias, Xosé Lluis. 1988. *Contribución a la gramática histórica de la lengua asturiana y a la caracterización etimológica de su léxico*. Uviéu: Universidá d'Uviéu.

García de Diego, Vicente. 1916. Dialectalismos. *Revista de filología española* 3.301-18.

García Rey, Verardo. 1934. *Vocabulario del Bierzo*. Madrid: Centro de Estudios Históricos.

Gessner, E. 1867. *Das Altleonesische. Ein Beitrag zur Kenntniss des Altspanischen.* Berlin.

Grammont, Maurice. 1939. *Traité de phonétique.* Paris: Delagrave.

Harris-Northall, Ray. 1990. *Weakening processes in the history of Spanish consonants.* London: Routledge.

Hartman, S. L. 1986. Learned words, popular words and 'first offenders'. En *Studies in Romance Linguistics,* ed. O. Jaeggli y C. Silva Corvalán, 87-98. Dordrecht: Foris.

Iglesia, Antonio de la. 1886. *El idioma gallego. Su antigüedad y vida.* La Coruña: Latorre y Martínez.

Krüger, Fritz. 1914. *Studien zur Lautgeschichte westspanischer Mundarten.* Hamburg: Mitteilungen und Abhandlungen aus dem Gebiet der romanischen Philologie. Seminar für romanische Sprache und Kultur.

Kuen, Heinrich. 1929. Kat. *colze. Butlletí de dialectologia catalana* 17.46-50. También en *Romanistische Aufsätze,* por Heinrich Kuen, 1970.12-15. Nürnberg: Hans Carl.

Ladefoged, Peter y Ian Maddieson. 1986. Some of the sounds of the world's languages (preliminary version). *UCLA Working Papers in Phonetics* 64.

Lamano y Beneite, José. 1915. *El dialecto vulgar salmantino.* Salamanca: Tipografía popular. (Reimpr. Diputación de Salamanca: Salamanca 1989).

Leumann, Manu. 1963. *Lateinische Laut- und Formenlehre.* München: Beck.

Lindsay, W. M. 1963. *The Latin language.* New York: Hafner.

Lorenzo, Ramón. 1977. *La traducción gallega de la Crónica General y de la Crónica de Castilla. II Glosario.* Orense: Diputación de Orense.

Machado, J. P. 1967. *Dicionário etimológico da lingua portuguesa.* 2ª ed. Lisboa: Confluência.

Malkiel, Yakov. 1946. Antiguo judeo-aragonés *aladma, alalma* 'excomunión'. *Revista de filología hispánica* 8.136-41.

_____. 1966. Form versus meaning in etymological analysis: Old Spanish *auze* 'luck'. In *Estudios dedicados a James Homer Herriott,* 167-83. Madison: Universidad de Wisconsin.

_____. 1975. En torno al cultismo medieval: los descendientes hispánicos de DULCIS. *Nueva revista de filología hispánica* 24.24-45.

Méndez Dosuna, Julián y Carmen Pensado. 1990. How unnatural is Spanish *Víctor → Vict-ít-or*? Infixed diminutives in Spanish. En *Naturalists at Krems. Papers from the Workshop on Natural Phonology and Natural Morphology (Krems, 1-7 July 1988)*, ed. Julián Méndez Dosuna y Carmen Pensado, 89-106. Salamanca: Universidad de Salamanca.

Menéndez García, Manuel. 1963. *El cuarto de los valles (un habla del occidente asturiano)*. Oviedo: Instituto de Estudios Asturianos.

Menéndez Pidal, Ramón. 1906. El dialecto leonés. *Revista de archivos, bibliotecas y museos* 10.128-72, 294-311. (Reed. Oviedo: Instituto de Estudios Asturianos, 1962).

_____. 1950. *Orígenes del español*. 3ª ed. Madrid: Espasa-Calpe.

Meyer-Lübke, Wilhelm. 1890. *Grammaire des langues romanes*. Paris: H. Welter.

_____. REW = 1935. *Romanisches etymologisches Wörterbuch*. 3ª ed. Heidelberg: Winter.

Millardet, Georges. 1923. *Linguistique et dialectologie romanes*. Montpellier: Société des Langues Romanes / Paris: Champion.

Morel Fatio, Alfred. 1875. Recherches sur le texte et les sources du Libro de Alexandre. *Romania* 4.7-90.

Munthe, Åke W:son. 1887. *Anteckningar om folkmålet i en trakt af vestra asturien*. Uppsala: Almqvist & Wiksell. Traducción española *Anotaciones sobre el habla popular de una zona del occidente de asturias*. Trad. de Mª. Berta Pallares, ed. de Ana Mª. Cano González. Uviéu: Universidá d'Uviéu, 1988.

Nandriş, Octave. 1963. *Phonétique historique du roumain*. Paris: Klincksieck.

Nolan, Francis. 1990. Who do phoneticians represent? *Journal of Phonetics* 18.453-64.

Nunes, José Joaquim. 1945. *Compêndio de gramática histórica portuguesa*. 3ª ed. Lisboa: Livraria Clássica.

Pattison, David G. 1973. The Latin suffix -ATICU in Early Old Spanish. *Vox Romanica* 32.60-65.

Penny, Ralph J. 1978. *Estudio estructural del habla de Tudanca*. Beihefte *Zeitschrift für romanische Philologie*, 167. Tübingen: Niemeyer.

Pensado, J. L. (ed.) 1979. Fr. Juan Sobreira. *Papeletas de un diccionario gallego*. Orense: Instituto de Estudios Orensanos 'Padre Feijoo'.

Piel, Joseph M. 1932. Da vocalização do 'l' em Português. *Biblos* 8.95-101.

Pope, Mildred K. 1934. *From Latin to Modern French with special consideration of Anglo-Norman: Phonology and morphology.* Manchester: Manchester University Press.

Rodríguez Castellano, Lorenzo. 1952. *La variedad dialectal del Alto Aller.* Oviedo: Instituto de Estudios Asturianos.

_____. 1954. *Aspectos del bable occidental.* Oviedo: Instituto de Estudios Asturianos.

Rodríguez González, Eladio. 1958/61. *Diccionario enciclopédico gallego-castellano.* Vigo: Galaxia.

Rohlfs, Gerhardt. 1966. *Grammatica storica della lingua italiana e dei suoi dialetti.* Torino: Einaudi.

Sas, Louis F. 1976. *Vocabulario del Libro de Alexandre. Boletín de la Real Academia Española,* Anejo 34.

Schuchardt, Hugo. 1866. *Der Vokalismus des Vulgarlateins.* Leipzig: Teubner.

Schürr, Friedrich. 1927. Sprachgeschichtliche-sprachgeographische Studien II. TALPA, MUS, RATTUS — *l* vor Kons. im Romanischen. *Zeitschrift für romanische Philologie* 47.492-513.

Seward, Thomas A. 1976. The peculiar Leonese dialectal forms *dulda, portalgo, selmana,* etc: A problem in diachronic phonology. *Hispanic Review* 44.163-69.

Smith, Harlie Lawrence, Jr. 1953. *The phonology of Arabic loanwords in Old Spanish.* Ph.D. University of Minnesota. Ann Arbor: University Microfilms.

Staaff, Erik. 1907. *Étude sur l'ancien dialecte léonais d'après des chartes du XIIIe siècle.* Uppsala: Almqvist & Wiksell.

Steiger, Arnald. 1932. *Contribución a la fonética del hispano-árabe y de los arabismos en el iberorrománico y el siciliano. Revista de filología española,* Anejo 17.

Straka, Georges. 1968. Contribution à la description et à l'histoire des consonnes L. *Travaux de linguistique et de littérature* 6.267-326.

Tuttle, Edward F. 1989. Ladinisch: Areallinguistik. En *Lexicon der romanistischen Linguistik,* ed. Günter Holtus, Michael Metzeltin y Christian Schmitt, 3.733-42. Tübingen: Niemeyer.

_____. en prensa. Considerazione pluristratica degli esiti di AU e AL + alveodentale nel Norditalia. Comunicación presentada al XVIII Congreso internacional de lingüística y filología románica (Trier, mayo 1986).

Ultan, Russell. 1970. Some sources of consonant gradation. *Working Papers on Language Universals.* Language Universals Project, Stanford, California, 2: Cl-C30.

Valladares Núñez, Marcial. 1884. *Diccionario gallego-castellano.* Santiago: Imprenta del Seminario Conciliar Central.

Vidos, B. E. 1939. *Storia delle parole marinaresche italiane passate in francese.* Firenze: Olschki.

Vignoli, Carlo. 1911. Il vernacolo di Castro dei Volsci. *Studj romanzi* 7.117-296.

Vigón, Braulio. 1955. *Vocabulario dialectológico del concejo de Colunga. Revista de filología española,* Anejo 63.

Wagner, Max Leopold. 1934. Etimologías españolas y arabigo-hispánicas. *Revista de filología española* 21.225-47.

Wells, J. C. 1982. *Accents of English.* 3 vols. Cambridge: Cambridge University Press.

Williams, Edwin B. 1938. *From Latin to Portuguese.* Philadelphia: University of Pennsylvania Press.

Zamora Vicente, Alonso. 1967. *Dialectología española.* 2ª ed. Madrid: Gredos.

The Spanish Suffix -*(i)ondo*

David Pharies

University of Florida

This article is meant to contribute toward a work that is sorely lacking in the field of Spanish historical linguistics, a work that might be entitled 'Orígenes de los sufijos españoles', or, since ideally the scope of the study will go beyond the question of origins, 'Historia de los sufijos españoles'. To date, the only book that might have legitimately laid claim to one of these titles, had it not included prefixation and compounding as well, is Alemany Bolufer's *Tratado de la formación de palabras en la lengua castellana* (1920), an outstanding achievement for its time, but hardly adequate today in light of the strides that have been made in allied fields such as dialect lexicography, dating, etymology, and morphological theory. What is needed now is a work that presents more than simply an etymon and a listing of transparent General Spanish derivatives for each suffix: it should also provide a more or less definitive list of derivatives from all Hispanic dialects (or, in the case of productive suffixes, a representative list), together with analysis of dialectal distribution, grammatical form-class, meaning, chronology, and comparative data, all woven into a succinct history focusing on the suffix's point or points of origin, and its subsequent stages of development, including documentation of levels of productivity, relationships with other suffixes or word-formational processes, and convergences with identical but nonsuffixal endings. This is the method that has been worked out over the last forty-five years by Yakov Malkiel in his masterful studies of Romance suffixation, and which I have tried to apply in my recent studies on Sp. -*aina* (Pharies 1989-90) and the Ibero-Romance -*nc-/-ng-* suffixes (Pharies 1990).

The data presented below were culled from reverse and etymological dictionaries, the *DRAE*, and from 16 dictionaries of regional

Hispanic dialects, both Peninsular and Insular.[1] Contrary to my practice in the works cited above, I present the data here by category, rather than in a dictionary-like format at the beginning of the essay.

The Base Layer

The base layer of Hispanic derivatives in -*(i)ondo* comprises eight Castilian deverbal adjectives, all of which, with the (no doubt arbitrary) exception of *moriondo*, were first attested between 1450 and 1735. They are, in order of appearance:

> **cachondo** Sp. adj. 'dícese de la perra salida' [1450], 'dominado del apetito venéreo' (*DRAE* 221), Argot adj. 'caliente, con excitación y deseo sexual', 'divertido, bromista', 'aplicado a una mujer, sexualmente atractiva', 'persona muy alegre, jovial, divertida', 'persona obsesionada por los placeres del sexo' (León 44), And. adj. 'guasón, persona aficionada a tomar el pelo' (Alcalá Venceslada 110). According to *DCECH* (1:728), *cachorro* 'puppy', 'cub' 'parece ser derivado de *cacho*, que hoy sólo subsiste en acepciones secundarias, pero que significaría primitivamente "cachorro"; es probable que proceda del lat. vg. *CATTULUS, por reduplicación afectiva y diminutiva del lat. CATULUS "id."' This same *cacho*, combined with -IBUNDUS, must have produced *cachondo*, 'reducción de *cachiondo* por absorción de la *i* en la otra palatal, formado como *torionda* ... '
>
> **botiondo** Sp. adj. 'dícese de la cabra en celo' [1475], 'dominado del apetito venéreo' (*DRAE* 198); vars. *butiondo* [1490] (*DRAE*), Ast. *bitonda*, *bitondia* 'id.' (Cano González 90). According to *DCECH* (1:608), these are derivatives of *bode*, Sor. *bote* 'billy goat', or possibly verbal derivatives of these, combined with the suffix -BUNDUS to indicate a female animal in heat.

---

[1] The reverse dictionaries were Faitelson-Weiser 1987 and Bosque and Pérez Fernández 1987; the etymological dictionaries were the *DCECH* and *DEEH*, and the dialect dictionaries were Andolz 1984 and Rohlfs 1985 for Aragonese, Guerra 1977 for Canary Island Spanish, Iribarren 1984 for Navarrese, Viudas Camarasa 1980 for Extremeño, Alcalá Venceslada 1980 and Cepas González 1985 for Andalusian, Alonso Garrote 1947 and Marcos Casquero 1979 for Leonese, Vigón 1955 and Cano González 1982 for Asturian, Goicoechea 1971 for Riojan, García-Lomas 1949 for Montañés, León 1980 and Oliver 1985 for Spanish Argot, and García Soriano 1932 for Murcian.

toriondo Sp. adj. 'dícese de la vaca en celo' [1492] (*DRAE* 1278); vars.: Rioj. *turionda* n. f. 'vaca en celo' (Goicoechea 169), Extr. *torrionda* (Viudas Camarasa 169), Nav. *torienda*, Gal. *touronda*, Sal. *torondia* 'id.' (*DEEH* 1013-14). Though the ultimate etymon is clearly *toro* 'bull', the *DCECH* (5:559) claims that this derives from **torir* 'montar el toro a la vaca', together with -BUNDUS.

hediondo Sp. adj. 'que arroja de sí hedor', 'molesto, enfadoso e insufrible', 'sucio y repugnante, torpe y obsceno', 'planta' (*DRAE* 698), Extr. adj. 'enfermo, dolorido' (Viudas Camarasa 95); vars.: archaic Sp. *fediondo, hidiondo* [1492], And. *heyondo* 'arbusto leguminoso' (Alcalá Venceslada 318), And. *jeyondo* adj. 'hediondo' (Alcalá Venceslada 344), Extr. *hiyonda* n. f. 'gallina' (Viudas Camarasa 99), Can. *jediondo* n. m. 'mala persona, despreciable, mujer ruin', 'insulto, ofensa semiseria', 'pobre de solemnidad' (Guerra 196). The word is a derivative of Lat. FOETĒRE 'to stink', often attributed to the Vulgar Latin stage (as *FOETIBUNDUS), even though the word is not represented elsewhere in Romania.

sabiondo Sp. adj., n. 'que presume de sabio sin serlo' [1512] (*DRAE* 1165); vars.: Sp. *sabihondo*, Nav. *sabirondo* (Iribarren 474). *DCECH* (5:114) remarks: 'Se trata de un derivado a la manera de *hediondo* ... (-IBUNDUS) y no de un compuesto con *hondo*.' The fact that the *-h-* of *sabihondo* is the result of a popular etymology is affirmed as well by *DRAE* (1165) and Alemany Bolufer (1920:88).

ardiondo Sp. adj. 'lleno de ardor o coraje' [ca. 1600] (*DRAE* 114). The word is traced by both *DRAE* and *DCECH* (1:318) to a hypothetical *ARDIBUNDUS 'id.' < Lat. ARDĒRE 'to burn'.

verriondo Sp. adj. 'aplícase al puerco y otros animales cuando están en celo' [1735], 'dícese de las hierbas o cosas semejantes cuando están marchitas, o mal cocidas y duras' [1735] (*DRAE* 1335), Argot adj. 'excitado sexualmente' (Oliver 307); vars.: Sp. *verrionda* 'ramera' [1631] (*DCECH* 5:791), Arag., Nav. *barrionda* 'cerda en celo' (Andolz 35, Iribarren 81), Arag. *barronda* adj. 'dícese de la cerda en celo' (Andolz 35), Extr. *berriondo* (Viudas Camarasa 21), Nav. *berranda, barrienda*, Salm. *berrondia, berreonda* 'id.' (*DEEH* 1058). The etymon is a lost reflex of Lat. VERRES 'boar', whence Sp. *verraco* 'id.'

moriondo Sp. adj. 'dícese de la oveja en celo' (*DRAE* 896); vars.: Leon. *marionda* n. f. 'oveja en celo', Sp. *murionda*, Gal. *maronda* 'id.' (*DEEH* 801), Ast. *marondia, marrondia* adj. 'aplícase a la oveja en celo' (Cano González 326, 327). *DCECH* (4:157) traces Sor. *murionda* to an unattested OSp. **marir* 'to be in heat (ewe)' + -BUNDA. As for the stem, *DCECH* points to a probable pre-Roman root as represented in Sp. *morueco, marueco* 'ram', cf. Basque, Nav. *marro, barro*, Alav. *marrón*, Sor. *mureco*, cat. *marrá*, Oc. *màrrou* 'id.'

The etymon of the formant *-(i)ondo* in these cases is clearly Lat. -I-BUNDUS, described by Kühner and Holzweissig (1966:1.994)[2] as a suffix for deriving, from verbs usually of the first, second, or third conjugations, adjectives synonymous with the verbs' present participles, with an added nuance of intensification and duration. Examples include ERRĀBUNDUS 'wandering' (< ERRĀRE 'to wander'), MĪRĀBUNDUS 'wondering' (MĪRĀRĪ 'to wonder, be astonished'), PUDIBUNDUS 'modest, bashful' (< PUDĒRE 'to be ashamed'), FURIBUNDUS 'raging' (< FURERE 'to rage'), FREMEBUNDUS 'roaring' (< FREMERE 'to roar'), MORIBUNDUS 'moribund' (< MORI 'to die'), LASCĪVĪBUNDUS 'wanton' (< LASCĪVĪRE 'to sport, be wanton'). One notes that whereas in the case of -ĀRE and -ĪRE, the respective theme vowel is used as a connector, both -ĒRE and -ERE employ -ĭ- for this purpose.

By all measures, the survival of -BUNDUS into Romance was precarious. Though Langlois (1961) lists ca. 150 Latin words in -BUNDUS, he considers only 11 to be 'usual', and even these failed to be popularly transmitted into Romance. The comparative grammars of Diez (1874:2.349) and Meyer-Lübke (1890:2.601) register new derivatives incorporating the suffix in only one Romance language other than Spanish, viz. Old Provençal,[3] which has only four: *desiron* 'desirous' (< *desirar*), *fadion* 'deceived', 'disappointed' (< *fadiar*), *sazion* 'satisfied' (< *saziar*), all cited by Diez, plus *gauzion* 'glad' (< GAUDIBUNDUS), cited in

---

[2] For further information on -BUNDUS, see Langlois (1961).

[3] Adams (1913:320) lists only two of these, while Ronjat (1937) lists none. It is even possible that some of the items listed may not derive from -BUNDUS. Whereas Diez had included OProv. *volon* among -BUNDUS derivatives, the *FEW* (14:616) traces this word directly to VOLUNTAS. Under *satiare* in the *FEW* (11:239), *sazion* is listed without reference to -BUNDUS.

REW (3703). The *REW* proposes three Rumanian derivatives in addition — *căscăund* 'stupid' (< *CASCĀBUNDUS 'striking'), *flămând* 'hungry' (< FLAMMĀBUNDUS 'burning'), and *plăpînd* 'tender' (< PALPĀBUNDUS 'fondling') — but these were all rejected by Cioranescu (1966). Rohlfs (1954: vol. 3) fails to mention -BUNDUS in his account of Italo-Romance derivation, while Darmesteter (1932:66) mentions the Latin suffix only to state that it 'n'a point passé en français'.

This last statement is meant to refer exclusively to popular transmission, as French, like most Romance languages, has its share of learned words whose etyma contained -BUNDUS, e.g., *nauséabond* 'nauseating', *vagabond, pudibond, moribond,* and *furibond.* Catalan, Spanish, Portuguese, and Italian all incorporate several more, including Cat. *errabund, meditabund,* Sp., Ptg. *sitibundo, furibundo,* Ital. *fremebondo, gemebondo.*

Considering the fact that none of the Classical Latin derivatives in -BUNDUS managed to be transmitted popularly into Romance, it is surprising that the suffix survived at all. That it did survive and enjoy a period of modest productivity is proven by the Provençal and Spanish reflexes, but there is some question about when this period of productivity might have taken place. The probably arbitrary fact that Diez formulated a hypothetical Latin base *FOETEBUNDUS (sic) for *hediondo* and not the others may explain why Hanssen (1913:148) claimed that the ending spread at the Romance stage from *hediondo* to *sabiondo, toriondo, verriondo,* and *cachondo*; it may also explain why the *REW* felt no need to formulate Vulgar Latin etyma for these words. The selection of *hediondo* for leader-word distinction is not easy to justify, however, as it is not the earliest to appear (1492, later than *cachondo, botiondo, toriondo*), and does not belong to the semantic core of the group, which refers to female animals in heat. Corominas (1941:156), in contrast, referred to the form -BUNDU as 'productiva ya en latín, y así nacieron *hediondo, sabiondo,* y los numerosos (sic) que indican animales en celo ... ' Here again, the phrase 'ya en latín' seems a bit exaggerated, in view of the lack of documentation of such words in Latin texts or correspondences with Provençal. One might more reasonably conclude that some of the original -BUNDUS words remained viable in the local vernacular well into the Proto-Romance stages of Provençal and Castilian, long enough to motivate new derivations of an idiosyncratic nature, after which the original derivatives died out.

The Castilian derivatives are eccentric in several respects. Formally, we notice that they apparently no longer admit stems in -ĀRE, so common in Latin and exclusive in Provençal, judging by the universal presence of -i- as a connecting vowel, except in *cachondo*, where, Corominas argued (1941:156), it was absorbed by the palatal consonant. Corominas further reasoned that, since -BUNDUS served to derive adjectives from verbs in Latin, 'todos estos adjectivos vienen de antiguos verbos en -*ir* con el significado de "cubrir el macho a la hembra" como cat. *boquir* (cabríos), *marrir* (ovinos), aran. *taurí* (bovinos). En castellano estos verbos han sido sustituidos por vocablos en -*ecer*: *morecer*, *verrecer* (Lamano), arag. *abuquecer* "cubrir el macho cabrío a la cabra".'

Several aspects of this account may be inaccurate. First, I question the assumption that all of these adjectives are deverbal. The fact that the alleged verbal stems are unattested in Castilian is problematic, and this, coupled with the fact that each of the core group of -(I)ONDO derivatives is easily identifiable with a noun stem, leads to the suspicion that the Hispano-Romance incarnation of -BUNDUS may have expanded its grammatical scope to include nouns as input. This is the case with the further development of the suffix, as I will show below, and it is also suggested by the fact that the stems of the two words that appeared earliest — *cachondo* and *botiondo* — are of non-Latin origin, and have left no trace of verbal derivatives of any kind.

Even admitting deverbal derivation, I cannot accept Corominas's assertion that all such stems must have been -*ir* verbs. One wonders if he forgot *ardiondo*, *hediondo*, and *sabiondo*, all transparently derived from -*er* verbs. If this claim was made, as seems likely, to explain the -*i*- connecting vowel, it is unnecessary, since, as shown by the Latin data cited above, both -Ē- and -Ĕ- verbs also employed -Ĭ- (which in hiatus would have closed to -*i*- in Romance) in this position.

My final objection concerns Corominas's semantic account. A hypothetical verbal stem meaning 'to cover a female animal (said of a male animal)', combined with -BUNDUS, would have produced the meaning 'covering a female animal constantly', not 'desiring to be covered by a male animal', which is in fact the meaning of such words as *toriondo*, *moriondo*, etc. Rather, the verb would have to mean 'to desire to be covered by a male animal'. Cat. *boquir* does indeed mean 'cubrir el boc (les cabres)', but, significantly, it has no -BUNDUS derivative.

Subsequent Derivatives

There is a second group of derivatives in *-(i)ondo*, all first attested in 20th-century lexicographical works. Although the actual date of coinage is impossible to determine, the assumption that they appeared subsequently to those of the base layer is supported by formal and grammatical differences between the two groups. The ten words are presented below:

bajonda Nav. adv. (*Allá* -) 'allá abajo' [Aguilar de Codés, para sus habitantes, todo pueblo vecino está 'allá bajonda'] (Iribarren 74). The etymon is *(a)bajo* 'down'.

bolondro[4] Mont. adj. 'torpe, negado, cabezota' (García-Lomas 59), (Alcalá Venceslada 93); derivs.: And. *bolondrón* n. m. 'tolondrón, porrazo, chichón', 'bola grande que los niños emplean en sus juegos' (Alcalá Venceslada 93), And. *borondo* 'cáncamo que llevan las jábegas para poder tirar de ellas' (Cepas González 45), And. 'canto rodado' (Alcalá Venceslada 96), And. *rebolondo* adj. 'esférico' (*DRAE* 1414), And. *rebolondo, reborondo* adj. 'redondo, persona o animal pequeño y grueso' (Alcalá Venceslada 528). Although in some cases the link is substantially obscured by confusion of liquid consonants, all of these words are derivatives of *bola* 'ball' (< OProv. *bola* 'id.' < Lat. BULLA 'bubble', 'ball', per *DCECH* 1:616): All are semantically derivable from the concept of 'ball', especially in terms of 'roundness'. The *DRAE* considers that *rebolondo* involves a blend with *redondo*, but this complication is unnecessary once the presence of the suffix *-ondo* is recognized.

cacarrondo Nav. n. m. 'despectivo que se aplica a personas y a cosas' (Iribarren 105). This definition is insufficient to allow certainty of identification, but there is little doubt that the stem is *caca* 'excrement', cf. the Nav. derivatives *cacarruta* 'cagarruta: bolita de excremento del ganado lanar y cabrío', 'despectivo de personas y objetos', *cacarrutiar, -ciar* 'arrojar cacarrutas las ovejas y cabras' (ibid.)

---

[4] The *-r-* in cases such as these is epenthetic, and general enough for Coromines to refer to it, on several occasions (e.g., *DCECH* 4:126, regarding *molondro*), as '*r* repercusiva'. I hope to investigate this phenomenon further in the near future.

echondo Nav. n. m. 'solanar, paraje soleado' ['He oído preguntar por una persona y contestar: "está en el echondo de tal sitio", porque en estos pueblos suele haber dos o tres, donde la gente toma el sol en invierno.'] (Iribarren 216). The etymon is the verb *echar* 'to lie down', cf. Sp. *echadero* 'sitio a propósito para echarse a dormir o descansar' (*DRAE* 502).

esfarrondón Extr. n. m. 'desconchado en la pared' (Viudas Camarasa 67). This word, along with Arag. *esfarachar* 'quebrantar el lino', Zam. *esfaragullar* 'deshacer', Gal. *esfarrapado* 'con harapos', Cast. *farpa* 'cortadura en el borde de las telas', Extr. *farrajar* 'romper, partir' (*DEEH* 170), Extr. *esfarrajar* 'rasgar una tela', Ast. *(d)esfarrapar* 'estrapar, estrujar, aplastar' (*DCECH* 3:318) all derive from a single root which is most clearly represented in *harapo* 'rag, tatter'. For the suffixoid *-apo* see Wagner (1943:329-47) where he discusses 'die *-p-* und *-f-*-haltigen suffixartigen Bildungen'.

golondro Sp. n. m. 'deseo y antojo de una cosa' (*DRAE* 669), Mont. 'chichón, tolondro' (García-Lomas 159); var.: *golondrón (de)* Ast. 'dícese cuando se bebe algo a tragos muy grandes, de tal manera que es muy fácil atragantarse' (Cano González 297). These are derivatives of *gola* 'throat' < Lat. GULA 'id.', whose Basque reflex, *gura*, has the meaning 'deseo de comer o beber', 'deseo' (*DEEH* 717). The Mont. meaning is the result of confusion with either the formally similar *tolondro* 'lump, swelling', or the family of *golondrina*, cf. *golondrino* 'swallow', 'tumor under the armpit', the latter explained by *DCECH* (3:165) as 'colgado ahí como el nido de la golondrina bajo el alero'.

pediondo And. adj. 'que se pee mucho, pedorrero' (Alcalá Venceslada 463); var: And. *pellondo* 'sucio, maloliente' (Cepas González 243). Both are reflexes of Lat. PĒDERE 'to fart', the latter either simply misspelled by Cepas González (cf. *hediondo*, And. *heyondo*), or associated with *pellejo* 'skin' by popular etymology.

pisondera Mont. n. f. 'nevatilla (motacilla alba)', 'muchacha presumida y pizpireta que anda con ligereza y pasitos cortos' (García-Lomas 238). The direct reference to the typical gait of the wagtail indicates that the origin is Sp. *pisar* 'to tread on', cf. the derivatives Sp. *pisón* 'piece of wood used to crush gorse', Arag. *pisadera* 'loom pedal' (*DCECH* 4:565).

porrondo Arag. adj. 'desastrado, que va enseñando las carnes' (Andolz 227); derivs.: Arag. *porrondón* adj. 'demostración de cariño, esp. a los niños' (Andolz 227), Nav. *porrondoco* n. m. 'tronco o rama de árbol que no puede hacerse astillas y se destina a la lumbre' (Iribarren 426). *DCECH* (4:677) identifies *porro* as a regional variant of *puerro* 'leek', a plant whose bulb-like appearance explains Sp. *porra*, Sant. *cachiporra* 'club, truncheon', and presumably Nav. *porrondoco* 'tree trunk'. The reference to nudity is explained by Corominas through the expression *en porreta* 'desnudo', where *porreta* refers to the green leaves of the leek. The endearment 'little leek' is self-explanatory.

verdiondo Mex. adj. 'se dice del fruto en sazón, cuando no llega todavía a la madurez perfecta' (Santamaría 1959:1111). This word, derived from *verde* 'green', and phonetically similar to *verriondo*, is synonymous with *serondo*. One wonders whether the latter two factors figured in its formation.

Formally, it is notable that only two of the 10 have the full form *-iondo*.[5] This is a first indication that the strict standards of the OSp. rule might be (further) deteriorating, something that is confirmed by the grammatical analysis. In the first place, the output of *-(i)ondo* is no longer solely adjectival. Though *bolondro*, *pediondo*, *porrondo*, and *verdiondo* are adjectives, *bajonda* is an adverb, and the remaining five are nouns. Granted, adjectives convert to nouns quite easily in Spanish, and it is easy to imagine this function for **esfarrondo* 'flaking', **posondo* 'tail-wagging', and *cacarrondo* ***'filthy'. The expansion of input categories I alluded to above is very much in evidence here. Of the ten examples, only *pediondo* fits the classical 'verb > adjective' pattern. Three others have verbal stems, i.e., *pisondera*, *echondo*, and *esfarrondón*, whose *es*-prefix indicates a probable etymon **esfarrondar*. All other stems are nonverbal, including three nouns (*cacarrondo*, *golondro*, *bolondro*), one adjective (*verdiondo*), and one adverb (*bajonda*).

Semantically, the new derivatives are notable for the absence of the strong connection with the concept of animals in heat, or any other

---

[5] Of course it could be argued, as Corominas did for *cachondo* (see above), that the palatal consonants of both *echondo* and *bajonda* absorbed the yod.

aspect of animal life (exception: *pisondera*). On the other hand, despite the lack of verbal stems, the nuance of intensification seems to have remained intact. *Allá bajonda* must be particularly far down there, *bolondro* unusually blockheaded, and *cacarrondo* quite disgustingly unpleasant. The pejorative nuance attached to many of these emanates from the stems (*caca*, *peder*, *porro*) rather than the suffix, which merely intensifies the traits of the input denotation.

In terms of dialectal distribution, the suffix is strongest in the north, where six of the ten have arisen (Nav. *bajonda*, *cacarrondo*, *echondo*; Arag. *porrondo*, Mont. *bolondro*, *pisondera*). *Golondro* is the sole Castilian contribution, the southern dialects of Extremadura and Andalusia have one each (resp. *esfarrondón*, *pediondo*), while *verdiondo* is the one American contribution.[6]

Convergences

It has been repeatedly demonstrated (e.g., in Pharies 1989-90, 1990) that the task of separating words that actually incorporate a given suffix from words that involve an identical but nonsuffixal sequence can be very difficult indeed, since it may be complicated by such things as borrowing, template modeling, nontransparent root-forms, and suffix substitution. In this section I will attempt to sort out these strains as they apply to *-(i)ondo*.

The concentration of derivatives in Navarrese alerts the analyst to the possibility that the Basque language may be involved in some way, and this is indeed the case. Three of the *-ondo* words in Iribarren (1984) are direct borrowings from Basque:

bestondo Nav. n. m. 'voz vasca que significa "después de la fiesta", pero que se aplica al estado de desmadejamiento, sequedad de boca, sueño y mal temple que sigue a una noche o a un día de juerga' (Iribarren 86). Azkue (1:160) cites Basque *bestondo* 'malestar del cuerpo o desmadejamiento después de un

---

[6] The dearth of American examples may be due, to some extent, to the less intensive coverage of American Spanish in my data. Faitelson-Weiser (1987), however, is heavily slanted toward American Spanish, since its database includes a dictionary of Americanisms plus individual lexicons of the dialects of Panama, Texas, Cuba, Venezuela, Colombia, Bolivia, Peru, and Argentina.

día de extraordinaria comida', probably a derivative of *besta* 'party' (presumably < Lat. FESTA 'id.'[7]) and *-ondo* 'consequence of', 'afterwards' (on which see below).

garondo Nav. n. m. 'nuca' (Iribarren 269) < Basque *garondo* 'cerviz, nuca' (Azkue 1:331).

sutondo Nav. n. m. 'tronco grande que arde en el hogar' (Iribarren 495). The word is Basque, cf. Azkue (2:239) *sutondo* 'junto al fuego'.

It turns out that *ondo* is a Basque word that, as is often the case in this language, can function as a suffix. Azkue (1905:2.113), whose information is supplemented by López Mendizábal (n.d.:482) and Villasante (1974:113), discerns, among others, the following suffixal meanings for *-ondo*, which closely parallel its functions as a separate word: (1) 'near to' (*ibayondo* 'near the river' < *ibai* 'river'), (2) 'after' (*bazkalaondoan* 'after eating lunch' < *bazkaldu* 'to eat lunch'), and (3) 'plant, trunk' (*sagarrondo* 'apple tree' < *sagar* 'apple'). The Navarrese words cited above exemplify 'near to' (*sutondo* 'near the fire', cf. *sutalde* 'brazier', *sutoi* 'forge'), and 'after' (*bestondo* 'after the party' < *besta* 'party'). I am unsure of the function of *-ondo* in *garondo* 'nape of the neck', which Azkue (s.v. *garando* 'id.', 2:327) derives from *gara*, which means, among other things, 'height'. The presence of these borrowings, plus especially the case of *bestondo*, whose root is possibly of Latinate origin, raises the possibility that Basque *-ondo* might have made its way into Romance, to converge with -BUNDUS. I would maintain that it has not, since none of the functions of Basque *-ondo* are discernible in the words clearly derived within Romance, including, significantly, Navarrese *bajonda, cacarrondo,* and *echondo*.

The next convergent category comprises a set of words in which *-ond-* is, in my opinion, not a suffix, but a template-determined sequence. The following words pertain to this class:

cabirondo And. n. m. 'raquis de la mazorca del maíz' (Alcalá Venceslada 107). Referring as it does to the tip of the corncob, this word must be traceable to And. *cabirón* 'id.' (ibid.), probably an elaboration on Sp. *cabo* 'end'.

---

[7] I have the editors of this volume to thank for this suggestion.

corrondilla Arag. n. f. 'corredilla, ventaja que se da a otro en las carreras, bien de distancia o de tiempo' (Andolz 78); var.: Arag. *correndilla* (ibid.). *Corredilla* derives transparently from *correr* 'to run, to race' (cf. *DCECH* 2:209), and actually appeared first with the epenthetic nasal consonant [16th cent.]. In *corrondilla* we see the effects of vocalic harmony, executed by the template.

dingolondango Arag. n. m. 'expresión que significa el balanceo de una cosa y también el parrandeo, de un lado a otro' (Andolz 101). As I explained in *Structure and Analogy* (Pharies 1986: 176), this word derives from an onomatopoeic root *din, dan* 'sound of bells', cf. the synonymous Cat. *dinc-danc*, Ital. *dindon*, Prov. *din-dan*, Gasc. *din-dàn*, *dingou-dangou*, and Basque *dingilin-dangolo* 'limping'. The sequences *-olo-* and *-nd-* are products of two different templates.

florondón Arag. n. m. 'forúnculo, divieso' (Andolz 142), probably from *florón* 'large flower' (*EI* 2023), with template extension *-ón* > *-on-d-ón*.

haronda Extr. n. f. 'cerda' (Viudas Camarasa 94). In view of the archetypal laziness of pigs, this is a probable expansion of Sp. *harón* 'lerdo, perezoso', itself < Ar. *ḥarûn* 'balky horse'.

pichorrondón Arag., Nav. adj. 'aplícase a la persona mostrándole que se le quiere mucho' (Andolz 220, Iribarren 413). In Navarrese, *pichorro* is a local variant of *pitorro* 'spout'. The endearment amounts, therefore, to 'little spout'.

pingolondangas Mont. n. f. 'forma familiar del cast. *pingo*' ['La culpa de ello la tienen esas pingolondangas de mis hermanas.'] (García-Lomas 236); var.: Mont. *mingorondangos* 'se refiere a los vestidos llamativos' (García-Lomas 205). Template modeling can explain a change *pingo* + *-angas* > *pingolondangas* (see below). As for the variation *p-* / *m-*, cfr. Murc. *mindango* 'good-for-nothing'/ Sp. *pindanga* 'whore', Col. *mirringo* / *pirringo* 'small (boy)'.

zamborondón Sp. adj., n. 'zamborotudo, tosco, grueso y mal formado' (*DRAE* 1364). In *Structure and Analogy* (Pharies 1986:235) I derive this word from *zambo* 'knock-kneed' (*EI* 4231) 'cross-eyed' (*DCELC* 4:818), combined with *-ón* and a certain amount of template modeling.

This is not the proper place for a complete exposition of the template modeling process. For readers unfamiliar with the phenomenon, I refer to the introductions of Pharies 1986 and 1990, both of which contain extensive explanation. The particular template involved in most of these cases is covered in Chapter Eleven of *Structure and Analogy* and on pp. 9-16 of *Origin and Development*. Essentially, I argue there that a word such as *pichorrondón* is to be segmented as *pich-orr(o)-on-d-ón*, i.e., without any unit *-ond-*. The function of the dental stop in such words, I claim, is esthetic, in that it prolongs and emphasizes the syllable boundary, thereby altering the rhythm of the words in a way that Spanish speakers presumably find pleasing. The phenomenon is in no way limited to instances of *-ond-*, cf. Can. *fulandango* 'so-and-so' (< *fulano* 'id.' + *-ango*), And. *flojindango* 'slob' (< *flojo* 'lazy' + *-ango*), nor indeed to *-n-*; cf. *zarabutear* / Cub. *zarambutear* 'to muddle'; Sor. *titirivaina* / Murc. *titirimbaina* 'idiot'; *moñiga* / Cub. *moñinga* 'cowchip'. Other words in this same subcategory are *zamb(o)-or(o)-on-d-ón* and *ping(o)-ol(o)-on-d-angas*, both of which involve another template as well, the same one found in *ding(o)-olo-n-dango*, where however it is the *-d-* that is etymological and the preceding *-n-* that is template motivated. *Cabirondo*, *florondón*, and *haronda* involve the simple addition of *-do* / *-da* to *-ón* to produce what is apparently, and might be mistaken for, *-ondo*. I cannot actually prove that *-ondo* is not present in a word such as *flor-ond(o)-ón*, of course, but I strongly doubt this, since *-ón* accounts for the augmentation, and since, in a case such as *haronda* (< *harûn*), the presence of *-ondo* is definitely ruled out. Finally, *corrondilla* belongs in this category even though both *-n-* and *-d-* are part of the *-end-* suffix, because here the change *-e-* > *-o-*, motivated by a variant of the same template seen in *dingolondangos*, has created an apparent *-ondo*.

A final convergence is purely structural, and appears to have been of minimal importance in this case. This is the membership of *-ondo* in a paradigm of suffixes featuring the consonantal nucleus *-nd-* in conjunction with any of the five tonic vowels of Spanish, viz., *-ando*, *-endo*, *-indo*, *-ondo*, *-undo*. Though, as we have seen, this paradigm did not figure in the creation of *-(i)ondo*, there remains the possibility that it may have encouraged the productivity, or at least the continued existence, of the suffix. The primary function of both *-ando* and *-(i)endo* is to form gerundives, and one wonders whether the existence of *echando*, *bajando*, *pisando*, and dialectal *pediendo* might have encouraged the formation of *echondo*, *bajonda*, *pisondera*, and *pediondo*. This prospect is enhanced by the fact that -*ando* and -*endo* have shown signs of going beyond the verbal function (Ynduráin 1962, Náñez Fernández 1973:60-63). As for -*indo*, it deserves a study parallel to the present investigation, while -*undo* appears to be almost completely learnèd (e.g., *jocundo* 'jocund', *fecundo* 'fecund'; exception: *bara(h)únda* 'row, uproar').

Miscellaneous

There remains a number of Hispanic words containing a sequence -*ond*- that fit into none of the preceding categories, and which for the most part are irrelevant to the history of -*(i)ondo*. In most of these, -*ond*- forms part of the root, e.g., in *mondar, redondo, hondo*. In some cases, certain modifications have masked the identity of the stem in such a way that instances of the suffix -*ondo* might seem to occur, as in the following:

> **curondia** Ast. n. f. 'cada una de las cuatro piezas planas y redondeadas que van encima de los pegoŝos' (Cano González 160). Like Sor. *colonda*, Ast. *colondra, coronda* 'post', *curondia* derives from COLUMNA 'column' (*DEEH* 591).
> **golondrina** Sp. n. f. 'pájaro' (*DRAE* 669), a direct descendant of some form of Lat. HIRUNDO -INIS 'id.' (*DEEH* 727, *DCECH* 3:165).
> **lirondo (mondo y -)** phr. 'limpio, sin añadidura alguna' [1735] (*DRAE* 890). According to *DCECH* (3:667), *lirondo*, which is used only in this phrase, 'parece resultar de un cruce de *liso* con *morondo* "pelado, sin cabellos"'.
> **morondo** Sp. adj. 'pelado o mondado de cabellos o de hojas' (*DRAE* 896), *molondra* Murc., Rioj. n. f. 'cabeza grande y rapada' (García Soriano 85, Goicoechea 117, *DRAE* 888); vars. and derivs.: Murc., Rioj. *molondrón* n. m. 'golpe dado con la cabeza, o a la cabeza', 'trasquilón' (García Soriano 85, Goicoechea 117), Sp. *molondro* 'hombre poltrón, perezoso y torpe' (*DRAE* 888), Mont. 'cabezón, cabezota' (García-Lomas 207), Arag. 'bebé' (Andolz 192), Extr. *melondrongo* 'tocino de cerdo, añejo' (Viudas Camarasa 115), And. *borondanga* 'vulgar por *morondanga*' (Alcalá Venceslada 96), Extr. *birondango* *(sopas de -)* 'sopa de tomate, pimienta, etc.' (Viudas Camarasa 22), Extr. *molondrosco* 'picadillo de chorizo, morcilla, etc.,

aliñado y dispuesto para ser embutido' (Viudas Camarasa 118), And. *molondrusco* 'pedrusco, pedazo de roca' (Alcalá Venceslada 408). See the article on *morondanga* in *Origin and Development* (Pharies 1990:48-50) for a complete explanation of how all these words derive ultimately from *mondar* 'to clean an object by removing all impurities and superfluous parts'.

orondo Sp. adj. 'aplícase a las vasijas de mucha concavidad, hueco o barriga', 'hueco, hinchado, esponjado', 'lleno de presunción y muy contento de sí mismo' [16th cent.] (*DRAE* 951), And. 'refiriéndose a la cosecha, bondad y abundancia de ella' (Alcalá Venceslada 439). *DCECH* (4:304) is unable to identify the origin of this word, but offers the following: 'la idea central parece ser la de "ancho, abultado, hinchado", y variantes como ... la andaluza y americana *fróndi(g)o*, y la portuguesa *fronho*, muestran que la palabra básica debía empezar por F o aspiración.' Later it is suggested that Lat. FUNDULA 'little bag' < FUNDA 'bag' may be the etymon.

torondo Sp. n. m. ant. 'chichón, tolondro' [13th cent.] (*DRAE* 1279); derivs.: Sp. *torondón* 'id.' [1492] (ibid.), Can. 'bulto de las cosas o del físico: así de un colchón duro se dice que tiene torondones; o como la persona que tiene un divieso' (Guerra 286), Sp. *tolondro* adj. 'aturdido, desatinado, y que no tiene tiento en lo que hace' [1553] (*DRAE* 1273), Sp. *tolondrón* adj. 'aturdido, desatinado, tonto', 'dícese de la vaca en celo', Sp., And. n. m. 'chichón', adj. 'torpe' (*DRAE* 1273, Cepas González 313), Nav. *tolondorro* adj. 'atontado, alelado, simple, sin sentido, mareado, tolondro' (Iribarren 514). From an original *torondo* < Late Latin TURUNDUS, var. of Lat. TURUNDA 'ball of paste', 'kind of cake', 'roll of lint for wounds' (*DCECH* 5:534, *DEEH* 1041). The *-ondo* suffix is not involved here, though in the meaning 'said of cows in heat', the influence of *toriondo* 'id.' may be seen.

The remaining *-ondo* words are either of unknown or uncertain origin, or else the single example of a category. I present them here, in any case, for the sake of completeness.

carburondo And. n. m. 'carborondo' (Alcalá Venceslada 132); var.: Extr. *caburondo* 'instrumento de los canteros para alisar la piedra de granito' (Viudas Camarasa 32). These are variants of Sp. *carborundo* 'carburo de silicio' (*DRAE* 258) < Eng. *carborundum* 'id.'

cohondongo Extr. n. m. 'ensaladilla de pimientos, tomates, y pepino', 'gazpacho especial de los hombres del campo' (Viudas Camarasa 45); var.: *cahandongo* (id., 33). There are several explanations for this word, including < OSp. *cohonder* < Lat. CONFUNDERE 'to confuse'; cf. other names for hash such as *chanfaina* < SYMPHONIA 'harmonious mixture (of sounds)', and Murc. *rinrán* (García Soriano 113), whose form is suggestive of a mishmash. The variant *cahandongo* (Viudas's spelling of *cajandongo*) suggests that *caja* 'box' might be involved, in which case *-ondo* might be present. This leaves *cohondongo* unexplained, however.

dorondón Arag. n. m. 'niebla', 'escarcha' (Andolz 103); vars.: Murc. *dondorondón* 'personaje fastuoso y ridículo' (García Soriano 44), Arag. 'escarcha diurna que se acumula cuando hay niebla' (Andolz 102), Extr. *dolondón* 'ruido del cencerro' (Viudas Camarasa 63), Extr. *dondolondón* 'chisme o invención falsa atribuida al rumor público' (Viudas Camarasa 63). Though the last two of these could easily derive from an onomatopoeic root *don* depicting the ringing of a bell (cf. *dolondón* 'sound of a cowbell'), the connection with fog and frost escapes me. In any case, there is very little chance that the suffix *-ondo* is involved in these words.

repaminonda Argot n. f. 'el colmo, el no va más, lo insólito o inaudito' (León 136, Oliver 266). Oliver remarks that the expression *la monda lironda* is synonymous with *repaminonda*, whose origin I cannot identify.

sarrondija Rioj. n. f. 'lagartija' (Goicoechea 154); var.: Rioj. *serrondija* 'id.' (ibid.). *DCECH* (2:858, s.v. *fardacho*) mentions *sarrondija* only to remark that 'irá con *sabandija*', which is of pre-Roman origin (*DCECH* 5:105).

serondo Sp. adj. 'aplícase a las frutas tardías, seruendo' (*DRAE* 1196); vars.: Ast. *seronda* n. f. 'otoño' (Cano González 456), Extr. *zorondo* adj. 'tardío, se dice de los cereales' (Viudas Camarasa 179), Sal. *ceriondo* adj. 'aplícase a los cereales que empiezan a sazonarse tomando color amarillo' (*DRAE* 294). This family of words is attributable to Lat. SERŌTINUS 'late (fruit)', itself derived from the adverb SĒRŌ 'late' (DCECH 5:226).

sumirondón Arag. n. m. 'canto y baile típicos de Gotor e Illueca' (Andolz 263); var.: *semerendrón* (id., 256). More information about this custom is needed before an accurate etymology can be proposed.

trapisonda Sp. n. f. fam. 'bulla o riña con voces o acciones' [1739], desus. 'agitación del mar' (*DRAE* 1289), Nav. adj. 'trapisondista, que arma trapisondas' (Iribarren 520). According to *DCECH* (5:592), 'en realidad se trata del nombre del Imperio de Trapisonda en Asia Menor, sonadísimo en los libros de caballerías y en el *Quijote*, y que gracias al ambiente de estos libros y por su aparente relación con *trápala* y *trapaza* tomó en el lenguaje del vulgo las acepciones de estas palabras'.

To summarize: the Latin suffix -BUNDUS, which functioned to derive intensifying adjectives from verbs, survived in popular form only in Castilian and Old Provençal. While none of the attested Latin derivatives appears in Romance, one or more of them must have persisted long enough to prompt new coinages. In Castilian, a semantic core associated with female animals in heat developed early on. Later, the contours of the derivational model became steadily fuzzier, in that the semantic effect returned to a vague connotation of intensity, and both sides of the 'verb > adjective' equation were abandoned. The 18 genuine derivatives in -*(i)ondo* must be scrupulously differentiated from several other classes of words exhibiting this ending.

References

Adams, Edward L. 1913. *Word-formation in Provençal*. New York: MacMillan.

Alcalá Venceslada, Antonio. 1980. *Vocabulario andaluz*. 2nd ed. Madrid: Gredos.

Alemany Bolufer, José. 1920. *Tratado de la formación de palabras en la lengua castellana*. Madrid: Suárez.

Alonso, Martín. 1958. *Enciclopedia del idioma*. Madrid: Aguilar.

106   David Pharies

Alonso Garrote, Santiago. 1947. *El dialecto vulgar leonés hablado en Maragatería y Tierra de Astorga.* 2nd ed. Madrid: CSIC.

Andolz, Rafael. 1984. *Diccionario aragonés.* 2nd ed. Zaragoza: Librería General.

Azkue, Resurrección María. 1905. *Diccionario vasco-español-francés.* 2 vols. Bilbao.

Bosque, Ignacio and Manuel Pérez Fernández. 1987. *Diccionario inverso de la lengua española.* Madrid: Gredos.

Cano González, Ana María. 1982. *Vocabulario del bable de Somiedo.* Oviedo: Instituto de Estudios Asturianos.

Cepas González, Juan. 1985. *Vocabulario popular malagueño.* Barcelona: Plaza y Janés.

Cioranescu, Alejandro. 1966. *Diccionario etimológico rumano.* La Laguna, Tenerife: Biblioteca Filológica.

Corominas, Juan. 1941. Aportaciones americanas a cuestiones pendientes: *orondo. Anales del Instituto de Lingüística* 1.154-60.

_____. 1954-57. *Diccionario crítico-etimológico de la lengua castellana.* 4 vols. Madrid: Gredos.

_____ and José A. Pascual. 1980-. *Diccionario crítico etimológico castellano e hispánico.* 5 vols. to date. Madrid: Gredos.

Darmesteter, Arsène. 1932. Traité de la formation de la langue française. In *Dictionnaire générale de la langue française,* ed. Adolphe Hatzfeld and Arsène Darmesteter. 9th edn. 2 vols. Paris: Delagrave.

DCECH = Corominas and Pascual 1980-.

DCELC = Corominas 1954.

DEEH = García de Diego 1985.

Diez, Friedrich. 1874. *Grammaire des langues romanes.* 3rd ed. 3 vols. Bonn: Franck.

DRAE = Real Academia Española de la Lengua 1984.

EI = Alonso 1958.

Faitelson-Weiser, Silvia. 1987. *Dictionnaire inverse et analyse statistique de la langue espagnole.* Québec: Presses de l'Université Laval.

FEW = von Wartburg 1922-.

García de Diego, Vicente. 1985. *Diccionario etimológico español e hispánico.* 2nd ed. Madrid: Espasa-Calpe.

García-Lomas, G. Adriano. 1949. *El lenguaje popular de las montañas de Santander.* Santander: Diputación Provincial.

García Soriano, Justo. 1932. *Vocabulario del dialecto murciano.* Madrid: Bermejo.

Goicoechea, Cesáreo. 1971. *Vocabulario riojano. Boletín de la Real Academia Española,* Anejo 61.

Guerra, Pancho. 1977. *Obras completas. III. Léxico de Gran Canaria.* Las Palmas: Plan Cultural.

Hanssen, Federico. 1913. *Gramática histórica de la lengua castellana.* Halle: Niemeyer.

Iribarren, José María. 1984. *Vocabulario navarro.* 2nd ed. Pamplona: Comunidad Foral.

Kühner, Raphael and Friedrich Holzweissig. 1966. *Ausführliche Grammatik der lateinischen Sprache. Erster Teil: Elementar-, Formen- und Wortlehre.* Hannover: Hahnsche Buchhandlung.

Langlois, P. 1961. Formations en -BUNDUS: index et commentaire. *Revue d'études latines* 39.117-34.

León, Victor. 1980. *Diccionario de argot español y lenguaje popular.* Madrid: Alianza.

López Mendizábal, Bera. n.d. *Diccionario vasco-castellano.* 3rd ed. Zarauz: Icharopena.

Marcos Casquero, Manuel-Antonio. 1979. *El habla de Béjar. Léxico.* Salamanca: CSIC.

Meyer-Lübke, Wilhelm. 1890. *Grammaire des langues romanes.* Vol. 2: *Morphologie.* 2nd ed. Paris: Welter. New York: Stechert, 1923.

_____. 1935. *Romanisches etymologisches Wörterbuch.* 3rd ed. Heidelberg: Winter.

Náñez Fernández, Emilio. 1973. *La lengua que hablamos. Creación y sistema.* Santander: Bedia.

Oliver, Juan Manuel. 1985. *Diccionario de argot.* Madrid: Sena.

Pharies, David. 1986. *Structure and analogy in the playful lexicon of Spanish.* Beiheft zur *Zeitschrift für romanische Philologie,* 210. Tübingen: Niemeyer.

_____. 1989-90. The Ibero-Romance suffix -aina. *Romance Philology* 43.367-99.

_____. 1990. *Origin and development of the Ibero-Romance -nc-/-ng-suffixes.* Tübingen: Niemeyer.

Real Academia Española de la Lengua. 1984. *Diccionario de la lengua española.* 20th ed. 2 vols. Madrid: Espasa-Calpe.

REW = Meyer-Lübke 1935.

Rohlfs, Gerhard. 1954. *Historische Grammatik der italienischen Sprache und ihrer Mundarten*. Vol. 3: *Syntax und Wortbildung*. Bern: Francke.

_____. 1985. *Diccionario dialectal del pirineo aragonés*. Zaragoza: Diputación Provincial, Institución Fernando el Católico.

Ronjat, Jules. 1937. *Grammaire istorique des parlers provençaux modernes. Tome III, Deuxième partie: Morphologie et formation des mots*. Montpellier: Société de Langues Romanes.

Santamaría, Francisco J. 1959. *Diccionario de mejicanismos*. Méjico: Porrúa.

Vigón, Braulio. 1955. *Vocabulario dialectológico del concejo de Colunga. Revista de filología española*, Anejo 63.

Villasante, Luis. 1974. *Palabras vascas compuestas y derivadas*. Oñate: Aranzazu.

Viudas Camarasa, Antonio. 1980. *Diccionario extremeño*. Cáceres: Universidad de Extremadura.

Wagner, Max Leopold. 1943. Ibero-romanische Suffixstudien. *Zeitschrift für romanische Philologie* 63.329-66.

Wartburg, Walther von. 1922-. *Französisches etymologisches Wörterbuch*. Bonn, Leipzig, Basel. 21 vols. to date.

Ynduráin, Francisco. 1962. Sobre un sufijo -anda. In *Strenae: Estudios de filología e historia dedicados al Prof. Manuel García Blanco*, 469-71. Acta Salmanticensia. Filosofía y letras, tomo 16. Salamanca: Universidad de Salamanca.

Metathesis of Yod and the Palatalization of Latin Medial /k'l/, /g'l/, /t'l/; /ks/, /ssj/, /sj/; /kt/, /ult/ in Hispano- and Luso-Romance

Joel Rini

University of Virginia

> Old theories — like the reptilian nature of dinosaurs — are accepted like old friends of the family. You don't yell at old Aunt Cecilia. So hundred-year-old dinosaur theories live on without being questioned, and too often they are assumed to be totally correct.
> (Robert Bakker 1986:27).

I. Introduction.

The development of two of the features which so clearly distinguished Old Spanish from Old Portuguese is, in all likelihood, and paradoxically, the furthest from being fully understood. On the one hand, Latin medial /kt/ (and /ult/), after evolving to /(u)i̯t/ in General Ibero-Romance, further developed to /(u)č/ in Hispano-Romance while remaining /(u)i̯t/ in Luso-Romance. Compare Latin NOCTE > Ibero-Romance */noi̯te/ > Ptg. *noite* vs. Sp. *noche*; MULTU > Ibero-Romance */mui̯to/ > Ptg. *muito* vs. Sp. *mucho*. On the other hand, after the voicing of Latin /-sj-/ to /-zj-/ in General Ibero-Romance, the yod proceeded to palatalize the voiced sibilant in Luso-Romance, but not in Hispano-Romance. Compare Latin BASIU > Ptg. *beijo* [bei̯žu] vs. OSp. *beso* [bezo] > Mod. [beso]. The picture is further complicated by the fact that nearly identical palatalizing effects of yod on other consonants are found in both languages. Much of the problem lies, I believe, in the way in which scholars have perceived the process of palatalization by yod in general, along with some deceiving textual and dialectal evidence.

Romanists have long held that palatalization of certain consonants by the off-glide semi-vowel [i̯] (e.g., [-i̯l-] > [-ḽ-], [-i̯t-] > [-č-], [-i̯s-]

> [-š-]) was not only possible, but was a fairly common phonological process in the history of Hispano- and Luso-Romance.[1] It is not surprising that scholars have operated with this assumption, in light of the following facts: (1) The yod produced in the case of Latin medial /k'l/, /g'l/, /t'l/, /ks/, /kt/, /ult/ developed from the respective implosive consonant, leaving it to precede the consonant which it was later to palatalize: [-kl-] > [-i̯l-], [-ks-] > [-i̯s-], [-kt-] > [-i̯t-], [-ult-] > [-ui̯t-]; (2) The result of Latin /-ks-/ in Portuguese apparently attests to palatalization of the sibilant first by [i̯], which was to coalesce with the preceding vowel later in Castilian: cf. Latin AXE > Ptg. *eixo* [ei̯šu], OSp. *exe* [ešε] (Mod. *eje* [exe]);[2] and (3) In the case of /-kt-/, thirteenth-century Leonese texts regularly offer forms such as *peyche, feycho,* which appear to attest to the same type of palatalization of /-t-/ by [i̯] before the monophthongization of the diphthong [-ei̯-] > [-e-] in Castilian.

However, by proceeding with the premise of palatalization by the off-glide [i̯], many pieces of the puzzle do not fit. First, it is difficult, if not impossible, to explain why [i̯] would have palatalized [l], [s] and [t] in Spanish, but only [l] and [s] in Portuguese (cf. OC'LU > Ptg. *olho,* Sp. *ojo;* MATAXA > Ptg. *madeixa,* OSp. *madexa;* but FACTU > Ptg. *feito,* OSp. *fecho*). Second, it is not clear why the off-glide [i̯] (after metathesis of [j]) would have palatalized both [s] and [z] (< Latin /-ss-/ and /-s-/ respectively) in Portuguese, but only the former in Castilian (cf. QUASSIARE > Ptg. *queixar,* OSp. *quexar;* but BASIU > Ptg. *beijo,* Sp. *beso*). Though it is true that a sound change which occurs in one language does not have to happen in another, one may question why two such closely related varieties of Ibero-Romance behaved so differently regarding palatalization by a preceding off-glide, when they behaved in a very similar fashion in the case of a following on-glide.[3] Perhaps one should question, not why an off-glide would palatalize in some cases and

---

[1] In the past decade alone, this view has been maintained by the following scholars: cf. Craddock (1980:63); Lapesa (1980:79 n. 14); Lathrop (1984:128-32); Pensado (1984:486); Torreblanca (1988:344).

[2] Other examples include Latin MATAXA > Ptg. *madeixa,* OSp. *madexa* (Mod. *madeja*) and Latin TAXU > Ptg. *teixo,* OSp. *texo* (Mod. *tejo*).

[3] Cf. the developments in Hispano- and Luso-Romance of Latin medial /tj/, /kj/, /ttj/, /kkj/, /ptj/, /ktj/, /ntj/, /nkj/, /rtj/, /rkj/, /ltj/, /lkj/, /wtj/, /dj/, /gj/, /nj/, /lj/. Of course, a major exception is /zj/ (treated below). Also different outcomes of /pj/, /bj/, /mj/, /rj/ in these two languages are the result of late metathesis in Portuguese (also discussed below).

not in others, but instead, whether the off-glide was ever actually capable of palatalizing at all. It remains unclear exactly how, physiologically, palatalization can occur from a preceding yod.[4] It might be beneficial to examine exactly how some scholars have envisioned such palatalization.

During the past decade, most Hispanists, (with very few exceptions — to be discussed below), have operated exclusively with the premise of palatalization by off-glide [i̯], without examining closely how the process might have ensued. Pensado confirms the widespread acceptance of such palatalization regarding /-kt-/ and /-ks-/, and accepts it herself: 'Se adopta aquí la cronología más generalmente aceptada *kt* > *i̯t* > *i̯č* (como más adelante *ks* > *i̯s* > *i̯š*)' (1984:486). Earlier, in an important study of the various effects of yod on vowels, Craddock (1980:63) had mentioned in passing: 'Note that in Spanish, the glide [i̯] palatalized the following consonants [t] and [s], while in Portuguese, it palatalized only the latter.' And with regard to the development of Ibero-Romance /-sj-/ and /-zj-/, Torreblanca (1988:348) recently argued that metathesis occurred first, followed by palatalization by [i̯], and claimed that [-i̯z-] would have become [-i̯ž-] in Castilian as well had the diphthong [-ei̯-] lasted as long as it did in Portuguese.[5]

Earlier, a couple of scholars (Spaulding 1943 and García de Diego 1951:86, 88) simply attempted to repeat Menéndez Pidal's chronology. Spaulding, for example, wrote: '*T*, under the force of the prepalatal *c*, palatalizes into the affricate [č]: *feycho* (*Orígenes*, §15, 6).

---

[4] Most examples of Romance palatalization, as well as assibilation and affrication, have resulted from the combination consonant + yod. Moreover, in other languages, English for example, palatalization of /d/ and /t/ by an on-glide yod is common in everyday speech: e.g., 'Did you' [di̯džə]; 'Won't you' [wou̯ntšə]; 'indian' [i̯ndžən], etc. However, as a native speaker of English, I cannot say I have ever witnessed the palatalization of any consonant by a preceding yod, i.e., 'I told him' *[ai̯ tšou̯ld hi̯m], 'exciting' *[ɛksai̯tši̯ŋ].

[5] Torreblanca's argument is weakened by the fact that some items which to date retain [ei̯], have not undergone palatalization, e.g., Sp. *aceite, peinar, seis*, etc., (as well as Ptg. *coisa* (dialectal), *mais* + /V-/). Torreblanca himself (1988:344) accounts for OSp. *egrija* as a lack of metathesis, rather than keeping within his hypothesis of palatalization by the preservation of off-glide [i̯]: 'La antigua forma castellana *egrija* es anómala. En vez de pasar la yod de ECLESIA a la sílaba precedente, se mantuvo el grupo /zj/ por influencia culta (*iglesia*), palatalizándose la sibilante en contacto con la yod siguiente'. It is strange, then, that he should insist on the idea that palatalization of Luso-Romance [z] > [ž] resulted from [i̯] *after* its metathesis.

Lastly, the two palatals combine: *fecho*' (1943:97). It should be noted, though, that much of Menéndez Pidal's hypothesis regarding this point has been either overlooked or misinterpreted by most. Menéndez Pidal (1929:92) depicted for Spanish the evolution of /-akt-/ as follows:

> En Castilla **akt** ha evolucionado primitivamente aŷt > eŷt, y luego en vez de sonorizar muy temprano la articulación de la ŷ > i̯ como en Aragón y Navarra, la ŷ atrajo antes a sí la articulación de la t, haciéndola prepalatal dorsal t̢ que por su naturaleza es siempre algo africada, y luego completamente africada t̢ŷ, relajándose después la primitiva ŷ, así: eŷt > eŷt̢ > eŷt̢ŷ > eyĉ > ei̯ĉ, y absorbiéndose luego la i̯ en la palatal siguiente > eĉ.

In his *Manual de gramática histórica española*, Menéndez Pidal repeated this view of the development of /-kt-/ (1941:143), and posited similar stages of development for /-ult-/:

$$u\b{l}t > uyt > uy\b{t} > uy\b{t}j > uyĉ > uĉ \quad (1941:140)$$

In his account of /-kt-/ and /-ult-/, note that yod has been posited, not only before, but after the consonant as well — it appears to 'straddle' /-t-/. It is clear that Menéndez Pidal wanted to demonstrate that the actual palatalization did not occur until a following on-glide (represented as [ŷ] [1929:92], [ŷ] and [j] [1941:140, 143]) was present.[6]

For the development of /ks/, Menéndez Pidal intended the same type of analysis: 'Los grados sucesivos de asimilación mutua serán *lo mismo* que para la *ch*: Ḱs > ŷs > ys > yš > š' (1941:144, emphasis mine). Note, however, that although he may have intended to do so, he did not posit in his scheme a yod on each side of the sibilant. This possible oversight no doubt led to much of the misinterpretation of his view, as did his simplified scheme for /-kt-/: 'La monoptongación de AI > *ei* > *e* es posterior a la formación de la *ch* ... como lo indica la serie que hemos establecido LACTE > *lai̯te* > *leite* > *leiche* > *leche*'(1941:52; also repeated

---

[6] This sort of 'straddling' was earlier expressed by Meyer-Lübke (1890:414-15): 'Ou bien la formation du canal qui est nécessaire pour la production du rétrécissement persiste pendant l'articulation du *t*, de sorte que ce phonème passe à *í* et, comme tel, continue de se développer jusqu'à *č* ... Ou bien les deux processus se confondent, *ct* passe à *it* qui, ou bien persiste tout d'abord, cf. a.-franç. *afaitier* et plus tard devient *it* franç. mod. *fait*, ou bien passe à *ič*, *č* comme en espagnol'.

in 1950:82-83). It is, therefore, somewhat understandable how so many have missed the most important part of Menéndez Pidal's analysis (i.e., the stage ẙ t ẙ, or ẙ t j). Even Lapesa, one of Menéndez Pidal's own students, has taken part in the propagation of this oversight, extending it to /gn/:

> El término «yod» designará también la [i̯] semivocal que nació al evolucionar grupos como /c'l/, /ct/, /cs/, /g'l/, /gn/ y originó resultados con consonante palatal (/oc'lu/ > [oi̯lu] > /ol̡o/ > /ožo/, *ojo* ... /factu/ > [faXtu] > [fai̯to] > [fei̯to] > /feĉo/, *fecho*; /laxus/ > [laXsus] > [lai̯sus] > [lei̯šos] > [lešos], cast. ant. *lexos*; /pugnu/ > [pui̯nu] > /puŋo/, *puño*) (1980:79 n. 14).

In recent scholarship, only Lloyd has accurately described this process of palatalization (in terms similar to Menéndez Pidal's), stating that the /l/ of the groups /-k'l-/, /-g'l-/, /-t'l-/ and the /s/ of /-ks-/ '*absorbed the semivowel* early enough to produce a palatal consonant in most areas of the peninsula'(1987:253, emphasis mine) and that Castilian later distinguished itself from surrounding dialects by '*fusing the palatal into the occlusive* and producing an affricate /č/'(1987:253, emphasis mine). By 'absorbed' and 'fusing', Lloyd really suggests the same type of 'straddling' suggested by Menéndez Pidal, as is clearly shown in his repairing of Menéndez Pidal's earlier oversight regarding /-ks-/: 'TAXU "yew tree" > [tai̯sʲu] (> *texo*), AXE "axis" > [ai̯sʲe] (> *exe*)' (1987:189).

But do not Menéndez Pidal and Lloyd really suggest something very close to metathesis? Could it not be that indeed metathesis occurred in these cases, e.g., [tai̯su] > [tei̯su] > [tesju] instead of [tai̯su] > [tai̯sʲu]? Over a century ago, by the way, Diez (1882:215) suggested just that for the development of /-ks-/, though without referring to the process as 'metathesis':

> Der aus *cs* entstandene Zisch- oder Hauchlaut scheint auf einer ursprünglichen, allgemeineren, im Nordwesten noch vorhandenen Auflösung des *c* in *i* und inniger Verschmelzung desselben mit *s* zu beruhen, so dass aus *coxa* erst *cojsa*, sodann *cosja* und hieraus it. *coscia*, sp. mit Neigung zur Aspiration *coxo* hervorgieng.

Diez's proposed stage of metathesis, however, never really caught on. Not until recently has the idea once again surfaced. Lathrop, who has operated

with the assumption of palatalization by off-glide [i̯] (1984:128-32),[7] in
a recent article, recognizes metathesis as a solution for the consonant
sequence /-ult-/, (suggested independently from Diez's solution for /-ks-/):

> Ahora bien, el español normalmente rechaza el grupo *ui*, salvo cuando es
> inevitable, como en *buitre*. ¿Cómo rechazarlo? Por metátesis. Entonces vemos
> la evolución [ult] > [uyt] > [uty] > [uč] (1988:142).[8]

To this point in time, it appears that there are three ways to view
the development of these consonants: (1) One may continue to follow the
misinterpretation of Menéndez Pidal's description of the process, accepting
the premise of palatalization by off-glide [i̯], which does not explain the
presence and absence of palatalization in Spanish and Portuguese; (2) One
may choose to follow Menéndez Pidal, as has Lloyd, viewing the process
as a type of straddling of the consonant by the yods (called *acercamiento
mutuo* by Menéndez Pidal, absorption and fusing by Lloyd), e.g., [-i̯tj-],
[-i̯sj-], etc., which in effect rejects any notion of palatalization by [i̯],
since the palatalization of the consonant in question is not complete until
an on-glide [j] follows; or (3) One may opt for Diez's and Lathrop's
suggestions of metathesis, though this hypothesis would require some
enlarging and refining.

Since most, in recent years, have followed choice (1), and because
advances in the natural sciences have often resulted from taking not only

---

[7] It should be noted, however, that in Lathrop's original English version (1980), he
indeed operated with the notion of palatalization by the on-glide either as straddling
[-yt-], or after metathesis. With regard to /-ks-/, /-kt-/, and /-ult-/, Lathrop (1980:94, 96)
writes: 'The development of this cluster appears to have been: [ks] > [ys] > [sy] > [š] >
[x] ... The development of the [kt] seems to have been [kt] > [ky] ([sic], an apparent
typographical error for [yt]) > [yty] > [č] ... Here is the development of the cluster: [ult]
> [uyt] > [uty] > [uč].' Lathrop's clear view of this problem became muddied in his 1984
version: 'La posible evolución debió de ser algo parecido a esto: [ks] > [js] > [jš] > [š]
> [x] ... La evolución de [kt] parece haber sido: [kt] > [jt] > [ĉ] ... Ésta es aparentemente
la evolución de este grupo: [ult] > [ujt] > [uĉ]' (1984:129, 130, 132). While, over all,
Lathrop (1984) is without a doubt much improved, and superior to Lathrop (1980),
something (quite important, I might add), indeed got lost in the translation.

[8] Lathrop's proposed motive for the metathesis, though, — to avoid the diphthong /ui̯/
— seems circular. It would be preferable to claim some factor (e.g., an existing pattern
of /-CjV-/) as having motivated the metathesis which resulted in the elimination of /ui̯/
than to view the metathesis as resulting from a desire to eliminate a particular type of
diphthong. Diez, by the way, proposed no real motive either.

a different, but at times, an entirely opposing view of existing orthodoxy,[9] I have chosen to operate with view (3), incorporating into the scheme a stage of metathesis. I shall proceed below with the premise that palatalization of /l/, /t/, /s/, and /z/ in Hispano- and Luso-Romance never resulted from an off-glide [i̯] as has so often been claimed, but rather, always necessarily from an on-glide [j]. And although choice (2) may still seem desirable because of the remaining off-glide in forms like Leon. *feycho* and Ptg. *queixar*, again, it is not clear why, in the case of [-kt-] > [-i̯t-] and [-ult-] > [-ui̯t-], straddling of yod would occur with /t/ in Castilian, but not in Portuguese; nor, on the other hand, why, in Portuguese, yod would straddle both /s/ and /z/ but only the former in Castilian. Whether one wishes to call the process in question *acercamiento mutuo*, absorbing or fusing (i.e., what I refer to as 'straddling'), or whether one wishes to see it as a case of metathesis, it remains to be explained why the yod moved from pre- to post-consonantal position — i.e., why yod would pass from the coda of one syllable to the onset of the next. While it may be impossible to explain why *acercamiento mutuo*, or absorbing/fusing of yod occurred in some cases and not others, we might indeed be able to explain why metathesis of yod might or might not have occurred in the history of Hispano- and Luso-Romance. I shall also propose a new solution for the development of Latin /-ks-/ > Ptg. *-ix-* (/-i̯š-/), OSp. *-x-* (/-š-/), which involves the interaction of the sequences /-ks-/ and /-ssj-/. All cases of presence or absence of palatalization will be explained for both Spanish and Portuguese, as well as the retention of the off-glide in cases like Leon. *feycho* and Ptg. *queixar*. Finally, while new data can deepen our knowledge of a particular problem, so can a reinterpretation of the old. No new textual evidence has surfaced to warrant the present reassessment of the problem: the interpretation here presented is simply intended to make more sense out of the existing set of facts.[10]

---

[9] Take as a recent example, Bakker's (1986) *The Dinosaur Heresies*, in which the author suggests convincingly that, contrary to earlier views, the facts possessed make more sense if one views the dinosaurs as swift, warm-blooded, bird-like creatures rather than slow, cold-blooded, and lizard-like.

[10] The data have been collected primarily from Craddock (1980), Menéndez Pidal (1929, 1941), Williams (1962), Torreblanca (1988), Lathrop (1984), Pensado (1984), Lloyd (1987).

II. Procedure.

        Having rejected the notion of palatalization by off-glide [i̯], we
must somehow explain why [i̯] would have metathesized to [j] before
palatalization occurred. Without such an explanation this hypothesis would
advance our knowledge no further than that which claims palatalization
by [i̯] was (and is) possible. It would appear that, in the case of /t/ for
example, our claim that [-i̯t-] metathesized to [-tj-] to yield /č/ in Castilian
but not in Portuguese, was simply arbitrary or ad hoc. Although one could
argue that it is entirely possible that this metathesis just happened to occur
in Castilian and not in Portuguese, again we would have learned nothing.
And while metathesis may be considered a somewhat sporadic sound
change (as it has appeared at various periods, and to different degrees in
the history of Ibero-Romance),[11] it has also displayed, as Lloyd (1987:28)
notes, 'a certain degree of regularity, e.g., OSp. *miraglo, parabla, periglo*
> MSp. *milagro, palabra, peligro*.' Lloyd further suggests that there may
be governing factors of sporadic sound changes (1987:29):

> It may be argued that if sporadic changes come from slips of the tongue, *they*
> *may be subject to all sorts of interference from other words* [emphasis mine].
> The reasons for their acceptance in the standard forms of words would have
> nothing to do with their sporadic character or phonetic nature, but would have
> to be sought in the special historical development of each word or word group.

Since metathesis may be a more 'regular' sound change than we have
thought in the past, it is not inconceivable that some factor or factors have
regulated it. In the following pages, I shall demonstrate that certain extant
patterns in all likelihood governed the metathesis of yod in the
development of Latin /-k'l-/, /-g'l-/, /-t'l-/, /-ks-/, /-ssj-/, /-sj-/, /-kt-/, /-ult-/,
in Hispano- and Luso-Romance. Also, we can establish two relative time
periods of change: (1) Earlier developments, including /-k'l-/, /-g'l-/, /-t'l-/,
/-ks-/, /-ssj-/, /-sj-/; and (2) Later developments, when Castilian and
Portuguese split with regard to the phonological development of /-Vi̯-/
and /-i̯t-/. Also, though our primary concern at present is to explain the
discrepancies between Spanish and Portuguese, a broader look at other

---

        [11] It is common to refer to 'late' as opposed to 'early' metathesis of yod (cf. Williams
1962:29; Craddock 1980:63, 66; Pharies 1990:391). As will be seen below, earlier or later
metathesis of yod seems to have had important consequences on the development of
Hispano- and Luso-Romance /-zj-/.

Romance dialects (when appropriate), will, in fact, sustain the claims made below.

EARLY DEVELOPMENTS

We may establish that there were two general patterns in Early Ibero-Romance (and, in general, Western Romance), which would affect the behavior of yod: (1) Latin primary /-lj-/, resulting from /-liV-/ or /-leV-/ with a loss of hiatus; and (2) /-Vi̯(C)-/, resulting primarily from the development of the sequences /-ks-/, /-kt-/, and /-ult-/ to /-i̯s-/, /-i̯t-/, and /-ui̯t-/ respectively, and also from either a loss of hiatus (e.g., LAICU > *lai̯cu*), or a lost consonant (e.g., AMAVI > *amai̯*).[12]

III. Metathesis and the development of Latin /-k'l-/, /-g'l-/, /-t'l-/.

The Latin sequences /-k'l-/, /-g'l-/, and /-t'l-/ all produced a lateral-palatal /ḽ/ in Ibero-Romance (preserved in Modern Portuguese), which evolved in Old Spanish to a palatal [ž], later devoicing to [š], and finally velarizing to [x] (or [h]) in Modern Spanish:

Latin	Late Latin	Ibero-Rom.	O. Spanish		Mod. Sp.
OCULU	oc'lu	[oḽo]	[ožo]	[ošo]	[oxo]
REGULA	reg'la	[r̄eḽa]	[r̄eža]	[r̄eša]	[r̄exa]
VETULU	vec'lu	[βeḽo]	[bježo]	[bješo]	[bjexo][13]

Regarding the development from the Late Latin to Ibero-Romance stage, most agree that syllable-final /k/ or /g/ (with /-t'l-/ > /-k'l-/) weakened to a fricative [x] or [ɣ], and later to the off-glide [i̯]. Traditionally, this off-

---

[12] This broad pattern of /-Vi̯-/ in early Ibero-Romance could conceivably be responsible for other instances of metathesis, e.g., -ARIU > *-arju* > *-ai̯ru* > Ptg. *-ei̯ro*, Sp. *-ero*.

[13] Other examples from Latin to Spanish include APIC(U)LA > *abeja*, ARTIC(U)LU > *artejo*, CUNIC(U)LU > *conejo*, GENUC(U)LU > *hinojo*, ORIC(U)LA > *oreja*, LENTIC(U)LA > *lenteja*, COAG(U)LU > *cuajo*, TEG(U)LA > *teja*; ROTULARE > *roclare* > *(ar)rojar* (from Lathrop 1984:128-29).

glide has been accredited with the subsequent palatalization of [l], yielding the lateral-palatal [ḷ] as depicted in the following scheme:

Late Latin			Ibero-Romance
oc'lu	[oxlo]	[oi̯lo]	[oḷo]
reg'la	[r̄eɣla]	[r̄ei̯la]	[r̄eḷa]
vec'lu	[βexlo]	[βei̯lo]	[βeḷo]

Operating with the notion that palatalization can result only from the combination consonant + yod, however, requires an additional step of metathesis:

Late Latin				Ibero-Romance
oc'lu	[oxlo]	[oi̯lo]	[oljo]	[oḷo]
reg'la	[r̄eɣla]	[r̄ei̯la]	[r̄elja]	[r̄eḷa]
vec'lu	[βexlo]	[βei̯lo]	[βeljo]	[βeḷo]

Such a proposed stage of metathesis should be seen as neither unwarranted nor sporadic. It is easily explained as analogical to the great Latin lexical stock which originally had the combination /l/ + yod (examples modified from Lathrop 1984:128):

Latin	Late Latin	Ibero-Rom.	Old Spanish	Modern Spanish
ALIENU	[aljenu]	[aḷeno]	[aženo]	[axeno] *ajeno*
ALIU	[alju]	[aḷo]	[ažo]	[axo] *ajo*
CILIA	[ŝilja]	[ŝeḷa]	[šeža]	[θexa] *ceja*
CONSILIU	[konselju]	[konseḷo]	[konsežo]	[konsexo] *consejo*
FILIU	[filju]	[fiḷo]	[fižo]	[ixo] *hijo*
FOLIA	[folja]	[foḷa]	[foža]	[oxa] *hoja*
MULIERE	[muljere]	[muḷer]	[mužer]	[muxer] *mujer*
PALEA	[palja]	[paḷa]	[paža]	[paxa] *paja*
TILIU	[tilju]	[teḷo]	[težo]	[texo] *tejo*

Thus the development of Latin /-k'l-/, /-g'l-/, and /-t'l-/, after vocalization of the syllable-final consonant, [i̯l], with metathesis to [lj] was swept up in the change of Latin primary /lj/.[14]

In Eastern Romance no such development occurred. Like the retention of voiceless stops, there was a tendency to maintain a cluster here, even if altered in form: NOCTE > It. *notte*, Rum. *noapte*. Consequently no yod was produced in this case and thus no possible metathesis. Rohlfs (1966:349), for example, writes: 'In posizione mediana *cl* passa a *kki̯* sia in Toscana che nel resto dell'Italia centrale e meridionale: cfr. *occhio, macchia, orecchio, specchio, ginocchio, vecchio, secchia, mucchio, Pracchia* (Pratula); il napoletano *uocchio, arecchia, denucchio* "ginocchio", *viecchio*'. (Cf. also the Rumanian development: Late Latin /oc'lu/, /auric'la/ > Rumanian *ochiu, ureche* [Bourciez 1956:175]).[15]

IV. Metathesis and the development of Latin /-ks-/ and /-ssj-/.

The development of /-ks-/ in Castilian could be easily explained independently, within the framework of palatalization by [j], as follows: Latin MATAXA [mataksa] > [mada i̯sa] > [made i̯sa] > [madesja] > OSp. [madeša] > MSp. [maðexa]. However, this scheme leaves unexplained why Portuguese developed the same palatal consonant but retained the off-glide, i.e., Latin MATAXA [mataksa] > [mada i̯sa] > [made i̯ša]. But if we take into account that Latin /-ssj-/ produced the same palatal consonant, e.g., Latin *QUASSIARE > Ptg. *queixar*, OSp. *quexar* > MSp. *quejar*, we find that perhaps an interaction between the two sequences, /-ks-/ and /-ssj-/, could account for the respective developments in Spanish and Portuguese.

I wish to point out first that the development of Latin /-ssj-/ > /-š-/ in a few Castilian lexical items must be seen as having occurred without

---

[14] Lathrop (1984:128) comes very close to suggesting what I have suggested here, but never mentions a stage of metathesis: 'Los grupos *c'l* y *g'l* evolucionaron de la misma manera que los grupos *lj*. Después de caer la vocal átona, *c* y *g* se convirtieron en yod y los dos grupos dieron [ž]. Este nuevo grupo se incorporó a la evolución de *lj*'.

[15] Perhaps the vocalization of /l/ in /-k'l-/ and /-g'l-/ to /-kj-/ and /-gj-/ in Italian was due to the pattern /-lj-/ exemplified above.

any metathesis whatever, e.g., Latin *BASSIARE[16] > [basjar] > [bašar]; and Latin RUSSEU > [rosjo] > [rošo] (with early absorption of [j] into [š] to account for the lack of vowel raising, for example, to *[rušo]). However, in most other lexical items descending from Latin forms with /-ssj-/, metathesis of [j] into the preceding syllable undoubtedly occurred, as reflects the vocalic inflexion of /a/ to /ei̯/ (later /e/ in Castilian and Catalan), e.g., *CAPSEU > Ptg. *queixo*, OSp. *quex(-ada)*, Cat. *queix*; *QUASSIARE > Ptg. *queixar*, OSp. *quexar*. Also, note that this metathesis occurred relatively early, as it is found, from east to west, across the Iberian Peninsula (Portuguese, Castilian, Catalan).

The development and interaction of /-ks-/ and /-ssj-/ in Ibero-Romance is seen here as follows. The implosive velar consonant of /-ks-/ first vocalized, as it did in other environments (/-k'l-/ > /-i̯l-/, /-kt-/ > /-i̯t-/), yielding /-i̯s-/. Meanwhile, Ibero-Romance [-sj-] (from Latin /-ssj-/) was beginning to palatalize, i.e., *quasjar > *quašjar. In some cases, before the on-glide [j] was completely absorbed into the new palatal [š] (as it apparently was in Hispano-Romance *basjar > bašar), it metathesized into the preceding syllable: hence, *quasjar > *quašjar > *quai̯šar. The impetus for this metathesis is found in the model /-i̯s-/ < /-ks-/, e.g., MATAXA > *madai̯sa, thus showing the first step in the interaction of medial /ks/ and /ssj/. Supporting models for this metathesis of on-glide [j] to the preceding syllable, of course, were /-i̯t-/ < /-kt-/ and /-ult-/ (and perhaps /-i̯l-/ before its metathesis to /-lj-/), as well as other categories of /-Vi̯-/, resulting from the loss either of hiatus or of a

---

[16] Some might wish to posit the etymon BASSARE, without yod, as Latin medial /ss/ is known to have yielded /š/ in a couple of cases: PASSERE > [pášaro] > [páxaro], VESSICA > [βešiga], as did initial /s/: SAPONE > [šabón] > [xaβón], SEPIA > [šibia], SUCU > [šugo], SYRINGA > [šeriŋga], etc. However, the etymon *BASSIARE is certainly legitimate, and necessary for Ptg. *(a)baixar*. As Walsh (1988:21-22 n. 2) explains, regarding the problem of verbs reconstructed with adjectival or past participial bases plus a hypothetical suffix -IARE: 'The great majority of such reconstructed verbs with reflexes in several Romance languages were in reality derived from comparative stems (e.g., ALTIOR/ALTIUS → ALTIARE "to make higher" [Sp. *alzar*]) or from deverbal abstract nouns in -IO (e.g., CAPTIO → *CAPTIARE [Sp. *cazar*]). In instances in which an -IARE base was reconstructed to account for a verb characteristic of a single Romance language, a better explanation is usually available involving descent from an amply recorded base in -ARE, with subsequent a) interference from another — often semantically related — word family, b) dialect borrowing, or c) lexical polarization.' The change from BASSARE > *BASSIARE would likely have resulted from lexical polarization: ALTIOR/ALTIUS → ALTIARE (Sp. *alzar*) — *BASSIARE (> Ibero-Romance *basjare > Ptg. *(a)baixar*, OSp. *baxar*).

consonant (e.g., LAICU > *lai̯cu*; AMAVI > *amai̯* etc.). The next step in the interaction of medial /ks/ and /ssj/ is the extension or spread of the palatalized sequence /-Vi̯š-/ (< /-ssj-/) to the non-palatalized /-Vi̯s-/ (< /-ks-/). Thus **quai̯šar* types served as a model for a sound substitution of /-Vi̯š-/ for /-Vi̯s-/ in types like **madai̯sa*, yielding **madai̯ša*. Given the apical nature of [š] in Ibero-Romance (Torreblanca 1988:347), it is quite understandable how the non-palatalized sequence /-Vi̯s-/ would have merged with the palatal sequence /-Vi̯š-/.[17] The entire interaction can be sketched as follows:

Latin	Ibero-Romance	Ptg.	OSp.
MATAXA [mataksa] > [madai̯sa] > [madei̯sa] > [madei̯ša] > [madeša]
QUASSIARE [kwasjare] > [kwašjar] > [kai̯šar] > [kei̯šar] > [kešar]

This view accounts for the palatal consonant, the vowel inflexion (with the exception of cases like Sp. *bajar* and Ptg. *(a)baixar*), as well as the retention of the off-glide in Portuguese, without attributing any palatalization to the off-glide [i̯].

V. The Development of /-sj-/.

The different results of Latin /-sj-/, Ibero-Romance [-zj-], in Hispano-and Luso-Romance (e.g. BASIU > Ptg. *beijo*, Sp. *beso*), too may be explained in terms of how metathesis of yod behaved in each case. Since Castilian is known to have been a bit more innovative in its development than Portuguese, it is possible that the former metathesized the on-glide [j] early, before palatalization could occur, while the latter either metathesized [j] late, or, as attests the lack of vocalic inflexion in some cases, not at all. Late (or complete lack of) metathesis would then allow time for palatalization. Examples from Latin to Portuguese include BASIARE > *beijar*, BASIU > *beijo*, CARISIA > *careja*, CASEU > *queijo*, CERESIA > *cereja*, CERVESIA > *cerveja*, COLOCASIA > *carqueija*, ECLESIA > *igreja*, SEGUSIU > *sabujo* (Torreblanca 1988:344). As in the case of [-sj-], the metathesis of [-zj-] to [-i̯z-] in Hispano-Romance occurred

---

[17] I owe this observation to one of my students, Matthew Juge.

presumably by analogy to /-it-/, /-is-/ (as well as -AVI > -ai, etc.). However, it remains to be explained why such metathesis was either later or thwarted in Luso-Romance. Also, if we are to claim that the on-glide in [-sj-] and [-zj-] metathesized during roughly the same period in Hispano-Romance (which is indeed necessary to account for similar vocalic inflexions, e.g., the /-ai-/ > /-ei-/ > /-e-/ in both QUASSIARE > Sp. *quexar* and BASIU > Sp. *beso*), we must explain as well why palatalization occurred in Hispano-Romance [-sj-] but not [-zj-], before the metathesis to [-iš-] and [-iz-].

One reason why metathesis of yod may have occurred later in Portuguese than in Castilian might be found in the genesis of the yod itself. Though it is generally accepted that the creation of the on-glide through loss of hiatus is an early development in Spoken Latin, and indeed I have claimed this above with regard to [-sj-], it is likewise widely accepted that when a sound change begins, not all words are affected simultaneously. Some words, morphemes, or grammatical categories are affected first, while others later, or not at all.[18] It is not out of the question, then, that hiatus may have been lost in Luso-Romance words with /-siV-/ patterns before those with /-ziV-/ patterns, especially in light of the fact that sound change also spreads gradually from one phonetic environment to another (see Lloyd 1987:21 on conditioned and unconditioned change). Furthermore, since we are dealing with two different varieties of Ibero-Romance, it seems even more likely that /-zi-/ would not develop to /-zj-/ in both Hispano- and Luso-Romance at the same time, especially since the former is known to have been the more innovative of the two. There is, in fact, a small bit of evidence for a later genesis of [j] (produced from a loss of hiatus) in Portuguese in certain environments. Upon close examination of some cases of late metathesis of [j] into the preceding syllable in Old Portuguese (e.g., *rabia* > *raiba*, *chuvia* > *chu(i)va*, etc.), one observes that, not only did late metathesis occur, but in the case of Latin /-pi-/, voicing of /p/ also occurred, yielding /-bi-/, whereas in Hispano-Romance it did not. If we accept that voicing did not occur in the latter because of an early loss of hiatus and resultant on-glide [j], so that /p/ was not truly intervocalic (nor in the environment -V_r-

---

[18] This, of course, is the 'lexical diffusion' hypothesis, originated and championed by Wang (1969) and Chen (1972). For a concise overview, see Lloyd (1987:21-26). For a few examples of studies in Hispano-Romance which adopt this view, see Wright (1982:16-18, 33, 40), Dworkin (1988), Harris-Northall (1990) and Rini (1991).

or -V_l-), i.e., Latin APIU > /apju/ > Sp. *apio*; Latin CAPIAT > /kapja/ > /kai̯pa/ > Sp. *quepa*; Latin SAPIAT > /sapja/ > /sai̯pa/ > Sp. *sepa*), we might also accept that the voicing in Luso-Romance, as well as the late metathesis, was due to a relatively late loss of hiatus and later production of the on-glide [j] itself: thus, Latin CAPIAT > /kapia/ > /kabia/ > /kabja/ > /kai̯ba/, Ptg. *caiba*; Latin SAPIAT > /sapia/ > /sabia/ > /sabja/ > /sai̯ba/, Ptg. *saiba* (but Ptg. *aipo*). If this is true for these cases, it could also be true for the sequence of phonemes /-zi-/. This conservation of hiatus in Luso-Romance fits well within the overall scheme of the conservative nature of this variety of Ibero-Romance.

The reason [-sj-] palatalized in Hispano-Romance while [-zj-] did not may be due to the voiceless feature of the former. Torreblanca (1988:348) suggested that palatalization would most likely have occurred first with the unvoiced sibilant /-sj-/ because it was more tense: 'la palatalización hubo de ocurrir con la sibilante sorda ... antes que con la sonora'. Thus QUASSIARE and BASIU, for example, would develop as follows: **quasjar* > **quašjar* > **quai̯šar* vs. **bazju* > **bazju* > **bai̯zu*.

The relatively early genesis and metathesis of [j] from Latin /-si-/ in Hispano-Romance, combined with Torreblanca's proposed factor of voiced [-zj-] resisting palatalization for some time, resulting in the lack of palatalization of [-z-], can be sketched as follows.

Latin	Hispano-Romance			Old Spanish	Spanish
BASIU	[bazju >	bai̯zu >	bei̯zo >	bezo] >	*beso*
CASEU	[kazju >	kai̯zu >	kei̯zo >	kezo] >	*queso*
CERESIA	[k̃erezja	> šerei̯za	>	šereza] >	*cereza*
CERVESIA	[k̃erbezja	> šerbei̯za	>	šerbeza] >	*cerveza*

The later genesis of [j] in Luso-Romance, resulting in a later and perhaps longer duration of [-zj-] with subsequent palatalization of the voiced sibilant is depicted below. Note too that [j] was either completely absorbed when the preceding vowel was /e/, or metathesized later, when the preceding vowel was /a/.[19]

---

[19] It is worth noting that Hispano-Romance [j] metathesized no matter what the vowel, while in Luso-Romance it did not in the case of /-ezja-/. Again, this demonstrates the well-known innovative vs. conservative nature of these two varieties of Ibero-Romance. Also, if the preceding vowel was /i/, it appears as though [j] metathesized and was absorbed into the /i/ in both Hispano- and Luso-Romance; e.g., Latin CAMISIA > Sp. *camisa*, Ptg. *camisa*.

Latin	Luso-Romance	Old Portuguese	Portuguese
BASIU	[baziu >	bazju > bažju > bai̯žu > bei̯žu]	> *beijo*
CASEU	[kaziu >	kazju > kažju > kai̯žu > kei̯žu]	> *queijo*
CERESIA	[ǩerezia >	šerezja > šerežja > šereža]	> *cereja*
CERVESIA	[ǩervezia >	šervezja > šervežja > šerveža]	> *cerveja*

The above hypotheses of earlier and later genesis of yod should not seem totally objectionable in view of the fact that we are still talking about developments in Early Ibero-Romance. However, since one cannot prove that the above scenario actually ensued, I wish to point out that the different developments of Ibero-Romance /-zi-/ in Hispano- and Luso-Romance can still be explained within the present framework of palatalization by [j]. Consider the following alternative solution.

In the case of Hispano-Romance /-sj-/ and /-i̯s-/ (< /-ks-/), it was demonstrated above that the unvoiced palatalized sequence /-Vi̯š-/, after metathesis of [-šj-] spread to the unvoiced non-palatalized /-Vi̯s-/ (from Latin medial /ks/). Apparently, it was not immediately associated with the voiced counterpart /-Vi̯z-/. Before the palatalized /-Vi̯š-/ could spread to /-Vi̯z-/, the descending diphthong monophthongized, yielding /-Vš-/ and /-Vz-/ respectively. These two sequences were now different enough to avoid any sort of influence from one to the other. Catalan evidence supports this claim; as in Castilian, one finds both a reduction of /-Vi̯-/ to /-V-/ and lack of palatalization of /z/: cf. Ptg. *beijar*, Cast. and Cat. *besar*; Ptg. *beijo*, Cast. *beso*, Cat. *bes*. However, in Luso-Romance, monophthongization did not occur, preserving a greater similarity between the pair /-Vi̯š-/ and /-Vi̯z-/, which could have led to the eventual spread of the feature [+ palatal] of the former to the latter. In this manner, Torreblanca (1988:348) may have been correct to a degree when he wrote: 'En castellano y catalán, la pérdida o reducción temprana de los diptongos decrecientes dio lugar a que la palatalización sólo ocurriera con la sibilante sorda, la más tensa. Consecuentemente, al portugués *beijo* corresponde el castellano *beso* y el catalán *bes*'. However, if the longer retention of the descending diphthong was responsible for the subsequent palatalization of /-z-/, it was because of association with palatalized /-i̯š-/, and *not* because of any palatalizing effect of [i̯].

However, this change of -IA to -*a* could be explained as a case of dissimilation, before the loss of hiatus from /-ia/ to /-ja/.

The reason for having presented two different hypotheses for the respective developments of /-zj-/ in Hispano- and Luso-Romance is not to create confusion. I believe that either is possible. My point is to demonstrate alternatives to the traditional view of palatalization by [i̯], which seems to be the least plausible of the three.

The proposed stages of metathesis for the development of /-ks-/, /-sj-/ and /-zj-/ in Old Spanish and Old Portuguese may at first appear ad hoc. However, upon examining the broader Romance picture, one finds, on the one hand, a correlation between the development of /-ks-/ > /-i̯s-/ and metathesis of /-šj-/ and /-zj-/ (or /-žj-/) > /-i̯š-/ and /-i̯z-/ (or /-i̯ž-/) in the West (as outlined above), and, on the other, the lack of vocalization of implosive [k] to [i̯] and subsequent lack of metathesis of yod in the East. Even outside of Iberia, where the development of implosive /k/ in /-ks-/ and /-kt-/ resulted in /-Vi̯C-/, metathesis also occurred: '... dans l'Ouest, d'ordinaire à *yz* par transposition du *y* (fr. *baiser* = basi̯are, prov. *baisar*, esp. *besar*, ptg. *beijar*). Lorsque *ss* était double, on a eu *ys* en Gaule (prov. *baissar*, fr. *baisser* = *bassi̯are), mais *yš* ou *š* en Ibérie (ptg. *baixar*, esp. *bajar*)' (Bourciez 1956:172). Conversely, in the East, /-ks-/, in general, underwent assimilation to /-ss-/, or /-šš-/ by way of mutual assimilation of */-çs-/ (Lausberg 1965:380), affording thus no model of /-i̯s-/ for metathesis. Assimilation also regularly occurred in the case of Eastern Romance /-kt-/ (with the exception of Rumanian, where /k/ was altered to /p/), e.g., NOCTE > Sardinian, Italian *notte*, Rumanian *noapte*; DIRECTU > Sardinian *derettu*, Italian *diritto*, Rumanian *drept* (Lausberg 1965:380). Bourciez (1956:177) writes: 'En Italie (mais non au Nord, sauf en Émilie et en Vénétie), dès la fin de l'époque impériale, le premier élément de *ct* s'est assimilé au second (it. *fatto*, *notte* = factum, noctem)'. Therefore, since neither /-i̯s-/ nor /-i̯t-/ (i.e., /-Vi̯C-/) existed in the East, no metathesis of yod in the sequences /-ssj-/ and /-sj-/ occurred either: 'Le group *sy* aboutit par fusion des deux éléments à *š* ou *tš* en Orient et en Italie (roum. *cireaşă* = *ceresi̯a, it. *bacio* = basi̯um)' (Bourciez 1956:172).

LATER DEVELOPMENTS

The further development and virtual elimination in an earlier Hispano-Romance period of descending diphthongs, mainly /-Vi̯-/ > /-V-/, likely played a role in the later governing of metathesis and subsequent palatalization of /-t-/, distinguishing Early Castilian even further from other Ibero-Romance dialects.

VI. Metathesis and the development of Latin /-kt-/, /-ult-/.

After the vocalization of /-kt-/ and /-ult-/ to /-i̯t-/ and /-ui̯t-/, the respective presence or absence of palatalization of [t] in Hispano- and Luso-Romance can be explained as follows. In Luso-Romance the abundant conservation of falling diphthongs from other environments (e.g., -AVI > -ai̯ > -ei̯; -ARIU > -arju > -ai̯ru > -ei̯ro; -URIU > -urju > -oi̯ro, etc.) provided a pattern or template for the retention of /-Vi̯t-/ (where [-V-] = any vowel other than /i/). In Castilian, on the other hand, the falling diphthong [-ei̯-] generally simplified to [e] (e.g., -ei̯ru > -ero; améi̯ > amé, etc.) while [oi̯] was replaced by the more common rising diphthong [we] (cf. CORIU > *coi̯ru > cuero; DURIU > *Doi̯ru > Duero; MORIOR > *moi̯ro > muero; DORMIO > *doi̯rmo > duermo). Eventually, then, a template of falling diphthongs no longer existed in Ancient Castilian, and the diphthongs [ei̯] and [oi̯] when followed by [t] were eliminated in Castilian by metathesis: e.g., [fei̯to] > *[fetjo] > [fečo]; [mui̯to] > *[mutjo] > [mučo].

One may question, however, why metathesis occurred in the environment of /t/, instead of simplification of [ei̯] to [e] and replacement of [oi̯] by [we]. As was the case of Latin /-k'l-/, etc., where [-i̯l-] metathesized to [-lj-] because of the broad extant pattern of primary /-lj-/, it is not inconceivable that the innovative Castilian dialect metathesized /-Vi̯t-/ to /-Vtj-/ by analogy to another broad pattern of Hispano-Romance, namely /-CjV-/ (where C = any consonant, V = any vowel other than /i/). In addition to the developments of /-tj-/, /-kj-/ > /-ẑ-/ (or /-ŝ-/), and the medial supported variants /-ttj-/, /-kkj-/, /-ptj-/, /-ktj-/, /-skj-/, /-nkj-/ etc., > /-ŝ-/, in which the yod was absorbed into the preceding consonant (e.g., PUTEU > pozo, CORTICEA > corteza; PETTIA > pieça, BRACCHIU > braço, CAPTIARE > caçar, COLLACTEU > collaço, FASCIA > haça, LANCEA > lança), the on-glide [j] was also preserved. Note the following cases: /-bj-/ — RUBEU > ruvio, RABIA > ravia, PLUVIA > lluvia, NOVIU > novio, CAVEA > gavia, SUPERBIA > sobervia, NERVIU > nervio, GU(L)BIA > gu(r)bia, guvia, SALVIA > salvia; /-mj-/ — VINDEMIA > vendimia, PRAEMIA > premia; /-prj-/ — CAPREU > cabrio; /-trj-/ — VITREU > vidrio. Furthermore, all weak preterite third person singular and plural forms of the second and third conjugations show the same /-CjV-/ pattern. And although primary Latin /-tj-/ had evolved to /ẑ/ or /ŝ/, the crucial template /-tj-/ of Hispano-Romance was by no means non-existent. Any second or third conjugation verb whose lexical morpheme ended in /t/

would provide a new template of /-tj-/ in the 3rd person singular and plural of the preterite (i.e., [-tjó] and [-tjeron]) and in the present active participle (i.e., [-tjendo]), as would have any primary Latin /tę́/ (e.g., /tę́ra/ > [tjeřa], /tę́mpu/ > [tjempo], /tę́nes/ > [tjenes], etc.), where palatalization of /t/ did not occur. This template of /-CjV-/, especially where /C/ = /t/, would then serve as an impetus for the metathesis of /-Vi̯t-/ to /-Vtj-/, providing an alternative solution to the reduction of /-ei̯-/ to /-e-/ or replacement of /-oi̯-/ and /-ui̯-/ by /-ue-/; hence, *feitu, noite, muitu*, etc. > **fetjo,* **notje,* **mutjo,* etc.

Meanwhile, in Luso-Romance, the pattern /-CjV-/ was in fact diminishing, in favor of the conservative model of /-Vi̯t-/; hence, late metathesis of /-VCjV-/ to /-Vi̯CV-/ is found in many of the Portuguese counterparts of the aforementioned Castilian examples: *raiba, chu(i)va, noivo, gaiv-agem, goiva, vindima* (contraction of *-ii-* to *-i-* after metathesis), OPtg. *preima* > MPtg. *prema, caibro.* The pattern /-CjV-/, so common to Castilian, had become so rare in Old Portuguese that, when the on-glide [j] did not metathesize (because of a preceding consonant sequence), it was simply dropped; hence, SUPERBIA > OPtg. *sobervia* > MPtg. *soberb(i)a,* NERVIU > OPtg. *nervho* > MPtg. *nervo,* SALVIA > *salva,* VITREU > *vidro.* Also, in the weak preterite third person singular and plural forms — again as opposed to Castilian where one finds only rising diphthongs — in Portuguese, only falling diphthongs developed: /-ou/, /-aram/; /-eu/, /-eram/; /-iu/, /-iram/. Also, /tę́/ did not diphthongize in Luso-Romance. This variety of Ibero-Romance, then, virtually lacked any type of major /-tj-/ template, and consequently had no impetus for metathesis of yod in *feito, noite,* and *muito* types.

Another aspect of this problem which remains to be explained is why primary Latin /-tj-/ evolved, for the most part, in Ibero-Romance to an alveolar or prepalatal affricate ([ẑ] or [ŝ]), while in Hispano-Romance, the innovation /-Vi̯t-/ > /-Vtj-/ produced the palatal [č]. One might incorporate here the first stage of Menéndez Pidal's view (1941:143), whereby the tongue-height differed regarding the articulation of the [t] in each case.[20] If the point of articulation of Latin primary [tj] was dental,

---

[20] Menéndez Pidal (1941:143) describes the process as follows: 'la ŷ o y mantiene por más tiempo la energía de su articulación, con fuerza bastante para atraer a la t, haciéndola prepalatal: yt > yt̪ ... al retraerse, la t̪ pierde su extructura [sic] apical para hacerse dorsal y naturalmente algo mojada como la y, recibiendo con esta dorsalidad un elemento de africación t̪ŷ o t̪j que hace tomar a la t̪ un timbre más chicheante hasta resultar č: así

then, the palatal [j] would likely raise the entire articulation of [ŝ] (or [ẑ]) to the alveolar, or prepalatal ridge — an intermediate point. On the other hand, with the sequence /-Vi̯t-/, the dorsum or predorsum likely held a higher point of articulation, i.e., prepalatal. The palatal [j] in this case, then, would likely raise the entire articulation to the palate, resulting in [č] and not [ŝ].[21]

Finally, though the sequence of events in [fei̯to] > *[fetjo] > [fečo], for example, may, to this point, seem reasonable enough, how does one explain the Leonese forms *peyche*, *feycho*, which suggest either palatalization by [i̯], or by the type of straddling proposed by Menéndez Pidal, rather than by a metathesized on-glide [tj]? Zamora Vicente (1967:151) recognized these as intermediate forms: 'una forma intermedia con palatalización y conservación del diptongo es conocido por el leonés en el siglo XI: p a c t e t > *peiche*; f a c t u > *feicho*. Esta fase está viva hoy en alguna zona de Teberga (*seicha* "surco"; *feichu* "hecho" ... de León (Ribera del Orbigo) y de Zamora (Villarino Tras la Sierra): *feicho*, *leichuga*'. It is not clear though what Zamora Vicente meant by 'forma intermedia', i.e., an intermediate stage of development or an intermediate form resulting from dialectal mixture. I prefer to interpret these as did Hanssen, who viewed these forms as dialectal mixtures: 'Las formas de la clase *feycho* ... no son invenciones de los copistas, tuvieron existencia real y todavía la tienen ... Pero no presentan el desarrollo natural de *factum*, sino que son "formas de compromiso" originadas por la mezcla de dos dialectos' (1913:57). To account for Leonese forms like *peyche* and *feycho* without attributing the palatalization of /t/ to the off-glide [i̯], I suggest that Leonese may have gone through the steps [fai̯to] > [fei̯to], like Portuguese (and Castilian), later acquiring the palatalized /č/ by way of Castilian influence: *feyto* X *fecho* = *feycho*, which has both the Castilian innovation [t] > [č] and the conservative Gallego-Portuguese diphthong [ei̯]. In fact, according to Menéndez Pidal (1941:52), Leonese offered both /-ei̯t-/ and /-ei̯č-/ types, e.g., *leyte*, *leyche*.

---

tenemos y t ẙ > yĉ > i̯ĉ que luego se simplifica en ĉ = *ch*'.

[21] It is worth noting too that in some areas of Zamora (Fermoselle, Cibanal) and Cáceres (Zarza la Mayor, Garrovillas) Latin medial /kt/ evolved to [ŝ] or [î] as in [peŝu] 'pecho', [leîuga] 'lechuga' (Zamora Vicente 1967:151 n. 70), which might suggest that [-i̯t-] > [-tj-] first produced [ŝ] which later evolved to [č]. It is also possible, though, that dialectal [ŝ] is a later fronting of [č].

In general, though, one does not find /-Vi̯č-/ types in Romance, but rather, /-Vi̯t-/ or /-Vč-/, or reduction of /-Vi̯t-/ to /-Vt-/, e.g. Catalan *fet* (except of course in Brazilian Portuguese where palatalization resulted from final /-i/, e.g., *noite* [noi̯či]. Cf. *verdade* [verdadži]). Compare the following examples from Zamora Vicente (1967:151-52): 'La vocalización es la forma única y viva en mirandés: *feito, uito* "ocho"; *nuite* "noche"; *fruita, lluitar*, etc.', and Menéndez Pidal (1941:144): 'Así f a c t u > arag. y port. *feito*, cat. *fet*, fr. *fait* ... prov. *fach*; ... l a c t e arag. *leit*, cast. *leche* ... l a c t u c a , port. y gascon *leituga*, fr. *laitue*, catalán *lletuga*, cast. *lechuga*, prov. *laichügo, lachügo'*.[22] Similarly, Bourciez (1956:178) observes: 'La plupart des régions qui viennent d'être énumérées en sont restées à *yt*: ainsi le N. de la France (*fait, nuit*), l'Auvergne, la Gascogne, et en Italie l'Ouest du Piémont (*fayt*); de même dans la péninsule ibérique, la Catalogne (*feit*, plus tard *fet*), l'Aragon (*nueyt*) et le Portugal (*feito, noite*). Ailleurs, au contraire ... au Centre de l'Ibérie (esp. *hecho, noche*), au Sud de la France dans le Limousin, le Languedoc, une partie de la Provence (*fach, nuech*), au Nord de l'Italie dans l'est du Piémont et en Lombardie (*fatš, nœtš*)'. As these examples clearly demonstrate, the yod as a preceding off-glide did not palatalize the following /t/ in Mirandese, Aragonese, Portuguese, French, Gascon, or western Piedmontese, in Northern Italy. There is no reason, therefore, to assume that palatalization must have occurred from a preceding off-glide in Castilian either. And while some may justifiably argue against the above reasoning, claiming that innovation must begin somewhere (i.e., in this case, in Castilian), in the present view, the innovation is seen in the stage of metathesis, *not* in any sort of palatalization by [i̯]. It is likely, too, that in those Romance dialects which underwent palatalization like Castilian, some factor (perhaps a common pattern of /-tj-/) motivated the metathesis of [-i̯t-] to [-tj-], before [i̯] could affect the preceding vowel (cf. Provençal and Lombard *fach*).[23]

---

[22] Palatalization of /t/ in the latter examples could conceivably be due to the following palatal /ü/ rather than the preceding [i̯]. Though the antiquity of the /u/ > /ü/ change has been debated (see von Wartburg 1971:47-63), von Wartburg concluded that this change was early, and in fact contemporaneous with /kt/ > /Xt/, both of which resulted from a Celtic substratum (1971:74). If one follows von Wartburg, then, positing the palatalization of /t/ by /ü/ in this case is not anachronistic.

[23] The investigation of this aspect of the problem, however relevant, remains beyond the scope of the present article.

VII. Conclusions.

Though certainly not every issue raised here has been resolved, I have attempted, nevertheless, to lay to rest the notion that the off-glide [i̯] was responsible for the palatalization of certain consonants in the history of Hispano- and Luso-Romance. I should think the same would be true for the behavior of [i̯] in other languages, and that the views here presented could be put to test against other varieties of Romance. I have also attempted to point out that such a notion actually resulted from a misinterpretation or over-simplification of Menéndez Pidal's analysis. It is certainly preferable to follow what Menéndez Pidal truly intended (as did Lloyd), i.e., 'straddling' of the consonant in question. This view automatically precludes any notion of palatalization by off-glide [i̯]. But if one is to go this far, (which one at least should), why should there be any objection to the positing of an additional stage of metathesis? No one, by the way, seems to object to the idea of metathesis of yod into the preceding syllable in the cases of Ibero-Romance [-sj-] and [-zj-] (nor in cases involving other consonants). In fact, this step of metathesis is necessary to explain the vocalic inflexion of /-a-/ > /-ai̯-/ > /-ei̯-/, in examples like QUASSIARE > Ptg. *queixar*, OSp. *quexar*, Mod. Sp. *quejar*; BASIU > Ptg. *beijo*, Sp. *beso*. By the same token, I believe the stage of metathesis which provides the on-glide [j] is necessary to account for the palatalization of the consonant in question.

Even if one is still to insist on Menéndez Pidal's view, I believe I have helped uncover the factors that motivated the straddling or extension of [i̯] to [j] (i.e., FACTU > *fai̯tu* > *fei̯to* > *[fei̯tjo]*). It appears that, in any case, either metathesis of yod (as presented in this study) or if one insists, 'straddling', in Hispano- and Luso-Romance was not simply a sporadic, unmotivated development, but was governed by extant broad patterns of either consonant + yod, or yod + consonant.

The implications of the present view are various. If adopted and applied, much of the relative chronology of the developments involved will automatically change. For example, in the case of /-kt-/, the simplification of the diphthong /ei̯/ to /e/ in Hispano-Romance must now be seen as anterior, rather than posterior to the palatalization of /t/. In Luso-Romance, on the other hand, palatalization of /-zj-/ is now seen as anterior rather than posterior to the metathesis of yod. And though it may seem a bother to rethink the chronology of certain developments, (no less, to re-teach them to our students), the present view of palatalization by [j] only may provide solutions to individual problems in the historical grammar of Spanish, such as that proposed here for the presence or absence of palatalization of Ibero-Romance [-(u)i̯t-] and [-zj-]. Other cases will undoubtedly arise, such as that of Latin TAM MAGNU > *[tamai̯nu], in which the lack of vocalic inflexion to *[tamei̯nu] can be explained as a result of early metathesis to [tamanju] (by analogy to extant /nj/ patterns), followed by palatalization to [tamaɲo]. It makes no sense otherwise, that [i] would inflect the vowel and palatalize the consonant in the sequence /-ai̯t-/ (as in FACTU to *fecho*), but not in /-ai̯n-/. Latin CICONIA presents another problem which might be solved with the present view, given that the traditional account of palatalization by an off-glide states that [i̯] could not have endured long enough in an environment such as [ŝegói̯ɲa] to undergo a substitution of /oi̯/ by /ue/ (see Craddock 1980:66-67). Certainly, upon altering our view of these and other problems like them, we may advance our knowledge and understanding of the complex historical development of Ibero-Romance.

References

Ariza, Manuel, Antonio Salvador and Antonio Viudas (eds.) 1988. *Actas del I congreso internacional de historia de la lengua española.* Madrid: Arco.

Bakker, Robert T. 1986. *The dinosaur heresies.* New York: William Morrow.

Blansitt, Edward L. and Richard V. Teschner (eds.) 1980. *A Festschrift for Jacob Ornstein. Studies in general linguistics and socio-linguistics.* Rowley, Mass: Newbury House.

Bourciez, Édouard. 1956. *Éléments de linguistique romane.* 4th ed. Paris: Klincksieck.

Chen, Matthew. 1972. The time dimension: Contribution toward a theory of sound change. *Foundations of Language* 8.457-98.

Craddock, Jerry R. 1980. The contextual varieties of yod: An attempt at systematization. In Blansitt and Teschner 1980.61-68.

Diez, Friedrich. 1882. *Grammatik der romanischen Sprachen.* Vol. 1. 5th ed. Bonn: Weber.

Dworkin, Steven N. 1988. The interaction of phonological and morphological processes: The evolution of the Old Spanish second person plural verb endings. *Romance Philology* 42.144-55.

García de Diego, Vicente. 1951. *Gramática histórica española*. Madrid: Gredos.

Hanssen, Friedrich. 1913. *Gramática histórica de la lengua castellana*. Halle: Niemeyer.

Harris-Northall, Ray. 1990. The spread of sound change: Another look at syncope in Spanish. *Romance Philology* 44.137-61.

Lapesa, Rafael. 1980. *Historia de la lengua española*. 9th ed. Madrid: Gredos.

Lathrop, Thomas A. 1980. *The evolution of Spanish*. Newark, Del: Juan de la Cuesta.

_____. 1984. *Curso de gramática histórica española*. Barcelona: Ariel.

_____. 1988. Č: un extraño desarrollo. In Ariza, Salvador and Viudas, 1988.139-42.

Lausberg, Heinrich. 1965. *Lingüística románica. Tomo I. Fonética*. Madrid: Gredos.

Lloyd, Paul M. 1987. *From Latin to Spanish*. Philadelphia: American Philosophical Society.

Menéndez Pidal, Ramón. 1929. *Orígenes del español*. 2nd ed. Madrid: Espasa-Calpe.

_____. 1941. *Manual de gramática histórica española*. 6th ed. Madrid: Espasa-Calpe.

_____. 1950. *Orígenes del español*. 3rd ed. Madrid: Espasa-Calpe.

Meyer-Lübke, Wilhelm. 1890. *Grammaire des langues romanes*. Vol 1. Paris: Welter.

Pensado Ruiz, Carmen. 1984. *Cronología relativa del castellano*. Salamanca: Universidad de Salamanca.

Pharies, David A. 1990. The Ibero-Romance suffix *-aina*. *Romance Philology* 43.367-99.

Rini, Joel. 1991. The diffusion of /-ee-/ > /-e-/ in Ibero-Romance infinitives: *creer, leer, veer, preveer, proveer, seer, poseer*. *Neuphilologische Mitteilungen* 92.1-9.

Rohlfs, Gerhard. 1966. *Grammatica storica della lingua italiana e dei suoi dialetti. I: Fonetica*. Torino: Einaudi.

Spaulding, Robert K. 1943. *How Spanish grew*. Berkeley: University of California Press.

Torreblanca, Máximo. 1988. Latín BASIUM, castellano *beso*, catalán *bes*, portugués *beijo*. *Hispanic Review* 56.343-48.

Walsh, Thomas J. 1988. The etymology of Span. *cejar* 'to move back, go back; to weaken or give ground in an undertaking or discussion'. *Zeitschrift für romanische Philologie* 104.20-24.

Wang, William S.-Y. 1969. Competing changes as a cause of residue. *Language* 45.9-25.

Wartburg, Walther von. 1971. *La fragmentación lingüística de la Romania.* 2nd ed. Madrid: Gredos.

Williams, Edwin B. 1962. *From Latin to Portuguese.* 2nd ed. Philadelphia: University of Pennsylvania Press.

Wright, Roger. 1982. *Late Latin and Early Romance in Spain and Carolingian France.* Liverpool: Cairns.

Zamora Vicente, Alonso. 1967. *Dialectología española.* 2nd ed. Madrid: Gredos.

Isoglosas riojano-castellano-leonesas en la Edad Media

Máximo Torreblanca

University of California, Davis

Con relación a la Época Contemporánea, Menéndez Pidal pensó que toda la provincia de Santander (o Cantabria, como se dice hoy día) pertenece al dominio lingüístico leonés, a pesar de ofrecer pocos rasgos exclusivamente leoneses (1962:14-15, 33). Para Penny (1969:31), el habla santanderina es castellano-leonesa, es decir, presenta una mezcla de rasgos propiamente castellanos con otros propiamente leoneses. La clasificación lingüística de Santander hecha por Penny es indudablemente menos arbitraria que la de Menéndez Pidal. No obstante, ambas presentan un grave inconveniente. Aunque generalmente con menos frecuencia que en Santander, se han encontrado en el norte de la provincia de Burgos rasgos lingüísticos 'leoneses' (García de Diego 1916, 1950). Además de ello, los documentos medievales procedentes de la mitad septentrional de la provincia de Burgos ofrecen rasgos lingüísticos que unían esta región con la santanderina y la riojana, separándola de la comarca de la ciudad de Burgos, del castellano normativo medieval. Daré algunos ejemplos.

En el leonés moderno, está muy extendida la vocal final /-u/ procedente de la terminación latina -UM (Menéndez Pidal 1968:54-56), *maridu, pradu, manu,* etc. Este fenómeno se ha registrado por toda la provincia de Santander (García-Lomas 1949: LII), y en comarcas adyacentes de la provincia de Burgos (González Ollé 1964:14-15; Penny 1969: mapa 4). Los documentos medievales señalan un área más extensa. Menéndez Pidal (1968:172) recogió formas como *sulcu, pedaçu, conceju* y *unu,* en escrituras notariales de fines del siglo XII y primera mitad del XIII, procedentes de Santander, Campoo y Castilla del Norte (Oña). También se dan más al sureste, desde la comarca burgalesa de la Bureba hasta la frontera riojana: *cantu, nietu,* Pedro *Couu,* el *couellanu,* Pedro *Brauu, nietu, blandu, pedaçu* (a. 1228, 1272, 1275 y 1265-95; Pérez de Tudela 1977:81, 84, 87); *omezillu,* la serna del *Carrascu,* el *Diaconu,* con mio *conventu,* Diag Lopez de *Faru, maridu, sulcu,* el *cuchillu mangu negru, pedazu* (a. 1182, 1190, 1195, 1200, 1213, 1214 y 1246; Cantera 1970:114, 118-19, 121, 124-26).

Menéndez Pidal (1968:342) encontró las formas pronominales *elli* 'él' y *li(s)* 'le(s)', y los demostrativos *esti* 'este' y *esi* 'ese' en documentos medievales procedentes de la Rioja Alta, Álava, Castilla del Norte y Campoo. En Castilla del Norte también existió la forma *aquelli* 'aquel' (a. 1292; Oceja 1986:142). Todas estas formas también se dan en documentos medievales procedentes de León (Staaff 1907:215, 272). En escrituras medievales de Navarra se encuentran *li(s)* y *esti* (Ciérvide 1972:65-66; Saralegui 1977:173, 186). En el leonés medieval se documentan algunos ejemplos de *isti* 'este' (Staaff 1907:215). En el habla moderna de Asturias se han recogido las formas *elli, esti, esi* y *aquelli*, además de *illi, isti, isi* y *aquil*. En las últimas, el paso de /é/ a /í/ se debe seguramente al influjo metafónico de la /-i/ final de palabra (Zamora 1967:107, 176). Con relación al habla de Tudanca (oeste de la provincia de Santander), Penny (1978:48) indica la existencia de *iste* 'este' e *ise* 'ese', formas procedentes de *isti* e *isi*, con paso posterior de la *-i* final a *-e.* Penny también ha recogido *iste* e *ise* en el valle santanderino de Pas, e incluso en algunos valles septentrionales de Espinosa de los Monteros (Burgos), limítrofes con la provincia de Santander (1969:115, 392-93). Tenemos noticias de la existencia de *esti* 'este', en el siglo XX, en el valle de Mena, al nordeste de la provincia de Burgos (González Ollé 1960:71). Formas similares a las actuales asturianas y santanderinas, con paso de /é/ a /í/ pero generalmente con apócope de la vocal final, se dan en documentos medievales procedentes de Castilla del Norte: 'et el otro [solar] en que moraua *il* [él]' (a. 1231; Pérez de Tudela 1977:49); 'et vendio *il* [él] mismo' (a. 1232; Pérez de Tudela 1977:51); 'una façuela que tiene en *ist* [este] pedaço' (mediados del s. XIII; Pérez de Tudela 1977:101); 'el conviento *dis* [de ese] mismo logar' (a. 1245; Álamo 1950:619); 'et al conviento *dis* mismo logar' (a. 1245; Álamo 1950:620); 'el conviento *disi* mismo logar' (a. 1245; Álamo 1950:621); 'al conviento *dis* mismo logar' (a. 1249; Álamo 1950:631); 'e(t) nos conviento *dis* mismo logar' (a. 1250; Álamo 1950:632, 633; a. 1251 y 1254; Oceja 1983: 130, 136); 'e nos conviento *daquis* (de aquese) mismo logar' (a. 1254; Oceja 1983:135).

Según Menéndez Pidal (1968:286-90, 294), la reducción del grupo consonántico *mb* a *m* (LUMBU > *lomo*) en la Península Ibérica se dio en el oriente de León, toda Castilla (incluso Santander), Navarra, Aragón y Cataluña. Dentro de esta gran área geográfica, la única excepción fue, en la Edad Media, la región riojana. Para García de Diego (1951:93; 1978:30-39), la evolución *mb* > *m* fue, en Castilla, un fenómeno originalmente burgalés, el cual se extendió hacia la Castilla del Norte y Santander. Lo característico de estas dos regiones de Castilla fue la conservación de *mb*. La divergencia de opiniones expresadas por Menéndez Pidal y García de Diego radica en la mayor o menor importancia dada a las hablas modernas y a los documentos medievales. En *El dialecto leonés*, Menéndez Pidal (1962:79) señala la conservación del grupo *mb* en Santander: *lomba, lamber, relambíu, camba* 'cama o pina de rueda'. Pero en *Orígenes del español* (1968:294), incluye un mapa en que toda la provincia de Santander, excepto el extremo más occidental, pertenece al área de la evolución *mb* > *m*. Históricamente, toda la actual provincia de Santander ha pertenecido a Castilla, excepto la comarca de Liébana, limítrofe con Asturias. Inicialmente podríamos suponer que los casos de conservación santanderina de *mb,* mencionados por Menéndez Pidal, proceden únicamente de la zona tradicionalmente leonesa, pero nos equivocaríamos.

En Tudanca, Penny (1978:65) ha recogido las formas *ambuesta* (< AMBOSTA), *camba* (< CAMBA) 'pieza de la rueda del carro', *cambera* 'camino carretero', *lamber* (< LAMBERE) 'lamer', *lambión* 'goloso', *lumbiyu* (LUMBU) 'pila larga de hierba' y *eslumbiyar* (LUMBU) 'tender la hierba segada'. Para el valle de Pas, Penny (1969:80) señala *lamber, lambión, lambiana* 'golosina', *lambiá* 'lamedura', *lumbiá* y *lumbiyu* 'pila de hierba', *cambá* (CAMBA) 'ringlera de gavillas', *camberón* (CAMBA) 'camino carretero' y *escarrambar* 'desvencijar'. Históricamente, la población de Tudanca ha sido siempre del Reino de Castilla y ha formado parte de la región de Santillana. Más interesante es el caso del valle de Pas. Aunque hoy día se encuentra en la provincia de Santander, en la Edad Media pertenecía a Espinosa de los Monteros (Burgos), y formaba parte de Castilla del Norte (Penny 1969:27-28). Teniendo en cuenta esta circunstancia, no tiene nada de extraño que en el habla contemporánea del norte de la provincia de Burgos, García de Diego (1950:108, 110) recogiera *lamber, lambión* y *ambugas* (< SAMBUCA). Menéndez Pidal (1962:79) señaló la existencia actual de *camba* (< CAMBA) 'cama o pina de rueda' en Asturias y Santander. También existe *camba* en la comarca burgalesa de la Bureba (González Ollé 1964:86). A juzgar por las hablas contemporáneas, no parece infundada la creencia de García de Diego sobre la conservación del grupo *mb* en el romance medieval de Santander y Castilla del Norte, caractererística lingüística que unía esta región con la Rioja. Veamos los hechos que llevaron a Menéndez Pidal a pensar lo contrario.

En documentos antiguos procedentes del este de Santander (Santoña) y Castilla del Norte (Oña), Menéndez Pidal (1968:287) recogió algunos casos de la evolución *mb > m: concamiauimus, concamiatone* (a. 1056); *conkamiatone, conkamio, conkamiatonis* (a. 1086); *camiet, camiare* (a. 1107). Como el lector podrá observar, todas estas formas proceden del latín CAMBIARE. Curiosamente, el mismo origen tienen los casos más antiguos de *mb > m* recogidos por Menéndez Pidal en León y en la región de Burgos (1968:286-87). Para el riojano medieval Menéndez Pidal (1968:286-87) señaló la conservación sistemática del grupo *mb*. No obstante en un documento riojano del año 1059 se da la forma *camium* < CAMBIUM (Ubieto 1960:99). Según Ciérvide (1972:41-42), en el romance navarro medieval la reducción del grupo latino *mb* a *m* fue más frecuente que la conservación, pero los únicos casos mencionados del resultado *m* proceden de CAMBIARE O CAMBIUM. Para Saralegui (1977:80, 140-41) la norma medieval navarra fue la conservación de *mb (camberos, palombar)*, añadiendo que las únicas excepciones encontradas en los documentos de Irache se remontan a CAMBIUM y CAMBIARE: *camium* (a. 1076), *camium* (a. 1084), *camio* (a. 1143 y 1141-57), *camiata* (a.1222). Con relación al Fuero General de Navarra, Ynduráin (1945:43) observó la conservación sistemática del grupo latino *mb*, con una sola excepción: *camio*.

Resultan curiosos los resultados de CAMBIARE/CAMBIUM en español puesto que en la lengua moderna se conserva el grupo *mb (cambio, cambiar)*, mientras que en la antigua se reducía sistemáticamente a *m*, incluso en regiones donde *mb* se conservaba ante vocal. Para la lengua moderna, podríamos suponer un origen dialectal o, más probablemente, un préstamo del latín eclesiástico medieval. Para la antigua, parece ser que el grupo latino *mb* seguido de yod, fue más propenso a pasar a *m* que cuando iba seguido por vocal. Si prescindimos del caso de CAMBIARE/CAMBIUM, la historia del grupo latino *mb*, en Castilla, fue distinta de la expuesta por Menéndez Pidal.

Menéndez Pidal (1968:287) recogió algunos casos castellanos antiguos procedentes de LUMBU: *lombo, lomba* (a. 1011); *lu lombu* (a. 1072); *Lombana* (a. 1074). A ellos podemos añadir los siguientes: *lombo* (a. 932 y 964; Serrano 1910:334, 367); *lomba* (a. 972, Serrano 1910:6); *Palomeiro, Palomero* (a. 972; Serrano 1910:335, 380). Las dos últimas formas no se encuentran en documentos originales, sino en copias hechas a fines del siglo XI. Ambos proceden de la comarca burgalesa. Aunque *Palomeiro* se dé en una copia, la conservación del sufijo -*eiro* nos permite suponer que tal vez *Palomeiro* ya se encontraba en el manuscrito original del siglo X (Torreblanca 1988). Por otro lado, las formas *lombo* y *lomba*, del siglo X pero conservadas en copias de fines del XI, también se dan en documentos burgaleses. Todo cambio fonético ocurre primeramente en un individuo o grupo de individuos, y luego puede o no extenderse gradualmente, palabra por palabra, al resto de la comunidad lingüística. En un momento determinado, convivieron en la comarca burgalesa un grupo innovador de hablantes que tendía a reducir a *m* el segmento fonético *mb*, y otro grupo que favorecía la conservación de *mb*. Es probable que el paso de *mb* a *m* ya se diera en la comarca burgalesa del siglo X, pero todavía no se había extendido a todo el léxico o a toda la comunidad lingüística.

No existe evidencia documental alguna anterior al año 1100 de la evolución *mb* > *m* (más vocal) en Castilla del Norte. Las formas *lombo* y *lomba*, del año 1011, y *lombu*, de 1072, mencionadas por Menéndez Pidal, proceden de Castilla del Norte. La forma toponímica *Lombana*, del año 1074, corresponde modernamente a *Lomana*, en el norte de la provincia de Burgos.

Hay más casos de *mb* en el siglo XI no mencionados por Menéndez Pidal: 'per illo *lombo* de Petrafita ... et per illo *lombo* de Cereseda ... et per illo *lombo* de Cantabrana ... et ad *lombo* que dicunt Galliello' (a. 1011; Álamo 1950:30); 'inter *ambos lombos* et per illa uia de illo *lombo*' (a. 1035; Álamo 1950:53). Los primeros casos de reducción a *m* en Castilla del Norte se dan en documentos del siglo XII: *loma* (a. 1114, 1156 y 1165; Álamo 1950:170, 266, 277). Pero también se documenta la conservación: 'el *lombo*' (a. 1169; Álamo 1950:281). Como indicó García de Diego (1978:38), es bien probable que la forma *loma* del siglo XII, como *lomo* y *paloma* en la lengua actual del norte de la provincia de Burgos, no sean autóctonas de esta región sino importadas de la comarca de Burgos. De cualquier modo, es seguro que la tendencia a reducir el grupo latino *mb* a *m* fue mucho más intensa en la zona central de la provincia de Burgos que en Castilla del Norte.

Del latín SARCULARE proceden las formas verbales españolas *sachar* y *sallar*. La primera presenta la evolución 'normal' castellana del grupo /k'l/ tras consonante, como en MASCULU > *macho* y AMPLU > *ancho*. Según Corominas (1954:4, 115-16), el segundo resultado se encuentra en Vizcaya, Santander, parte de Asturias y Burgos. No tengo noticias concretas de la existencia de *sallar* en toda la provincia de Burgos, pero sí se ha recogido esta forma en dos comarcas del norte de Burgos: el valle de Mena (González Ollé 1960:83) y la Bureba (González Ollé 1964:200). De MASCULU se derivan la forma medieval riojana *masl(l)o* 'macho', empleada por el poeta riojano Gonzalo de Berceo, y la santanderina moderna *mallo* 'tronco de la cola de los cuadrúpedos' (García de Diego 1950:122; Corominas 1954:175-76). Según Corominas (1954:4, 417), las formas *tiempla* y *tienlla* 'sien, pómulo', que aparecen ambas en Berceo (primera mitad del siglo XIII), proceden del latín TEMPORA 'sienes'; el mismo origen tienen *tenllera* 'carrillo', del Libro de Alexandre, *tenlleira,* 'mejilla' en gallego y *te(n)llerada* 'bofetada' en Asturias.

Los documentos medievales de Castilla del Norte complementan los datos anteriores. En una escritura notarial del año 1228 se menciona a un labrador de Vileña (Bureba) llamado 'Ennego *Tienlla* Pegada' (Pérez de Tudela 1977:34). El apellido de este labrador era la misma forma *tienlla* empleada por Berceo (o sus copistas riojanos). En una escritura notarial del año 867, procedente también de la Bureba, se menciona el lugar siguiente: 'in valle *amplam*' (Ubieto 1976:18); y en 870, *Balle Ampla* (Pérez Soler 1970:20). En un documento de 1063, no original sino copiado en la Rioja a comienzos del s. XIII, este mismo lugar aparece bajo la forma *Valle Anlha* (Ubieto 1976:320); en otro documento escrito en la Bureba a mediados del siglo XIII, *vall anlla* (Pérez de Tudela 1977:99). De CONCHULA (> esp. *concha*) proceden las formas toponímicas *Conlla* (a. 1131; Oceja 1983:39) y *Concha* (a. 1290; Oceja 1986: 106), las cuales designaban un lugar situado cerca de Valdivielso (partido de Villarcayo). La primera de estas formas representa el resultado, o un resultado, autóctono de CONCHULA en el romance de Castilla del Norte; la segunda pudiera ser un préstamo venido de la comarca burgalesa, a menos que ambos resultados se hubieran dado espontáneamente en el norte de Castilla, en grupos distintos de hablantes.

En el norte y noroeste de la Península Ibérica, hubo dos resultados principales de los grupos /-k'l-/ y /-pl-/ tras consonante: a) una consonante palatal africada sibilante, *ch*; b) una consonante palatal lateral, *ll*. El primero fue el más frecuente, y se estableció como norma lingüística de Castilla y Portugal. El segundo se dio, como hecho autóctono, en la Rioja Alta, Castilla del Norte, Santander y Asturias, e incluso se extendió a Galicia.

Una característica del leonés antiguo y moderno es la diptongación de la ŏ tónica latina seguida de yod (Menéndez Pidal 1966:39-40): *nueche* 'noche', *mueyo* 'mojo', *fueya* 'hoja', etc. Lo mismo ocurre en aragonés (Zamora 1967:218): *güello* 'ojo', *ruello* < RŎTULU, etc. La diptongación existió también en el romance navarro medieval (Ciérvide 1972:34; Saralegui 1977:64, 109): *fuoia* 'hoja', *Pueio* 'poyo', *huey* 'hoy', *fuellas* 'hojas', *nueites* 'noches'. Con relación a la Rioja, García de Diego señaló las formas *luejo* < LŎLIU y *huey* 'hoy' en la lengua moderna (1978:363), y *duecho* < DŎCTU en la medieval (1951:47). También existe *ruejo* < rŏtulu en la Rioja, además de Álava, centro y sur de Navarra, suroeste de Aragón y Soria (Velilla Barquero 1971:17; Alvar 1979-80: mapa 226; Iribarren 1952:455; Manrique 1956:44). García de Diego señala *nuétiga* 'lechuza' (< NŎCTUA), *bisuejo* 'bisojo', *cuejo* 'cojo' y *muejo* 'mojo' en el habla moderna de Santander (1978:194-95), y *cuejo* 'cojo' en el norte de Burgos (1916:302). Para García de Diego (1951:47), la no diptongación castellana de la ŏ tónica latina, ante yod o una consonante palatal, fue originariamente un fenómeno propio o exclusivo de la comarca burgalesa, pues tanto la Rioja como Castilla del Norte y Santander pertenecieron al área lingüística de la diptongación.

Menéndez Pidal (1968:143) insinuó la posibilidad de que la forma *cuejo* del norte de Burgos sea 'un vulgarismo como *cuerro, ruempo,* ajeno a la diptongación ante yod.' Añadió que sólo había encontrado un ejemplo de diptongación medieval de la ŏ tónica latina seguida de yod en documentos medievales de Castilla, *cuejan* 'cojan', forma que se da en una escritura notarial redactada en el año 1244 en Pancorbo. Según Menéndez Pidal (ibidem) esta escritura 'parece tener influencias orientales'.[1] Prescindiendo de la forma medieval *cuejan,* Menéndez Pidal (ibidem) llegó a la conclusión de que 'en Castilla faltó siempre esta diptongación [ante yod], según comprueba un nombre toponímico como Campóo < CAMPŎDIUM. La falta de diptongación ante yod en muchas voces del leonés y aragonés moderno es un efecto debido principalmente a la influencia castellana, y su falta al Sur de la Península es debida a la total castellanización del territorio reconquistado por Castilla.'

Menéndez Pidal expuso su opinión sobre la evolución de la ŏ tónica latina, ante yod, en *Orígenes del español,* una obra primeramente

---

[1] He examinado con detenimiento este documento, el cual fue publicado por Menéndez Pidal (1919:86-87). Si prescindimos de la forma *cuejan,* no ofrece ninguna influencia oriental.

publicada en 1926. Por entonces, la única forma moderna conocida por los lingüistas de la diptongación en el territorio de la primitiva Castilla, que incluía toda la provincia de Santander excepto la comarca de Liébana, en el extremo occidental, era *cuejo,* del valle de Losa (García de Diego 1916:302). Consecuentemente, es muy comprensible que Menéndez Pidal le quitara toda importancia a esta forma 'aislada'.

El verbo español ofrece casos no etimológicos de diptongación o falta de diptongación de vocales latinas, debidos a la influencia analógica de unos verbos sobre otros o de unas formas verbales sobre otras de un mismo verbo (Menéndez Pidal 1966:288-90): *siembran* (ant. *sembran*), *friega* (ant. *frega*), *cuelo, consuelo, veda* (ant. *vieda*), *conforta* (ant. *confuerta*), etc. Por sí sola, una forma como *cuejan,* en la lengua moderna o en la medieval, no prueba absolutamente nada respecto a la evolución de la ŏ tónica latina ante yod. No obstante, puede ser útil si se da acompañada por otras formas espontáneamente diptongadas.

El valle de Losa, donde García de Diego encontró la forma *cuejo,* se encuentra en el extremo septentrional de la provincia de Burgos. En el valle de Pas, el cual perteneció históricamente a Castilla del Norte, Penny (1969:60) ha recogido *cueju* 'cojo' (del verbo 'coger'), junto a *nueche* 'noche', *biscueju* 'bisojo' y *uy* < *huey* 'hoy'. Las tres últimas formas no pueden explicarse por analogía morfológica. La forma *cuejan* del año 1244, recogida por Menéndez Pidal, se encuentra en un documento escrito en la población de Pancorbo, del partido judicial de Miranda del Ebro, una comarca burgalesa limítrofe con Álava y Logroño. Tanto en Álava como en Logroño existe actualmente la voz *ruejo.* En cuatro documentos de los años 1287, 1290 y 1291, escritos en Valdegrún o Cerezo del Río Tirón, poblaciones de la antigua Rioja burgalesa (Madoz 1845-50:13, 485-88), se da la forma *fueia* < FŎLIA 'hoja' (Castro Garrido y Lizoain Garrido 1987:104, 126, 128, 139). El partido judicial de Belorado, donde se encuentran Valdegrún y Cerezo, limita al norte con Pancorbo. Las formas *cuejo,* del habla moderna del valle de Losa, y *cuejan,* de la medieval de Pancorbo, deben ser consideradas como dos ejemplos de diptongación espontánea de la ŏ tónica latina ante yod.

A juzgar por los datos disponibles, la ŏ tónica latina seguida de yod no diptongó en la comarca de la ciudad de Burgos, pero sí lo hizo en la Rioja (logroñesa y burgalesa), Castilla del Norte y Santander, como indicó García de Diego. En Castilla del Norte, la diptongación probablemente no se dio con mucha frecuencia.

El último rasgo lingüístico del que me ocupo en esta ocasión, el cual relaciona la lengua actual con la medieval, se refiere a unas palabras recogidas por Penny en Selaya y San Pedro del Romeral, dos poblaciones del valle de Pas (1969:59): *ajuogu* 'ahogo', *cuoju* 'cojo' (del verbo 'coger'), *iscuondu* 'escondo', *bisuoju* 'bisojo' y *salmuora* 'salmuera'. Penny se inclinó a pensar que el diptongo [wó], en estas palabras, era un arcaísmo fonético.

El diptongo español [wé], procedente de la ŏ tónica latina, tuvo como etapa anterior la secuencia fonética [wó], la cual existe todavía en algunas hablas leonesas (Zamora 1967:89-93). Según Lapesa (1984:20-21, 161), en el castellano del siglo XII y primera mitad del XIII, alternaban los diptongos [wó] y [wé], y el primero se podía representar gráficamente por *o*. Comparó este hecho gráfico-fonético con el existente en documentos medievales procedentes de una comarca asturiana (donde todavía se conserva el diptongo [wó]), los cuales apenas ofrecen la grafía *uo*, transcribiéndose normalmente por *o* (dominante hasta 1370), el resultado romance de la ŏ tónica latina.

Con relación al Fuero de Madrid, redactado en el año 1202, Lapesa (1984:160-61) observó que raramente se utilizan las grafías *ie* y *ue* para representar los resultados romances de las vocales tónicas latinas Ĕ y Ŏ, pues normalmente se dan las grafías simples *e* y *o*: *ferro* y *fierro*, *cutello*, *petra*, *uernes*, *parentes*, *foras* y *fueras*, *morto*, *morte*, *bonas*, *bolta*, etc. Según Lapesa, en formas como *ferro* y *morto* la permanencia gráfica de las vocales simples pudo responder 'a un hábito culto que se prolongó entre los notarios hasta mediar el siglo XIII y aún después dejó muestras aisladas. Sin embargo, hay también otra posibilidad, la de que en el sistema fonológico del romance hablado en el Centro peninsular los diptongos *ie, ue*, no fuesen todavía fonemas distintos de las vocales abiertas *e* y *o*, sino variantes expresivas de ellas.' Si, por la razón que sea, los escribas medievales, dentro de un período determinado, podían representar el diptongo [jé] con la grafía *e*, como en *ferro*, no hay seguridad absoluta de que la grafía *o*, en *morto*, corresponda al diptongo [wé], pero no [wó], o viceversa. Según lo dicho por Lapesa, todo dependería de que el diptongo procedente de la ŏ tónica latina, ya fuese [wó] o [wé], se interpretara como una mera 'variante expresiva' del fonema /ɔ/. De todos modos, es seguro que el diptongo [wó] todavía no se había perdido en la lengua castellana cuando se redactó el Fuero de Madrid.

En un documento de 1192, escrito en la región central de la provincia de Burgos, se menciona una serna llamada *Uolga,* la cual estaba situada entre Villanuño y Villadiego (Peña 1983:75); en otro de 1281, aparece bajo la forma *La Velga* (Lizoain Garrido 1987:124). Su etimología es la palabra prelatina ŎLGA (> esp. *huelga* 'huerta a la orilla del río'; Corominas 1954:2, 932). En la comarca burgalesa de la Bureba existe actualmente la aldea de Buezo, cuyo origen lingüístico desconozco. En un documento pontificio de 1216, escrito en Letrán, encontramos la forma *Buozo,* designando esta misma población (Garrido 1983:308). Se trata de un documento relativo a disputas territoriales existentes por entonces entre los obispos de Burgos y Osma, los cuales comparecieron ante el papa Inocencio III para que solucionara el pleito. Aunque este documento no se redactó en Castilla, la forma *Buozo* que en él aparece debe de reflejar la pronunciación, o una de las pronunciaciones castellanas de aquella época, del moderno Buezo. Al margen de una escritura notarial de comienzos del siglo XIV, procedente de Aguilar de Campoo, se da la frase siguiente: 'Don Yuannes el *buon* (bueno) II quartos e III eminas trigo e V eminas de ordio'. Este mismo documento contiene las formas *Foyolo* (3 casos) y *Foyuelo, Cozuelos, fuent, Uarriolo, uerto* (Merchán 1982:243-46, 251, 261-62). La teoría de Lapesa, según la cual los escribas castellanos utilizaron la grafía *o* con el valor fonético de [wó], tiene absoluta validez en esta escritura notarial de Aguilar de Campoo.

A juzgar por los datos disponibles, el diptongo [wó] se conservó o se ha conservado durante más tiempo en la mitad septentrional de Castilla (Castilla del Norte, Campoo y Santander) que en la meridional (incluida la comarca burgalesa). Los casos de [wó] hallados modernamente en el valle de Pas son, como sospechó Penny, verdaderos arcaísmos fonéticos.

En 1916 García de Diego publicó 'Dialectalismos', una colección de rasgos lingüísticos no pertenecientes al español normativo, y encontrados por él mismo en Castilla (la Vieja). En 1950 apareció otro estudio suyo, 'El castellano como complejo dialectal', donde aparecen más hechos lingüísticos no normativos, obtenidos por él mismo u otros investigadores. Posteriormente, en su *Grámatica histórica española* (1951), añadió datos procedentes de la lengua medieval. En esta obra, y en su *Manual de dialectología española* (1978), García de Diego intentó demarcar áreas lingüísticas, o trazar isoglosas, dentro de Castilla. El lector de estas dos obras de García de Diego debe de llegar a la conclusión de que la cuna de la lengua española se encontraba en la comarca burgalesa.

Esto no quiere decir, por supuesto, que el romance burgalés de los siglos XII y XIII fuese ininteligible para los habitantes de la Rioja y Castilla del Norte. En realidad, las hablas de estas comarcas castellanas tenían muchos rasgos comunes. Pero también había algunos rasgos que las diferenciaban, de los cuales encontramos restos en la época moderna.

Referencias

Álamo, Juan del. 1950. *Colección diplomática de San Salvador de Oña (822-1284)*. Madrid: CSIC.

Alvar, Manuel. 1979-80. *Atlas lingüístico y etnográfico de Aragón, Navarra y Rioja*. 12 vols. Zaragoza: CSIC.

Cantera, Francisco. 1970. El libro becerro de Bugedo de Campajares. *Revista de la Universidad de Madrid* 73.107-29.

Castro Garrido, Araceli y José M. Lizoain Garrido. 1987. *Documentación del monasterio de Las Huelgas de Burgos (1284-1306)*. Burgos: J. M. Garrido Garrido.

Ciérvide, Ricardo. 1972. *Primeros documentos navarros en romance (1198-1230)*. Pamplona: Diputación Foral de Navarra.

Corominas, Joan. 1954-57. *Diccionario crítico etimológico de la lengua castellana*. 4 vols. Madrid: Gredos.

García de Diego, Vicente. 1916. Dialectalismos. *Revista de filología española* 3.301-18.

_____. 1950. El castellano como complejo dialectal y sus dialectos internos. *Revista de filología española* 34.107-24.

_____. 1951. *Gramática histórica española*. Madrid: Gredos.

_____. 1978. *Dialectología española*. 3ª ed. Madrid: Ediciones Cultura Hispánica.

García-Lomas, G. Adriano. 1949. *El lenguaje popular de las montañas de Santander*. Santander: Excelentísima Diputación Provincial.

Garrido, José Manuel. 1983. *Documentación de la catedral de Burgos (1184-1222)*. Burgos: J. M. Garrido Garrido.

González Ollé, Fernando. 1960. Cáracterísticas fonéticas y léxico del valle de Mena. *Boletín de la Real Academia Española* 40.67-85.

_____. 1964. *El habla de la Bureba*. Madrid: CSIC.

Iribarren, José María. 1952. *Vocabulario navarro*. Pamplona: Diputación Foral de Navarra.

Lapesa, Rafael. 1984. *Estudios de lingüística histórica española*. Madrid: Paraninfo.

Lizoain Garrido, José Manuel. 1987. *Documentación del Monasterio de Las Huelgas de Burgos (1263-1283)*. Burgos: J. M. Garrido Garrido.

Madoz, Pascual. 1845-50. *Diccionario geográfico-estadístico-histórico de España y sus posesiones de Ultramar*. 16 vols. Madrid: Pascual Madoz.

Manrique, Gervasio. 1956. Vocabulario comparado de los valles del Duero y del Ebro. *Revista de dialectología y tradiciones populares* 12.3-53.

Menéndez Pidal, Ramón. 1919. *Documentos lingüísticos de España. I: Reino de Castilla*. Madrid: Centro de Estudios Históricos.

_____. 1962. *El dialecto leonés*. Oviedo: Instituto de Estudios Asturianos.

_____. 1966. *Manual de gramática histórica española*. 12ª ed. Madrid: Espasa-Calpe.

_____. 1968. *Orígenes del español*. 6ª ed. Madrid: Espasa-Calpe.

Merchán, Carlos. 1982. *Sobre los orígenes del régimen señorial de Castilla. El abadengo de Aguilar de Campoo (1020-1369)*. Málaga: Universidad de Málaga.

Oceja, Isabel. 1983. *Documentación del monasterio de San Salvador de Oña (1032-1284)*. Burgos: J. M. Garrido Garrido.

_____. 1986. *Documentación del monasterio de San Salvador de Oña (1285-1310)*. Burgos: J. M. Garrido Garrido.

Penny, Ralph. 1969. *El habla pasiega*. London: Tamesis.

_____. 1978. *Estudio estructural del habla de Tudanca*. Tübingen: Niemeyer.

Peña, F. Javier. 1983. *Documentación del monasterio de San Juan de Burgos (1091-1400)*. Burgos: J. M. Garrido Garrido.

Pérez de Tudela, María Isabel. 1977. *El monasterio de Vileña en sus documentos*. Madrid: Universidad Complutense de Madrid.

Pérez Soler, María. 1970. *Cartulario de Valpuesta*. Valencia: Anubar.

Saralegui, Carmen. 1977. *El dialecto navarro en los documentos del monasterio de Irache (958-1397)*. Pamplona: Diputación Foral de Navarra.

Serrano, Luciano. 1910. *Becerro gótico de Cerdeña*. Valladolid: Cuesta.

Staaff, Erik. 1907. *Étude sur l'ancien dialecte léonais.* Uppsala: Almqvist & Wiksell.

Torreblanca, Máximo. 1988. La fonología histórica española, los documentos y los diccionarios medievales. *Journal of Hispanic Philology* 12.139-49.

Ubieto, Antonio. 1960. *Cartulario de Albelda.* Valencia: Universidad de Valencia.

_____. 1976. *Cartulario de San Millán de la Cogolla (759-1076).* Valencia: Anubar.

Velilla Barquero, Ricardo. 1971. *Contribución al estudio del vocabulario alavés.* Vitoria: Diputación Foral de Álava.

Ynduráin, Francisco. 1945. *Contribución al estudio del navarro-aragonés antiguo.* Zaragoza: Institución Fernando el Católico.

Zamora Vicente, Alonso. 1967. *Dialectología española.* 2ª ed. Madrid: Gredos.

The Demise of Lenition as a Productive Phonological Process in Hispano-Romance

Thomas J. Walsh

Georgetown University

Little over a half-century ago, the Swiss Romanist Walther von Wartburg published in the *Zeitschrift für romanische Philologie* an article well known to all Romance historical linguists, titled 'Die Ausgliederung der romanischen Sprachräume', expanded fourteen years later into a full-fledged monograph. In that piece, the Swiss scholar articulated what could well be called the 'standard theory' of the classification of the Romance languages into Eastern and Western branches. The Eastern group was held to comprise Central and Southern Italian (including Sicilian), Dalmatian (a language whose last native speaker died toward the end of the last century), and Rumanian; while the Western group subsumed Gallo-Italian, French, Provençal, Catalan, Spanish, and Galician-Portuguese, with Sardinian, as befits its geographic position, occupying a sort of middle ground between the two main branches.

The criteria invoked by Wartburg in justification of that bipartite division were preservation vs. deletion of word-final /-s/, about which nothing further will be said here, and presence in the West vs. absence in the East of Lenition, or weakening of intervocalic obstruents. That weakening affected three distinct series of phonemes. Briefly, 1) the Latin voiced stops were spirantized and in some instances ultimately deleted, 2) voiceless obstruents were voiced (with subsequent spirantization in some varieties), and 3) geminate — or long — consonants were reduced to simple. All of this will seem accurate if, like Wartburg and most of his predecessors, we limit our purview to the Romance literary tongues, especially in their written forms. To illustrate the differing outcomes in East and West, I cite some Italian and Spanish words, alongside their Latin etyma.

Classical Latin	Italian	Spanish	
HABĒRE 'to have'	avere[1]	haber [ß]	
NĪDU 'nest'	nido [d]	nido [δ]	Spirantization
NEGĀRE 'to deny'	negare [g]	negar[2][γ]	
CAPUT 'head'	capo	cabo [ß]	
VĪTA 'life'	vita	vida [δ]	Voicing
CAECU 'blind'	cieco	ciego [γ]	
CAPPA 'cape'	cappa	capa	
MITTŌ 'I send'	metto	meto	Degemination
VACCA 'cow'	vacca	vaca	

However, such connoisseurs of Italian dialect speech as Heinrich
Lausberg and Harald Weinrich knew that Lenition — albeit of a typo-
logically distinct variety — was current in many Italian dialects spoken
to the south of the famous La Spezia-Rimini line, where, according to
Wartburg's vision, it is not supposed to occur. In most of Tuscany,
intervocalic voiceless stops are spirantized in all speech registers (the
well-known *gorgia toscana*), while their voiced counterparts undergo the
same process in conversational style (see Giacomelli 1934:197, Rohlfs
1949:342-45, Fiorelli 1952, Giannelli 1976:22). In ample regions of
southern Italy, intervocalic voiced stops are regularly spirantized and
voiceless ones voiced, while the geographically central dialects of Umbria
and Latium exhibit Voicing of voiceless stops and incipient geminate
reduction (see relevant sections of Rohlfs 1949). Fortunately for scholars,
it is not necessary to undertake mountain-climbing expeditions or trans-
desert treks to track down these features. To the contrary, one hears them
constantly in the speech of even highly educated Romans and Nea-

---

[1] All Romance languages exhibit a labial spirant as reflex of Latin intervocalic /b/,
a fact which has led comparatists to project spirantization of that phoneme onto proto-
Romance. Thus only the dental and velar, but not the labial voiced stop, can be invoked
for purposes of subclassification.

[2] Lat. intervocalic /d/ was deleted, presumably after an intermediate stage of
spirantization, in numerous Spanish and Portuguese lexemes. Intervocalic /g/ appears to
have suffered deletion in certain words at the proto-Romance stage. For details see
Grandgent 1908:110, Malkiel 1960, and Dworkin 1974.

politans. Within Italy itself, central and southern Voicing of intervocalic /p, t, k/ is so well known as to have achieved the status of a stereotypical feature in northern Italian caricatures of the southern accent.[3]

Lausberg (1956:31-32), evidently reluctant to project Lenition onto Late Spoken Latin, posited an historical link between Tuscan and Northern Gallo-Romance Lenition, on the one hand, and between the Central Italian and Sardinian types, on the other, a vision consistent with his earlier opposition of an archaic to an innovative ROMANIA. Weinrich (1958:140), assuming monogenesis of Central Italian and Western Romance Lenition, lowered the dividing line between Eastern and Western Romance down to south of Naples. Udo Figge (1966:453) went a step further and projected Spirantization and Voicing onto all primitive Romance varieties save Northeastern Sardinian and Southern Corsican, with fragmentation resulting from later phonological reactions to the Lenition process. In his view (1966:455), the West was characterized by phonologization (or phonemic restructuring), the Balkans (including Rumania) by loss or reversal of the process, and central/southern Italy and Sardinia/Corsica by preservation of the primitive state of affairs.[4]

All these attempts to establish an historical connection between Eastern and Western Lenition ultimately failed, however, when their proponents proved unable to offer linguistically plausible hypotheses to explain how the Western type emerged from the Eastern, something I hope to do in this paper. But before proceeding to outline my own hypothesis, I wish 1) to review briefly the most important differences between Eastern and Western Lenition, and 2) to explain why I find Lausberg's, Weinrich's, and Figge's accounts wanting.

The most significant difference between Eastern and Western Lenition, as attested in the modern tongues, goes right to the heart of its status as a phonological process. The Eastern type is a fully productive rule, responsible for the creation of synchronic alternations. Thus, in Roman speech, 'earth' is [térra], while 'the earth' is, in a relaxed conversational register, [la dérra] (not taking into consideration the fact that in

---

[3] I owe this observation to Thomas D. Cravens.

[4] Wüest (1979:231-40), who surveyed several Prague School accounts of Lenition, in the end reverted to Martinet's notion that Degemination was responsible for its demise as a productive process in the West — an hypothesis radically at variance with the one to be outlined here.

unguarded speech, /rr/ is realized [r]).[5] The name of the country, which in very careful speech may be pronounced [itálja], in more informal style is routinely pronounced [idálja].

In Spanish or French, by contrast, 'earth' is [tjérra] or [téR] in all phonetic contexts and the name of the neighboring country is invariably [itálja] or [italí], regardless of speech-style. In the West, operation of Lenition at a past historical stage can be inferred only through comparison of modern words with their Latin forerunners. Juxtaposition of Sp. *vida* 'life' to Lat. VĪTA proves that a voicing rule must have operated some time between Classical Latin and Modern Spanish. But from a synchronic standpoint, the medial consonant of the Spanish word must be assigned to the phoneme /d/. Likewise, the [t] of *meto* 'I put' is traceable synchronically to the phoneme /t/ despite its demonstrable descent from a Latin geminate. A truly productive voicing rule cannot be motivated for Modern Spanish, despite the best efforts of such generative theorists as Harris (1969:40-45). Somewhere along the way, Spanish, and all other Western Romance languages for that matter, restructured their phonologies and lexica in such a way that voiced stops were assigned to voiced stop phonemes and voiceless stops to simple voiceless stop phonemes, with the consequence that synchronic Lenition as a living phonological rule withered.

This brings us to the second major difference between East and West, which involves word-initial position. Eastern Lenition, including the Corsican, Sardinian, and Central/Southern Italian varieties, oblivious of its victims' position within the word, attacks all obstruents in the proper phonetic environment. In the West, by contrast, Lenition appears to have affected only word-medial consonants, with initials all but invariably preserved (e.g., Sp. [la pjéðra] 'the rock', [la tjérra] 'the earth', [la kása] 'the house').

Lastly, the final step of Lenition, namely Degemination, universal in Western Romance, appears only sporadically in Eastern leniting dialects. Most Central and Southern Italian, Corsican, and Sardinian dialects which routinely Spirantize voiced stops and voice voiceless obstruents nevertheless exhibit preservation of Latin geminates.

---

[5] Troncon and Canepari (1989:47) report that of every twenty occurrences, intervocalic /p t k/ are realized fully voiceless only once; four are fully voiced, while the remaining manifestations are 'otto sonore leni, quattro miste (o «intermedie» tra sorde e sonore perlopiù leni), tre sorde leni'.

Assuming with Weinrich and Figge that proto-Romance Lenition is continued in pristine form in Central/Southern Italy and Sardinia and that Western restructuring represents a later outgrowth, one is compelled to explain how the Western — and specifically the Hispano-Romance — type evolved out of the Eastern. Concretely stated, one must provide satisfactory answers to the following questions. 1) What factor, present in Hispano-Romance but alien to Eastern varieties, led to the phonological restructuring and relexicalization alluded to above? 2) Why are Latin word-initial voiceless stops preserved as such in Hispano-Romance, if those segments were indeed affected by Lenition during its productive phase? 3) What phonological development triggered Degemination in Hispano-Romance?

Lausberg, in his brief chapter on sandhi phenomena (1956:92-95), conjectured that in Western ROMANIA, as in Tuscany, intervocalic voiceless stops, before being voiced, underwent Spirantization. When, at a slightly later stage, those same segments were voiced, the phonetic distance between the allophones (i.e., absolute initial and postconsonantal voiceless stops vs. intervocalic voiced spirants) became intolerable, whereupon intervocalic voiceless stops were restored word-initially and Lenition collapsed. But there is no reason to believe that voiceless stops cannot alternate with voiced spirants. Lausberg himself (1956:93) reports the existence of just such an alternation in numerous Sardinian dialects (e.g., *su* δ*empu* 'the time' vs. *sos tempos* 'the times').

Weinrich's (1958:73-75, 134) analysis differs somewhat from that of Lausberg. For him, what seemed intolerable was the merger occasioned by the voicing of the formerly voiceless consonants. Once /t, k/ voiced, they became indistinguishable phonetically from original /d, g/.[6] The hearer, confronted with a phonetic sequence [la gáza] 'the house' would have been at a loss to determine whether it reflected an underlying /la kása/ or /la gása/. What Weinrich evidently failed to take into account — and this oversight is repeated a number of times in his book — is that prior to the Voicing of voiceless stops, the voiced stops had in all likelihood been transmuted into voiced spirants. Therefore, as Figge observed, no phonemic distinctions would have been lost. A phonetic sequence [la gáza] was, as in modern Corsican and Central/Southern

---

[6] According to Weinrich, merger would not have represented a threat in the labial series inasmuch as intervocalic /b/ had previously been spirantized and hence was not susceptible to confusion with [b] deriving from voicing of /p/.

Italian dialects, traceable unambiguously to an underlying /la kása/ inasmuch as an underlying /la gása/ would have surfaced as [la ɣáza].

Elsewhere in his book, Weinrich (1958:139, 155) was mindful that voiced stops had been spirantized in the West and even interpreted such Spirantization as a phonological reaction to the impending merger threatened by Voicing of the voiceless series. But when, having reached such an advanced stage of weakening, those voiced spirants began to suffer deletion, the phonemic contrast between underlying /d/ and /g/ was threatened. The predictable phonological reaction, if one accepts Weinrich's Martinetian model, was restoration of stable voiced stops to word-initial position. But this in turn led to potential confusion with surface voiced stops deriving from underlying voiceless, a situation which compelled speakers to devoice those segments. Like his teacher Lausberg, Weinrich cavalierly brushed aside the evidence of numerous Sardinian dialects in which, despite general deletion of underlying intervocalic voiced stops both word-initially and medially, communication has not collapsed.

Figge (1966:453-54), displaying better command of the data, postulated that the underlying distinction between voiceless and voiced stops was realized phonetically as voiced stop vs. voiced fricative, and charged Western restructuring to the inherent instability of the contrast between velar stop and fricative. For him, threat of loss of surface distinction between [g] and [ɣ], which entailed dephonologization of the underlying opposition of /k/ vs. /g/, was what compelled speakers to restore voiceless initials in the West. But Figge's appeal to a putative merger-avoidance mechanism, against which the seasoned diachronist can adduce dozens of counterexamples, renders his solution hardly more convincing than Weinrich's.[7]

Despite the lip service paid by the adherents of Prague School phonology whose views have just been discussed to systemic factors and structural pressures in phonological evolution, they failed to undertake a systematic reconstruction of the phonologies of Western Romance dialects in the period immediately predating lexical and phonological restructuring. The goal of such a reconstruction would be to identify factors present in the phonological systems of the West, but absent from their Eastern counterparts, that could potentially account for the radically diver-

---

[7] Vincent (1978) discusses some of the problems inherent in teleological accounts of phonetic change.

gent outcomes in the two domains. Since there is no a priori reason to believe that those factors were necessarily identical in all regions, the reconstruction at issue should be carried out separately for each of the Western Romance branches. In this paper, then, we shall focus attention exclusively on proto-Hispano-Romance, i.e., the ancestor of Modern Spanish and Portuguese.

We shall assume — on comparative grounds — that Spirantization of intervocalic voiced stops and Voicing of intervocalic voiceless ones were productive phonological rules of Late Spoken Latin and hence that they represented characteristic features of proto-Hispano-Romance.[8] The operation of both rules was conditioned only by phonetic context, with word-boundaries routinely ignored. Otherwise put, the proto-Hispano-Romance treatment of intervocalic simple stops was identical to treatment of those same phonemes in Modern Corsican or South/Central Italian.

Using the dentals to illustrate the relevant alternations, we may assume that speakers pronounced [dó] 'I give' and [non dó] 'I do not give', but [ɛo ðó] 'I give'; [tɛrra] 'earth' and [en tɛrra] 'on earth', but [la dɛrra] 'the earth'. Given the existence of those word-initial alternations, speakers would no doubt have analyzed word-medial [ð] (e.g., [núðo] 'nude') as an allophone of /d/ and [d] (e.g., [vída] 'life') as an allophone of /t/, despite the absence of alternations there, just as modern Corsican and South/Central Italian speakers do. Phonemic geminates, which occurred only in medial position, presumably continued to be pronounced as double or long consonants, e.g., [mɛt:o] 'I put'. For initial position, then, we must posit a phonemic distinction between voiced vs. voiceless stops, realized phonetically as voiced spirant vs. voiced stop, respectively, when the preceding word ended in a vowel;[9] while medially we assume a three-way phonemic contrast consisting of

---

[8] Harris-Northall (1990:6-36) provides an informative overview of attempts by generativists to attribute all processes comprising Lenition to the operation of a single complex phonological rule. He concludes that phonological strength hierarchies offer better possibilities for an accurate characterization of Lenition than do synchronic rules.

[9] I discuss briefly below the likelihood that syntactic doubling of the sort attested in modern Sardinian, Corsican, and central/southern Italian (see Rohlfs 1949:290-93, Loporcaro 1988) operated in proto-Hispano-Romance, a possibility first raised by Hall (1964).

voiced stop vs. voiceless stop vs. voiceless geminate, realized intervocalically as voiced spirant vs. voiced stop vs. voiceless geminate.

By the time of the earliest documents in Old Spanish, however, the situation had changed dramatically. Initial position had become invariable, with 'the rock', 'the earth' and 'the house' emerging as [la pjéðra], [la tjérra], and [la káza]. Medially, geminates had been reduced to simple (e.g., *capa* 'cape', *meto* 'I put', *vaca* 'cow'), and consequently were assigned to the simple voiceless stop phonemes, while phonetic voiced stops, previously derived from underlying voiceless, were reassigned to the voiced stop phonemes. Phonetic voiced spirants, now occurring only medially, are generally believed to have constituted independent phonemes, rather than being derived synchronically from underlying voiced stops. Most historians of Spanish (e.g., Alonso 1967:63-75) believe that a phonemic distinction in medial position between voiced stops (< Latin voiceless stops) and voiced spirants (< Latin voiced stops) persisted throughout the Middle Ages. In their view, medial voiced stops reflecting the Latin voiceless were spirantized in the fifteenth century and merged at that point with voiced spirants traceable to the Latin voiced stops.

Now given a) our assumption that Spirantization and Voicing operated as synchronically productive rules in Late Spoken Latin and b) our knowledge that phonemic restructuring had taken place before the emergence of written Old Spanish, it follows logically that something happened in the interval to trigger the restructuring. Since the vernacular tongue was not written during that period, direct documentary evidence bearing on the restructuring at issue is in principle impossible to obtain. Nonetheless, it makes good sense to study Latin documents from that period with an eye to identifying clues to developments affecting intervocalic stops.

For the purposes of this paper, I shall limit myself to the documents studied by Menéndez Pidal in his linguistic magnum opus *Orígenes del español*, while noting that his findings have been largely replicated by Díaz y Díaz (1957), Bastardas y Parera (1960:268), Gil (1970), Jennings (1940:51-65), and Vespertino Rodríguez (1985:345-55). First, the Spanish master observed frequent deletions of intervocalic *d* and *g*, e.g., *peones* for *pedones*, *Araon* for *Aragon*, *pao* for *pago* (1950:260-61). In certain manuscripts, the scribe would include the voiced stop in the first occurrence of a word and omit it thereafter. These facts should cause no surprise inasmuch as intervocalic /d/ and /g/ had been deleted in many words by the time of the earliest Old Spanish.

Far more significant for our purposes is increasingly frequent replacement of *p, t, c* by *b, d, g*, observed by Menéndez Pidal even in the earliest document he studied (*sebaratus* for Classical *separatus*), an Asturian charter dating from the year 775. Such orthographic blunders are especially prevalent in documents datable to the period 870-1040. Here are some typical examples cited by Menéndez Pidal (1950:241-49), with Classical forms in parentheses: *abidura* (HABITURA), *abut* (APUD), *acebit* (ACCEPIT), *artigulo* (ARTICULU), *ederna* (ÆTERNA), *episcobus* (EPIS-COPUS), *eredidade* (HEREDITATE), *excomunigatus* (EXCOMMUNICATUS), *exido* (EXITU), *mader* (MATER), *nebotes* (NEPOTES), *nodicia* (NOTITIA), *obtorigare* (AUCTORICARE), *pacifigas* (PACIFICAS), *plaguit* (PLACUIT), *prado* (PRATU), *probria* (PROPRIA), *rodundo* (ROTUNDU), *confirmada* (CONFIRMATA), *semedarium* (SEMETARIUM), *Stebano* (STEPHANU), *suber* (SUPER), *subra* (SUPRA),[10] *teridorio* (TERRITORIU), *tidulus* (TITULUS), *uindigare* (VINDICARE), and *uolumtade* (VOLUNTATE).

Menéndez Pidal, taking such orthographic slips at face value, interpreted them as evidence that originally voiceless stops were being voiced in the period at issue, i.e., the Early Middle Ages. It is important to recall, however, that by that time the Latin voiced stops had long since been spirantized intervocalically, with the result that any voicing of voiceless stops in the same environment would not have led to phonemic merger or loss of pertinent contrasts.

Adopting one of the graphemic principles developed by Herbert Penzl in a string of articles and books (1957:197-203, 1971:34-36, 1975:23), namely that orthographic confusion of previously discrete graphemes reflects dephonologization of an erstwhile phonemic contrast, we are forced to conclude that the data reported by Menéndez Pidal are indicative of something more than a mere incipient allophonic alternation. Following Penzl's principle, I submit that such large-scale confusion of the graphemes corresponding to the Latin voiceless and voiced stop phonemes constitutes conclusive proof that those phonemes were merging or had already merged by the late eighth century, the precise phonetic mechanism being a second round of Spirantization (henceforth labeled

---

[10] Menéndez Pidal (1950:247) analyzed *subra*, which no doubt represents Lat. SUPRA with the expected voicing of intervocalic /p/, as showing phonological influence from Umbrian.

Spirantization-2), this time affecting the phonetic voiced stops deriving from phonemic voiceless. It was this seemingly insignificant phonetic change which, in my judgment, set off the chain of events that culminated in restructuring and the demise of Lenition as a productive process in Hispano-Romance.

That sequence of events may be reconstructed as follows. First, recall that the Classical Latin system of stop phonemes was characterized by a two-way contrast in initial and postconsonantal position, but by a three-way contrast medially. Using the dentals for purposes of exemplification, we recall that /t/ contrasted only with /d/ initially, while medially those two phonemes were opposed by a third, namely /t:/. In intervocalic position, both initially and medially, assuming the operation of Lenition, /t/ would have been realized phonetically as [d] and /d/ would have surfaced phonetically as [ð].[11]

When, in the very early Middle Ages, [d] from underlying /t/ became a voiced *spirant*, merger with /d/ (realized phonetically as [ð]) was the only possible result in word-medial position since no alternations occurred there. Whereas GRĀTU 'pleasing' and GRADU 'step' were previously distinguished as [grádu] vs. [gráðu], after Spirantization-2 both words were realized phonetically as [gráðu]. At that point, the earlier three-term system of medial contrasts was reduced to two poles, namely a voiceless stop reflecting the Latin geminate, and a voiced spirant echoing the Latin simple voiceless and voiced stops. Otherwise put, once the medial voiced stop allophones of the voiceless stop phonemes became spirants and were obligatorily reassigned to the voiced stop phonemes, speakers had no choice but to associate the medial voiceless stops (from the Latin geminates) with absolute-initial and postconsonantal voiceless ones, and the intervocalic voiced spirants with the absolute-initial and postconsonantal voiced stops.[12]

Having offered an explanation for the phonemic reanalysis of stop contrasts in word-medial position in proto-Hispano-Romance, we must

---

[11] This is precisely the situation one finds today in much of central and southern Italy.

[12] This analysis also explains, incidentally, why one component of Lenition, namely Spirantization of voiced stops, survives in Spanish and certain other Western Romance languages. Whereas Spirantization-2 deprived the Latin voiceless stops of their medial voiced stop allophones, it greatly increased the statistical frequency of intervocalic voiced spirants, thereby strengthening the voiced stop/voiced spirant alternation. I will return to this important point below.

still account for the Hispano-Romance outcomes of the word-initial intervocalic stops. In South/Central Italian Lenition, as well as in the Sardinian and Corsican varieties of the process, we recall, a word-initial stop is lenited whenever the preceding word ends in a vowel (but see discussion of syntactic doubling below). Assuming that the same was true of proto-Hispano-Romance, we must wonder why all modern Hispano-Romance languages and dialects seem to preserve the Latin word-initial voiceless stops. (Since word-initial voiced stops are in fact lenited in the modern languages — e.g., Sp. [la ßóδa] 'the wedding', [la δúδa] 'the doubt', [la γérra] 'the war' —, the issue concerns only the voiceless stops.) Specifically, if proto-Hispano-Romance speakers pronounced *la piedra* 'the rock', *la tela* 'the cloth', and *la casa* 'the house' with voiced initials, then why do such lexemes exhibit voiceless initial stops in all contexts, including intervocalic, in the modern languages?

The following three factors contributed, in my judgment, to the restoration of invariable voiceless initials:

1) The voiceless stop/voiced stop alternation was severely undermined by loss, caused by Spirantization-2, of word-medial intervocalic voiced stop allophones. With the reassignment of those segments to the voiced stop phonemes, the alternation in question acquired the status of a strictly sandhi rule, operating exclusively at word boundaries, a type of phonological process toward which Hispano-Romance has at all stages shown a distinct aversion.

2) Preservation of certain particularly frequent word-final consonants in Hispano-Romance, along with creation of numerous others through apocope, both features which sharply distinguish Hispano- from central and southern Italo-Romance, occasioned a significant reduction in the statistical frequency of word-initial stops preceded by word-final vowels. The predictable effect was that the voiced stop allophones of the voiceless stops became increasingly scarce.

3) If we assume with Hall (1964), as seems entirely reasonable, that proto-Hispano-Romance, like South/Central Italian, Sardinian, and Corsican, exhibited syntactic doubling (It. *raddoppiamento sintattico*), then after Degemination had occurred, simple voiceless stops would be expected after lexemes formerly marked to trigger such doubling. From the point of view of the speaker, occurrence of the voiceless vs. the voiced allophone would have been an entirely fortuitous and arbitrary matter, dependent upon the presence or absence of a special marker in the lexical entry of the previous word. Complete avoidance of the voiced

allophone must have seemed, under those circumstances, an especially attractive solution.

The outcomes of the Latin word-initial voiced stop phonemes go a long way toward proving that Factor (1) was the most potent of the three just considered. Since in word-medial intervocalic position, under-lying simple voiced stops were invariably spirantized, those phonemes were subjected to the same treatment in word-initial intervocalic position, regardless of whether the previous word had at an earlier stage been lexically marked for syntactic doubling.[13]

The remaining unanswered question is why the Latin geminates were not preserved in Hispano-Romance. Degemination should not, to my way of thinking, be conceived of as an empirically verifiable and measurable sound change, but rather as a matter of the phonological analysis performed by the language learner. Phonological quantity, unlike, say, voicing or continuancy, is a relative feature. We cannot project long consonants or long vowels onto a language — even one in which the phones at issue may by measurably longer than in most other languages — unless those segments contrast in identical phonetic contexts with shorter counterparts. I contend that from the moment when the Latin voiceless stops were reassigned to the voiced stop phonemes, speakers could no longer have analyzed the erstwhile voiceless geminates as anything but simple voiceless stops. This interpretation, incidentally, may also explain why geminate sonorants appear to have outlived geminate stops in Hispano-Romance by a margin of several centuries.[14] Since the

---

[13] Another reason for believing that initial voiced stops in erstwhile syntactic doubling contexts promptly became voiced spirants has to do with the outcomes of medial geminate voiced stops — phonemes so rare in Late Spoken Latin as not to be mentioned in most scholarly treatments of Lenition. So far as I can determine, only five Latin words containing voiced geminates survived into Hispano-Romance, to wit: ABBĀTE 'abbot', *ABBATUŌ 'I beat', ADDŪCŌ 'I bring to', ADDORMIŌ/ADDORMISCŌ 'I fall asleep', and *INADDŌ 'I add to', yielding respectively OSp. *abad, abato, adugo, aduermo/adormesco*, and *eñado/añado*. The fact that the corresponding phones were represented ortho-graphically by *b* and *d* in medieval Spanish strongly suggests that they were pronounced as voiced spirants.

[14] The conclusion that long sonorants, with the possible exception of /m:/, outlived their obstruent counterparts by several centuries follows from application of the comparative method. If the Latin long obstruents are continued by simples in all Western Romance languages, then simple obstruents must have characterized proto-Western Romance. But the divergent outcomes of Lat. /l:/ and /n:/ in Spanish and Portuguese

proto-Hispano-Romance simple sonorant phonemes had undergone no phonological changes, speakers continued to analyze the geminate sonorants as long.

To sum up, I have argued that Lenition was a characteristic feature of Late Spoken Latin and that its demise in Hispano-Romance was occasioned by Spirantization of voiced stops deriving from the Latin voiceless series, a change which forced speakers to a phonological analysis in which synchronic Lenition no longer played a role.

References

Alonso, Amado. 1967. *De la pronunciación medieval a la moderna en español*. Vol. 1. 2nd ed. Madrid: Gredos.

Bastardas y Parera, Juan. 1960. El latín medieval. *Enciclopedia lingüística hispánica*. 1.251-90. Madrid: CSIC.

Díaz y Díaz, M. C. 1957. Movimientos fonéticos en el latín visigodo. *Emerita* 25.369-86.

Dworkin, Steven N. 1974. Studies in the history of primary -D- in Hispano-Romance. Ph.D. Dissertation. University of California, Berkeley. Ann Arbor: University Microfilms International.

Figge, Udo L. 1966. *Die romanische Anlautsonorisation*. Bonn: Romanisches Seminar der Universität Bonn.

Fiorelli, Piero. 1952. Senso e premesse d'una fonetica fiorentina. *Lingua nostra* 13.57-63.

Giacomelli, Raffaele. 1934. Controllo fonetico per diciassette punti dell'*AIS* nell'Emilia, nelle Marche, in Toscana, nell'Umbria e nel Lazio. *Archivum Romanicum* 18.155-212.

Giannelli, Luciano. 1976. *Toscana*. Profilo dei dialetti italiani, 9. Pisa: Pacini.

Gil, Juan. 1970. Notas sobre fonética del latín visigodo. *Habis* 1.45-86.

---

prove that those long sonorants were still long at the proto-Hispano-Romance stage. Portuguese simplification and Spanish simplification-cum-palatalization must be assigned to a period when the two languages had already split and were developing along independent lines. The phonemic distinction between /r/ and /r:/ persists in all Hispano-Romance varieties to this day.

Grandgent, Charles H. 1908. *An introduction to Vulgar Latin*. Boston: Heath.

Hall, Robert A. 1964. Initial consonants and syntactic doubling in West Romance. *Language* 40.551-56.

Harris, James W. 1969. *Spanish Phonology*. Cambridge, Mass: MIT Press.

Harris-Northall, Ray. 1990. *Weakening processes in the history of Spanish consonants*. London: Routledge.

Jennings, Augustus Campbell. 1940. *The Cartulario of San Vicente de Oviedo*. New York: Vanni.

Lausberg, Heinrich. 1956. *Romanische Sprachwissenschaft*. Vol. 2: *Consonantismus*. Sammlung Göschen, 250. Berlin: De Gruyter.

Loporcaro, Michele. 1988. History and geography of *raddoppiamento fonosintattico*: Remarks on the evolution of a phonological rule. In *Certamen Phonologicum. Papers from the 1987 Cortona Phonology Meeting*, ed. Pier Marco Bertinetto and Michele Loporcaro. 351-87. Torino: Rosenberg & Sellier.

Malkiel, Yakov. 1960. Paradigmatic resistance to sound change. The Old Spanish preterite forms *vide, vido* against the background of the recession of primary *-d-*. *Language* 36.281-346.

Menéndez Pidal, Ramón. 1950. *Orígenes del español*. 3rd ed. Madrid: Espasa-Calpe.

Penzl, Herbert. 1957. The evidence from phonemic changes. In *Studies Presented to Joshua Whatmough on his Sixtieth Birthday*, ed. Ernst Pulgram, 193-208. The Hague: Mouton.

_____. 1971. *Lautsystem und Lautwandel in den althochdeutschen Dialekten*. München: Hueber.

_____. 1975. *Vom Urgermanischen zum Neuhochdeutschen*. Berlin: Schmidt.

Rohlfs, Gerhard. 1949. *Historische Grammatik der italienischen Sprache und ihrer Mundarten*. Vol. 1: *Lautlehre*. Bern: Francke.

Troncon, Antonella and Luciano Canepari. 1989. *Lingua italiana nel Lazio*. Roma: Jouvence.

Vespertino Rodríguez, Antonio. 1985. La sonorización de las consonantes sordas intervocálicas en el latín de los mozárabes. In *Homenaje a Álvaro Galmés de Fuentes*. 1.345-55. Madrid: Gredos.

Vincent, Nigel. 1978. Is sound change teleological? In *Recent developments in historical phonology*, ed. Jacek Fisiak, 409-30. The Hague: Mouton.

Wartburg, Walther von. 1936. Die Ausgliederung der romanischen Sprachräume. *Zeitschrift für romanische Philologie* 56.1-48.

_____. 1950. *Die Ausgliederung der romanischen Sprachräume*. Bern: Francke.

Weinrich, Harald. 1958. *Phonologische Studien zur romanische Sprachgeschichte*. Forschungen zur romanischen Philologie, 6. Münster: Aschendorff.

Wüest, Jakob. 1979. *La dialectalisation de la Gallo-Romania*. Romanica Helvetica, 91. Bern: Francke.

Historical Syntax and Old Spanish Text Files

Dieter Wanner

The Ohio State University

The following considerations have principally programmatic and promissory character; they concern the difficulty of doing historical syntax, and they propose a procedure for recursive, yet efficient searches of an extensive Old Spanish data base, which could turn out to be helpful in overcoming some of the principled obstacles encountered.[1] Historical syntax in its various manifestations — syntax of a historical linguistic

[1] The idea for the syntactic data base had a significant prehistory in 1981-83 at the University of Illinois, involving also Elizabeth Pearce (U. of Wellington, New Zealand). A pilot project, underwritten by the Research Board of the Graduate College, University of Illinois at Urbana–Champaign, concerned a 15th-century Florentine text (the autograph letters of Alessandra Macinghi Strozzi, written in the rather spontaneous, unpretentious language of utilitarian business and family letters); it was eventually abandoned due to inordinate computer costs. While the mechanics of the analysis and most other details have changed, the basic motivation and outline of the project presented here owes much to Liz Pearce's endeavors, from programming to execution and improvement (Wanner and Pearce 1981-83).

The project described in this article has been made possible by a Seed Grant award from the Office of Research and Graduate Study of The Ohio State University. I would like to express my thanks for the generous help, support and encouragement which this pilot project on Old Spanish syntax files is receiving from the Seminary of Medieval Spanish Studies at the University of Wisconsin–Madison, and in particular from its director, John J. Nitti. I have been able to gain access to the transcriptions of the Alfonsine and Heredia corpora, and also to the larger file collections associated with DOSL. I also wish to thank Brian Dutton (University of Wisconsin–Madison) for offering me the use of his files containing the Berceo works. The Old Spanish samples contained in this article stem from these files. Special thanks go to the Graduate Research Associates from the Ohio State University who have helped me on this project so far: Vicent Barberà-Manrique, Richard Danford, Carla Davis, Luis Hermosilla, Carolyn Méndez, Frederick Parkinson, Roberto Perry. Prof. Terry Patten from the Department of Computer and Information Science has also contributed essential advice and effective help to the project. Finally I wish to thank the editors of the present volume for their valuable suggestions and stylistic improvements.

phase, developmental syntax over a period of perceived change, comparative syntax of related and commensurate linguistic phases, and syntactic reconstruction (cf. Hock 1986) — has always held a special status, ranging from benign neglect to laborious accumulation of mainly uninterpreted data (in the philological tradition; cf. e.g., Jensen 1990), and from theoretical indeterminacy (e.g., Lass 1980) to derivative status or full dependence on a specific formalized framework (e.g., Lightfoot 1979). The exact stance appears to depend on a combination of the framework employed and the temperament of the researcher.

1. Recent efforts have been quite numerous in the Romance and Germanic languages, working within prevalent formal syntactic frameworks, mainly Principles and Parameters.[2] They invariably bring a theory-driven analysis to bear on historical and diachronic data, deriving from such analyses considerable insight into the conditions of the historical material (cf. Lightfoot 1979 as a major statement in this vein). The approach is, however, severely limited as to the kinds of problems it can deal with successfully (cf. the principled criticisms in Lass 1980), due mostly to the nature of current syntactic investigation and conceptualization. The formal and crucially reductionist orientation of syntactic theory and Universal Grammar must rely on sophisticated grammaticality judgments by native speakers, applied to utterances with a very low index of probability of actual occurrence in any kind of corpus. With this test condition unavailable in historical phases, the sole resource must be the extant texts. But the written documentation typical of historical phases — e.g., Medieval Romance languages — is severely limited in breadth of expression and of register, often precluding the presence of examples required for formal argumentation. The crucial example to support a given syntactic principle simply may not be available, even if all sources could be put to full, unequivocal use. Most embarrassingly, the much cited concept of 'no negative evidence' from the language learning context is in full effect, since the absence of a construction from the corpus under investigation in no way implies its ungrammaticality, possibly leaving the question hanging.

---

[2] Cf. for Romance an arbitrary selection of recent contributions, e.g., Adams 1989, Hirschbühler 1989, Martineau 1991, Pearce 1990, Rivero 1986, forthcoming, Vance 1989, or the collection of articles concerning V2 in Germanic contained in Haider and Prinzhorn 1986.

A case in point is the noun complement clause of the type *la idea de que, el hecho de que,* quite common in the modern language. To my knowledge, it is not directly attested for the medieval language. From the similar constructions surrounding it, one could presume its existence without extending the formal capacity of the grammar in any way. One commonly finds *el fecho* in the meaning of 'this matter', the natural basis for the more schematic meaning of 'fact' present in the noun complement construction; cf. *sobre el fecho del prinçipado* (Heredia, *Morea* 267r2). There are complement structures with infinitive, e.g., *aquel fecho; de prender a Yssem so Rey.* (EE 101r2), or with a +QU element instead of the neutral complementizer *que,* e.g., *Ellos contaron le estonces tod el fecho; de como les acaesçiera con ell sobrel departimiento de los agueros.* (EE 88r1). In this construction the subordinate clause has the effect of afterthought specification, as if it were an apposition; these two traits characterize the semantic import of the noun complement clause in modern Spanish. In view of this field of close relatives, the question can be raised whether the Old Spanish data present us here with an accidental gap or with a more systematic void which will be filled only later in the development of Spanish syntax.

2. This situation implies not that historical syntax is impossible as an undertaking, but rather that the heuristics of formal syntax in the synchronic vein is not appropriate for historical phases. The program of formal syntax is oriented toward the discovery of the underlying principles characterizing the full range of idealized syntactic competence in formalizable terms. In this enterprise, actual syntactic data enter only tangentially as indicators of more abstract options. The investigative program — P&P, GPSG, LFG, RG, etc. — is not concerned with the full range of data available to support deductively formulated claims about syntactic structure. Having relegated this problem to one or more 'performance' modules, and having foresworn any interest in discovery procedures, the formal approach is normally correlated with a heuristics appropriate for the synchronic investigation of the boundary conditions enveloping each atomic principle. The resulting fixation on grammaticality judgments by an idealized native speaker is a heavily introspective test configuration. While recognizing the inherent danger of circularity, this judgment device can be made to conform tolerably well to the projected idealized performance standard, by choosing as

consultants speakers known to be sympathetic to the enterprise and sophisticated in extreme language use.[3]

The impossibility of applying this kind of procedure to historical data requires the field of historical syntax to be concerned with a complementary aspect of the total range of syntactic phenomena, more in tune with an orientation towards actual data and their contextually determined ambiguities, including the frequent lack of appropriate documentation. The questions surrounding theoretical constructs lose their primacy, without thereby falling away entirely. Any practice of historical syntax is reined in by an encompassing theory of syntactic phenomena (whatever form it may take), since insightful classification, description and explanation of data is possible only within such a constraining conceptual network. But historical syntax is not thereby relegated to an ancillary position with regard to the development of an adequate theory of syntactic phenomena. Rather, the apprehension of syntactic change over time and across systems is a major axis along which the internal constitution of a system can be put to the test. Dynamic operation provides a wealth of information on the articulation and interaction of components, while static analysis achieves greater precision by freezing an artificial state of grammar for purposes of observation: synchronic and diachronic perspectives complement each other.

The historical dimension added to a syntactic research program introduces a crucial second system of values and coordinates which are frequently orthogonal to the 'formal linguistic' aspects proper. The external circumstances of the language under study need to be taken into full account. In the present case, extralinguistic aspects, i.e., the material, economic, social and cultural situation of Castilian texts from the 13th to the 15th century, codetermine the possible results of the investigation. The primary documentation, texts of all kinds, are specific products of their times: period of linguistic composition, period of actual elaboration of a text, interferences from material culture, targeting of readership, etc., all are to be seen within the external historical frame of the kingdoms of

---

[3] The above description is in no way intended as ironic; rather, it is known to any syntactician consulting with native speakers that a certain amount of training — not in formal linguistics, but in stylistic expansion — is inevitable for meaningful consideration of the relevant utterances: hence sophistication. Of course, a cooperative spirit must be present also, if the (natural?) tendency to trenchant prescriptive attitudes or annoyed indifference is to be overcome: hence the sympathetic disposition.

Castile and Aragón in the two and a half centuries between 1200 and 1450.[4] Together with necessary care in deciphering and properly understanding the text, these sociolinguistic dimensions require the intervention of traditional philological skills. The preserved texts represent various registers and style levels which can be discerned with considerable accuracy from their content, language and presentation. The entire documentation of Old Castilian may thus be described as a varying number of prototypically clustered textual categories (in addition to chronological, regional and individual differentiations). This allows the investigator to counteract where necessary a premature null hypothesis of complete linguistic homogeneity for the extant corpus (cf. Wanner 1987:139-47 for some discussion).

In this context, the historical study of syntax can focus profitably on the major and more frequent patterns found in the available texts. Descriptions of change over time and in the comparative dimension will be concerned mainly with macroscopic features, detectable from written records and resistant to decay through the often long transmission lines of these texts. The dimensions active in change and cross-language variation can be identified as major factors in syntactic change and — barring crucial external conditioning — in synchronic syntactic structure as well. At the same time, the fine-grained and quite variable written documentation will always be useful for casting a healthy dose of skepticism on claims of simplifying categorical explanation. The low-level variation observed within a given text or in linguistically similar documents imposes the exercise of much care in the postulation of abstract bifurcations at higher levels of analysis: the solution must contain the entire range of variation.

3. The raw materials of historical syntax are texts which need to be regarded as samples of language in their own right, functional for the transmission of the thoughts intentionally contained in them. By their

---

[4] These two major historical entities are taken as encompassing the linguistically relevant territory, including the areas of Asturias, León, and the newly reconquered South for Castile (excepting Galicia), and Navarre and reconquered territories for Aragón (excepting Basque or Catalan speaking areas).

sheer survival (except for cases of accidental preservation[5]) they signal that these texts were regarded by contemporaries as intelligible, expressive of their main concern and worthy of archivation. Being written, in a society where writing (and reading) was not a primary means of communication, but was limited to more formal occasions, these language samples present relatively high stylistic levels, in which the language is set down with appropriate care and reflection. These texts may be considerably removed from spontaneous discourse, but they cannot thereby be regarded as divorced from the everyday linguistic reality of their period of composition and/or transcription. Their linguistic form must be considered as representing a genuine register of the language under consideration; the typical feature of massive intratextual and intertextual variation is expressive of a linguistic condition and a wilful communicative choice.[6] Such texts are open for minute interpretation of the available features and for their qualitative and quantitative analysis. In this way they become reflections of the language as actually practiced, even though they cannot directly reflect either the spontaneous register or the range of extreme options[7] afforded a linguistically sympathetic speaker by a fully activated system of syntactic principles.

In the morphological domain, alternations in the inflectional stems of certain verbs and forms may be at the low end of expressivity; cf.

---

[5] A case in point might be the early samples of (para-)Romance writing, e.g., the Indovinello veronese (Monaci 1955:1), the Parody of the Lex Salica (Väänänen 1974:326-28) or the Leonese list of cheeses (Menéndez Pidal 1950:24-25).

[6] Cf. in this connection Cerquiglini's (1989) notion that medieval French texts are constituted by *variance,* rather than that they merely exhibit *variantes.* This is fully applicable to the medieval Spanish situation, and to medieval European textuality in general.

The historical linguist must steer a course clear of the major obstacles of underplaying the possible significance of variant forms as different and of over-interpreting potentially insignificant allotropisms. A general principle that there cannot be any synonyms in language (at the lexical or constructional level; cf. the 'Principle of Contrast', Clark 1987) is too strong for the orthographic domain; the transformational equivalency between alternate string arrangements (perhaps even for a minor detail such as clitic pronoun interpolation; cf. Rivero 1986, Wanner forthcoming) may be heavy-handed. A highly promising approach to such questions can be found in Cognitive Grammar (Langacker 1987), capable of attributing differential meaning to different structures and of establishing functional equivalencies where appropriate.

[7] As required for formal syntactic argumentation.

vernie el monesterio por el a su estado (Berceo, *Santo Domingo* 207d) with metathesized *rn* from /ven∅r-/ vs. *Esperando la ora quand verrie el mandado* (Berceo, *San Millán de la Cogolla* 295a) with assimilation of the same group. But already at the still very formal level of clitic linearization, minor variations may contain significant, meaningful information, even if a strictly formal reconstruction of the conditions fails to point up a systematic correlation with an unequivocally detectable feature of expressivity. In Wanner (1990) it is argued that variable enclisis of the object clitic pronoun after a subject noun phrase cannot be linked to differential topicality of the subject and thus does not represent more than an optional formal, perhaps stylistic process. This applies to the contrast *et el te mostrara una albuhera* (EE §316, 184b7, f112r2) with proclisis vs. *Et ellos partieron se con sus huestes* (EE §293, 175b48, f107r1) with enclisis in the same formal and text dynamic context. It is quite possible that the actual usage of the two arrangements by a given writer may have been guided by subtle differences in conceptualization (of the role of the subject NP referent) which cannot be recaptured in the historical vacuum of the present vantage point.[8] At the high end of expressivity, the macroscopic variations in the order of major constituents are unquestionable signals of meaning differences at one or more levels of understanding.

The central heuristic question thus shifts from the constitution of a theoretical frame for syntax to the mediation between the concrete level of language use and the poly-abstract formal core of syntactic theory. Historical syntax is a valid enterprise in its own right in a view which grants an appropriate place to the formal aspect of syntactic theory, but which at the same time conceives of linguistic theory as dealing with the entire spectrum of language, from cognitive competence to actual performance. For syntax, formal matters are relevant only to the extent that they are connected to the task of expressing meaning on various levels. Given the relationship between meaning in general and the real world — material and mental — underlying it, the form-content pairings must be of primary importance to historical linguistics as a dimension of contingent history and its cognitive expression. Change will be located primarily in the functional-expressive domain due to its dependency on

---

[8] According to the precepts of Cognitive Grammar (Langacker 1987) this is even strongly predicted.

an external reality shifting along chronological, geographic, sociological and other axes.

The prime dimension for these changes is the lexicon, in the case of meaning shifts, e.g., the culturally dependent change from Lat. DOMUS to Proto-Romance *casa* as the lexical form for 'house' (CASA originally 'hut, primitive dwelling place'). The change from COGITARE 'to think, consider, ponder' to *cuidar* 'to worry' represents an anchoring of the more schematic Latin verb meaning to a narrower domain of thoughts anticipating difficulties. For syntax one might point out the slow development of the prepositional accusative (direct object marking) with *a*. The gradual progression of its distribution across linguistic dimensions (as well as its synchronic Modern Spanish constitution)[9] documents very clearly its manifest semantic foundation: a means of marking highly salient objects with which/whom the speaker empathizes (cf. Bossong 1991).

On the other hand, purely formal aspects of syntax, as exponents of deeply rooted cognitive properties of linguistic behavior, are not expected to change with ease. Such properties are more directly controlled by principles of UG and kept in place by the prevalent form of language. Any changes in formal principles can be assumed to be minimal, given the effect of major consequences at a higher level of organization stemming from minor modifications in basic, but inter-connected system components.[10] While semantically effective change thus appears foregrounded, the practical consequence is that historical syntax can be pursued in considerable isolation from the intractable dimension of purely interpretive meaning. Diachronic variation in meaning is not fully controlled in historical situations if it is not coupled with manifest (formal) change. On the other hand, the study of formal change in the situation where meaning can be assumed to be predictable becomes entirely possible in the absence of direct native speaker

---

[9] Cf. Menéndez Pidal 1944 for a classical Old Spanish situation, Keniston 1937 for the phase of the 16th century, and Butt and Benjamin 1988 for Modern Spanish.

[10] This does not amount to a claim of immutability of such subsystems. Changes in principles and parameter settings are definitely a possible expression of linguistic change, but they are more easily comprehended as consequences of change, not as causes. Furthermore, some system properties may vary from individual to individual due to the considerable plasticity and adaptability of cognitive functions (cf. Newell, Rosenbloom and Laird 1989).

reactions, i.e., in the historical context. The intense study of clitic pronouns in the development of Spanish illustrates very well the potential for
fruitful syntactic investigations largely independent of meaning and its
problems.[11] A highly topical question concerns the three variant place-
ment patterns for the clitic pronoun: in proclisis (*onde te ruego e te
conseio que te non vayas* (EE §59, 43a46-47, f29r2)), enclisis (*Onde
ruego te que pares mientes si fiz yo alguna cosa por ti* (EE §59, 43b8,
f29r2)), or 'interpolation', i.e., separation from the verb (*por conseio de
los sabios por quien se el guiaua* (EE 100v2)). Syntactic change in this
view refers to change in the phenotype, directly documented in the data,
accessible in varying degree to the sophisticated language user (copyist
or author) and thus a fortiori also to the investigating linguist. Such
changes allow the linguist to bridge the chronological, diastratic or
diatopic gap inherent to historical-comparative research.

   Is historical syntax thus feasible in the above sense, but external
to the limits of 'real' linguistics? The multiple performance dimensions
characterizing historical data — linguistic production, written expression
and secondary transmission — are not exceptional characteristics
exclusive to this domain. The basic aspects of real-world production
apply to all linguistic manifestations, diachronic as well as synchronic.

   The (one or more) microlect(s) embodied in a text represent(s) at
the level of written discourse a data situation which must have served for
speaker-writers of the period in one way or another as a learning
experience in the domain of written linguistic usage. The text is thus a
representative sample of the linguistic environment for acquisition/
expansion of competence in the written language, producing L(w)
acquisition akin to the learning of L1 in the spoken medium. Admittedly,
L(w) enters a speaker's cognizance on the basis of previous L1 internal-
ization, but not as an incompatible practice, given the foundation of L1.
Unless writing is viewed as a linguistic exercise totally removed from
'normal' knowledge of a language,[12] the characteristics of the written

---

[11] Cf. Ramsden 1963, Rivero 1986, forthcoming, Wanner 1982, forthcoming, for
discussion and relevant bibliography.

[12] This seems to be an implication of the thesis by Wright 1982 (cf. also Blake
forthcoming) that monoglossic writing practice can span a diglossic abyss, e.g., between
'Latin' and 'Romance' in Late Latin and early Romance writing (6th to 9th century in
France, to 11th century in Spain). It is not evident that the situation described there can
be regarded as an instance of writing a given language, and not rather one of using

language, spanning different registers, directly represent (some or even most) features of the spontaneous registers, especially those exempt from conscious control (stylistic and expressive devices such as word order may, however, be greatly affected by directed interference; cf. Wanner 1989). Written expertise is clearly dependent on cumulative practice and learning over extended periods of time, and it is based on the existing models of written discourse much more than on the formal instructions of any schooling program.[13] In this sense, written language learning resembles native L1 acquisition in significant aspects: it is cumulative, depends on modeling, and presents a non-discrete trajectory between basic and sophisticated command. The written documentation of a language can thus be regarded as a useful model of the relevant linguistic environment for (pre-)adult learning of this linguistic modality, in the

---

conventionalized written expression attached to the spoken language by a process of translation equivalence: a classical diglossia situation for the media of writing vs. spoken language (except that Wright does not allow for consciousness of the language-cum-register difference). The issue here seems to be the unresolved problem of the connection between more than one linguistic competence for an individual speaker: one or two grammars? Even if the answer lies within the range of a single grammar, it is to be assumed that a (more or less conscious) dedicated component for converting from one to the other domain needs to form part of the speaker's linguistic knowledge. In the process, the secondarily acquired domain, here the written language, is invested with the status of an effective linguistic system possessing a determined macroscopic degree of difference from the base system. Barring the terminological regress over what counts as a different language given L(i), the Old Romance situation (6th to 10th century) can be comprehended as a form of Romance-Latin diglossia regardless of the precise degree of diversity and pertinent consciousness separating the spoken and the written forms of the linguistic expressions practiced by a particular speech community. A parallel modern problem is found in the case of various 'minority language' speakers (Aragonese, Asturian, Galician) with regard to their practice of the switch between local/regional language and standard Castilian. In Italy the question has been subject to considerable debate and investigation with the three poles of local dialect (minority language) - regional variant of the Standard - Standard Italian (in one of its accepted versions); cf. De Mauro (1984, passim).

[13] This does not refer to the question of appropriate content exposition at the higher levels of text organization (creative writing programs, etc.), but rather to the mechanics of using written language with formal accuracy. Then again, the dichotomy between form and content is in no way sharp, especially not in the written domain. With much more assurance, one could concentrate on the gradualness of relative mastery and form-content codetermination, rather than on neatly exclusive categorizations.

same sense as the spoken register is accepted as the proper linguistic context determining the many stages of infant language learning.

For both spoken and written modes of discourse, the distinct linguistic environments (spontaneous speech, existing texts) serve as anchors holding the learning process to a given standard. In both situations, discrete change can be viewed as due to the discontinuous transmission of linguistic knowledge across individual generations (learning from example, rather than from systematic instruction about the production tool). Since the (spoken and written) environment is very rich with different microlects defining a broad band of acceptable variation for the speech community, the learning process would have to be extremely robust and independent of environmental influence if it were not to be shaped by such accumulated experience from different systems. Within a framework of continuous learning (without momentaneous major reorganization of previous analyses) this context-dependent language processing system will be affected by its further exposure to linguistic material, spoken or written, even after a putative early-puberty cut-off of 'native' language learning. In other words, it is to be expected that language change may take place not only in the transition from one individual to another, but also during the individual's lifetime, albeit at a pace much diminished compared to the rapid learning progress of infancy. This slow-down is a result of accumulated experience which stabilizes the language processing components in a relative equilibrium that will accept modification only through massive modeling of a new or variant pattern.

The given data pattern of the context explains the basic stability of language form which perpetuates itself. The social dimension of multiple microlects, across individuals and across generations, elucidates the inevitability of change at a slow pace, change affecting the adult speaker/writer. The generational gap of abductive grammar construction provides for the discontinuities in language over a short time span which introduce possible historical change over a larger period of evolution. As linguistic experience accumulates in spoken and written registers, the corresponding outputs will also reflect such added knowledge and experience. Both major dimensions of speech activity, spoken and written, are subject to the same kind of constraints and are produced by the same general processes of linguistic knowledge. While spoken language is a more basic aspect of linguistic activity, written expression as a closely related derivative may contain rather good indications of general linguistic conditions in the period(s) of text constitution. In the absence of the filtering perspective provided by the introspective native speaker on an open range of linguistic stimuli, the overall composition of a text and of the extant documentation of a period become crucial for gauging the relative grammaticality of a given utterance or construction. In such investigations, tracing the actual use of a construction (type or variant thereof) is a necessity for practical purposes; it is, however, also motivated by general considerations of language embedded in its realistic context of usage, and this usage is, in accordance with the above arguments, a weak equivalent of the linguistic learning environment of the (historical) native speaker.

According to prevalent psycholinguistic and learning psychological views, language acquisition (beyond the bootstrapping problem) is crucially dependent on performance dimensions of environmental language modeling.[14] In particular, learning seems to involve extensive frequency tracking of processes and/or phenomena, perhaps accomplished as in a connectionist model (Rumelhart 1989, Rumelhart and McClelland 1987). Here a given path is sensitive to weighting for probability of its activation based on a cumulative, near-inert imprint of past occurrences. This general approach to language learning primarily affirms the crucial 'performance' dependence of processable linguistic input. In the classical model of abductive grammar constitution (L(i) > G(ii)) the surface data of L(i), dependent on the internalized competence grammar G(i), permit infant language learners to abduct their next-generation grammar G(ii), which in turn will support their performance range L(ii) (Andersen 1973). The synchronic abstractions of G(i) or G(ii) are necessarily data-driven, even where a heavy layer of UG principles might narrow the available band width of variation to a level manageable by the infant learner. Given that psycholinguistic understanding points heavily toward gradual, rather than dichotomous reaction to input material, the constitution of grammar G(n) necessarily moves from special, localistic features to more integrated

---

[14] Summary statements of this position are found e.g., in Bates and MacWhinney 1987b, Braine 1988, MacWhinney 1987. Such a position contrasts with the more directly linguistic/formal approaches found e.g., in Wexler and Culicover 1980, Hyams 1986 or Roeper 1987. On the 'bootstrapping' problem, i.e., how the infant L1 learner manages to associate intended meaning with perceived sound, cf. Pinker 1987, 1989.

ones.[15] Speakers could potentially differ in their individual degree of extension or completion of the grammar with regard to the formally predicted generalizations. Unless UG principles are strong enough to induce maximal generalization at every appropriate juncture, individual grammars (of competence) will contain imprints of the nonoptimal data situations of the input. Input data of L(i) are never of a pure character; output data from G(ii) as L(ii) also document non-optimal analyses. It is enough to study any given language synchronically to find extensive areas where a deeper generalization should have been achievable by the speakers according to the predictions of linguistic logic.

An instructive case is the linearization of clitic pronouns in Modern Spanish: enclisis is obligatory with non-finite verb forms (*por hacerlo, diciéndoselo*), proclisis characterizes finite verbs (*lo haré, se lo dijeron*), affirmative imperatives show enclisis (*¡cállate!*), but negative commands have proclisis (*¡no me digas!*). The lack of effect by the negative particle with nonfinite verb forms (*de haberse dado cuenta* as well as *de no haberse dado cuenta*) differentiates nonfinite Vs from imperatives; imperatives cannot be subsumed under finite forms either, due to their partial enclisis. No formal system has been found so far which could describe this situation insightfully. For the medieval language, the problem of the imperative does not exist: it behaves like any other finite verb form, yet the nonfinite conditions are less clearly structured (cf. Wanner 1991).

Such grammars are thus not explained exhaustively with general principles.[16] In view of the prominent historical continuity of languages (both as L(n) and G(n)), it is almost inevitable to recognize a major role in grammar formation for the quantitative and qualitative configuration of the input data.

---

[15] For the general problem of categorization in (language) learning, cf. Levy and Schlesinger 1988, Smith 1989.

[16] The meta-principle of functionality sometimes invoked as a counterpole to the vector of generalization is not sufficient to hold overgeneralization in check (cf. Fodor and Crain 1987, Macken 1987 on over-generalization). The actual irregularity of data is primary and thus relegates the trend toward generalization to a lower level of importance. This is observable in L1 learning and in historical evolution (cf. Wanner 1979 for the loss of an overwhelming prosodic regularity in Late Latin).

While frequency profiles for the features under investigation are commonplace in historical studies of traditional stamp,[17] they are virtually banned from relevance in current (synchronic, but also recent diachronic) methodologies. This amounts to a serious curtailment of the reach and power of linguistic explanation. It may thus be justified to advocate a broader conception of what is admissible in synchronic syntactic investigation, transcending the purely formal domain. Such a stance, external to the formal core of syntactic competence, reveals itself as fruitful for the unification of synchronic and diachronic language studies into a coherent, but not necessarily self-contained (sub-)discipline of cognitive studies.

Historical change reveals itself to be closely related to L1 learning, driven as much by actual linguistic context as by general and formal principles. Language change, and thus also syntactic evolution, regard the entire breadth of language as a functional cognitive conglomerate of processing modules. Of these, formal syntax is an essential, but not exclusive component. Language, as manifested in its variance, may only be amenable to a comprehensive treatment, providing multiple perspectives, of which change of syntactic form is one facet and formal syntactic principles another.[18] In this way the various approaches complement each other in a meaningful way, rather than preempting the competing area of investigation.

A realistic heuristics of synchronic linguistic research needs to rely in part on the same kinds of data as historical research. The seemingly atheoretical, inelegant minutiae of research methods in historical syntax are actually quite compatible with synchronic investigation concentrating on syntactic phenomena fully embedded in actual language use. There does seem to be a difference, in that historical investigation depends on accidental materials, from limited registers, while the synchronic syntactician is able to explore the entire breadth of registers, styles and individual differences. In actual practice, however, this inherent advantage of synchronic syntax has only rarely been put to

---

[17] Cf. Keniston 1937 as a particularly elaborate example; serious consideration of quantification characterizes Hawkins 1983 for the determination of actual and possible word order types, while Wanner 1987 tries to operate with impressionistic 'massive' differences in distribution.

[18] Cf. Fasold and Schiffrin 1989 as a recent collation of current work regarding the connection between variation and change.

full use, and self-imposed limitation has not impeded the formulation of many insightful analyses where the data are sufficiently clear-cut. In this respect, historical analyses, based among other features on quantitative evaluation, find themselves in a natural advantage over studies based on absolute occurrence, in spite of the absence of formal depth. This suggests that diachronic syntax is a viable field of research in the perspective developed here. Its somewhat defective raw materials are far from ideal, but they have the merit of forcing the modeling of syntactic development in terms of real-world conditions of use, and thereby also of change. They must ultimately yield insights into historical change, determined by realistic constraints facing the language learner at any chronological point. Such linguistic analyses will, among other traits shared with formal studies, be characterizable as

- data oriented
- performance dependent
- co-determined by frequency profiles
- compatible with continuous, incremental learning processes
- admitting considerable variation, and
- responsive to truly formal generalizations only in the absence of any contrary indications of (linguistic) fact.

5. The question may now shift to the implementation of such feasible historical syntax. Extensive data collections are pivotal for the purpose, but their effective control is very laborious. In particular, unaided reading of texts for collating data is usually focused on a single feature. If the data collection later proves inadequate for any reason, the entire reading process must be repeated. An obvious solution is to take advantage of electronic storage for reading and recall of data. The qualitative improvement from such operational assistance derives from the automated recall capacity extending over a representative corpus of texts. The combination of such an extensive data base with its increased accessibility due to appropriate coding and with flexible data recall can be utilized as a (very weak) analog to the unavailable native speaker in his/her role as an intuitive judge of the relative grammaticality/acceptability of the strings under investigation. At the same time, the frequency profile inherent in such automated data searches can give important indications of the range of salient features characterizing the language.

In accordance with the theoretical arguments for the feasibility of historical syntax, the following description outlines a practical course of action. It will discuss some mechanical parameters in the creation of an electronically assisted data base for Old Spanish syntax. In its evolved state, such a data base should yield the sort of research tool required for effective and efficient investigation of an open-ended variety of syntactic problems in the medieval language.

The basic materials of choice should be already existing data files. This indicates the extensive corpus of Old Spanish texts assembled for the Old Spanish Dictionary Project at the University of Wisconsin-Madison. A specific subpart of this text corpus is the maximally authentic texts of (a) the Alfonsine production transcribed by the Seminary of Medieval Spanish Studies according to the manuscripts from the Cámara Regia of Alfonso X (†1284) and (b) the works of Juan Fernández de Heredia (†1396) prepared by the same institution. These large bodies of text represent two important aspects of the loose conglomerate known as Old Spanish prose: later 13th-century historiographic and scientific prose of Castilian stamp and later 14th-century historiographic and philosophical prose in Aragonese format. In both corpora, translation/recasting of an original from a variety of languages plays an important role.

6. These texts will be utilized in different forms according to distinct levels of text preparation. A large corpus of texts highly varied in chronology, provenience and genre will be accessible as simple text files with no other internal structuring than that provided by the edition or manuscript(s) utilized in establishing the original DOSL files (Dictionary of the Old Spanish Language; cf. Mackenzie 1986). In conjunction with a concordance creation program (key word in the context of the entire utterance) these files can be used for syntactic searches where the formal problem stands in close correlation to morpholexically identifiable forms.

An example is the syntax of the adverbial pronominals *y* and *ende*. Relevant data can be captured in a first approximation by reference to the simple occurrence of the lexical items *y, ende*.[19] Such searches will produce extensive data from which it is possible to gain an initial overview of the problem at hand. Specifically, comparison between the Alfonsine and Heredia corpora yields an accurate picture of the differential syntactic status of *y* and *ende* in the two subcorpora: full clitic status in Heredia, including shortened forms *en, ne* and *sen*, vs. variable

---

[19] Including any relevant spelling variants, highly dependent on the constitution of the text.

cliticness and lack of shortened forms in the Alfonsine texts. Subsequent searches will need to concentrate on more specific features once the outline of the syntactic problem has been formulated based on these loosely focused concordances. In the case of *y* and *ende*, the most efficient procedure is to tease apart the semantic domains in which the alternating *ende, en, ne* vs. *sende, sen* appear. The etymologically compound forms *sende, sen* are prevalently used with verbs of motion (*irsen*), but there does not seem to be a systematic distribution of full vs. shortened forms. In other cases, the narrower approach needed to produce a more focused concordance file may not be expressible in terms of simple text reference. Here the more precise data access can be assured through one of the analytical coding levels provided for a smaller set of text files: morpholexical and/or syntactic analysis.

A necessarily much more restricted corpus of texts will contain codings essentially representing word class information. Each word in the text will receive, in a preparatory phase of both manual and automated file preparation, a single letter coding representative of its word class (cf. Appendix, first column for a list). Texts prepared in this format allow for searches involving both morphological classification and overt word form, given that both aspects appear as regular components in linear arrangement. At this level of analysis, it would be possible to search, e.g., for all subject pronouns (#s#), QU words (#q#), articles (#d#), auxiliaries (#x#), subjunctives (#r#), gerunds (#g#), etc., all coded distinctively. The search can be narrowed by focusing on given lexical forms within these categories, and/or by proximity to other word classes and/or lexical forms. The result of such searches will be much more specific and to the point than in the simple word form concordances. However, the amount of work associated with the preparation of these files reduces the possible extent of the morphologically analyzed data base.

In addition to the morpholexical codings, the texts in the analytical data base should also contain a sketch of their essential syntactic articulation. The major surface constituent structure is indicated for the phrase and clause level (indicated by {...} and [...]) in a mixed identification of functional and structural categories. The main effect of this analysis is to identify constituents in terms of their constituent elements, e.g., a simple declarative clause consisting of verb, direct object and prepositional phrase [$_v$ #v# {$_d$ d} {$_p$ p} $_v$], or a prepositional phrase as containing a preposition followed by a determiner and a noun {$_p$ #p# #d# #n# $_p$}. It also identifies constituents which, when only their form is considered, may have unclear function (subject $\{_{ss}\}$ vs. direct object $\{_{dd}\}$, oblique PP of argument status $\{_{bb}\}$ vs. adjunct adverbial expressions $\{_{pp}\}$). Clauses are coded mainly for their function (declarative vs. imperative vs. question, etc., at the root level, or complement vs. relative vs. adverbial, etc., at the subordinate level) and for level of embedding (root vs. non-root). While this analysis is consciously held at a level of considerable naïveté — no empty categories at any level, no abstract constituents such as INFL — it has the advantage of remaining neutral with regard to the theoretical framework that an investigator might want to use for further analysis. The issues are not prejudged beyond the degree of bias introduced by the straightforward interpretation of the surface manifestations themselves.

The available search levels are greatly enhanced by the syntactic elaboration, since search strings may now refer to the less overt aspects. All three levels of analysis are concurrently and alternatively available for reference, given that the file contains the three elements in linear order in association with a given word:

form	#word class#	(syntactic boundaries, if any at this level), e.g.
et	#k#	
aqui	#a#	[v
fue	#x#	
co-"menc[']ada	#z#	
muy	#a#	{s
grant	#j#	
"batalla	#n#	s}
la	#d#	[r {q
qual	#q#	q}
duro	#v#	
lue\<n>-"gament	#a#	r] v]

(Heredia, Florilegio f15r2)

In particular, the search string may focus on a single constituent type (referring either to its initial or final boundary), to a sequence of such constituents, and also to a discontinuous pattern of constituents and other kinds of materials contained in the complete analysis. It would thereby be possible to search for all cases of clitic pronouns with nonfinite forms not enclitic to the infinitive or gerund, and to compare them to those that are enclitic (*por lo fazer* vs. *por fazerlo*).

The three degrees of analysis — text file, word class, phrase and clause level — provide considerable freedom in formulating search strategies; they can be adapted to the needs of the specific situation and to the interests of the researcher. The output of the searches will always be a file containing some useful and some inappropriate information; this imprecision is inevitable given the relatively wide mesh of categorizations compared to the intricacies of full-fledged syntactic structurations. It is also likely that the searches will tend to exclude some relevant material due to the restrictions of the search formulation. But it should be kept in mind that the entire undertaking is dependent on the interaction between the syntactician and the search procedures. Thus, manual input is essential for the creation of the files, and manual evaluation and correction of the search output is inevitable. From the rather approximate concordance files of a first search run, human based analysis of the result will permit formulation of a more directed search, and the winnowing process continues to the point of centering in on the search goal. The advantage of the automated concordance procedure for syntactic phenomena is the speed and mechanical precision with which such data collections can be established over the entire range of the prepared data base. Beyond the initial syntactic concordance in its amorphous arrangement according to relative position in the file, the further elaboration of the concordance file with a sorting utility permits high efficiency in the goal oriented manipulation of large data collections.

Once established, the coded data base will benefit a larger constituency, since it can be used by others in projects of varied focus. The annotated file sets (morpholexical and syntactic domains) have the potential of constituting a control corpus to delimit some dimensions of a linguistic norm within the rich spectrum of Old Spanish. That this can be a very useful aspect is demonstrated, among other places, in Keniston's frequency based grammar for the 16th century (Keniston 1937). Norm in this context does not refer to the purely externally imposed standard form of a language; rather the notion is akin to the concept proposed by Coseriu (1967). It can be understood as a prototype of grammaticality relative to a given corpus. The same relativity with regard to a base of experience (i.e., the corpus) and a comparable non-categorical status of grammaticality (i.e., prototypicality) characterizes the linguistic etiology of the native speaker in the view sketched above.

The data base offers the opportunity of adding to it in such a way as to make it possible to engage in truly diachronic syntactic study across the chronological phases of a given language. Similarly, a comparative dimension is easily introduced if comparable data bases are established for other languages. The accessible nature of the data base and its manipulation, including expansion, open the way to testing of theoretical syntactic predictions. Given the virtually theory-neutral stance of the data analysis, the fast-changing and multi-faceted scene of current theoretical studies does not pose a threat to the continued relevance of the evolving investigative tool. Rather, the tool will acquire a stability akin to the underlying data.[20]

7. In the context of the few considerations on historical syntax presented in the first part of the paper it is assumed that the practical approach

---

[20] At this point, only a few hints can be given about the creation of the data base files and the search functions. In general, the idea is to use the micro-computer environment for file preparation as much as possible, due to considerations of convenience, cost and efficiency. The syntactic analysis must segment the text into clauses and utterances, and this segmentation also serves as the citation context for concordance files. Preparation of morpholexically annotated files on the microcomputer is a rather mechanical process, involving the establishment of a word list on which base the word class markings are added to the right of the word form, following purely formal criteria. The reconstituted text is then edited manually to check for accuracy, especially to adjust the notorious ambiguities of homophonous function words (e.g., *la* as article vs. clitic pronoun). The coding process is operative at this point and produces rather consistent and accurate results. The addition of a syntactic analysis is a manual process, involving the experience of the linguist analyzing the utterances into their syntactic constituents at the phrase and clause levels. While the file is still in columnar format during preparation, the syntactic codings are joined to the relevant word in the rightmost column, after the location identifier, the text form, and the morpholexical coding. The two levels are distinguished by brackets — {x...x} for the phrase level, [x...x] for the clause level — and their functions are indicated by single letter labels, so [v ... v] for the opening and closing brackets of a declarative utterance (see the Appendix for a listing of the coding symbolization). The format chosen allows for considerable breadth in formulating search strategies, including certain negative conditions as permitted by the properties of regular expressions. A possible solution is the use of an existing Unix utility, EGREP. This has the advantage of putting to use a proven function instead of developing untested new programming. On the other hand, its drawback is the requirement of a Unix system, either a mainframe computer or a powerful microcomputer with the implication of high cost. At present, the project takes the form of a mini data base containing a number of fully analyzed text samples from the Alfonsine, Berceo and Heredia corpora. The next step would be to shift into full production of analyzed files.

delineated here will help raise the level of interest in historical syntactic studies, and in particular for Old Spanish, through its quantitatively enhanced results, leading to a qualitative gain in the long range. The decision of keeping the morpholexical and syntactic analyses as theory-neutral as possible acquires thus further importance. The foreseeable changes in syntactic theory can be expected to be decisive over a period of five to ten years, even within a homogeneous research framework (a rather daring assumption in itself). A data base will yield its full potential only after some years of constitution, expansion, utilization and refinement. It is thus essential to leave the theoretical overlay to be decided by each individual investigator and to provide a base which is as 'surface true' as possible.

While this is a promissory note on what needs to be implemented with considerable energy, the projections of the thought experiment justifying renewed concentration on historical syntax as distinct from a simple extension of formal synchronic syntax are quite encouraging. Its potential validation with the help of Old Spanish syntax files stands to provide a new means of dealing with the management of historical syntax data and with putting them to use in the investigation of the cognitive processes determining the form and use of language.

References

a. Texts

Gonzalo de Berceo. *La vida de Santo Domingo de Silos*, ed. Brian Dutton. London: Tamesis, 1978 [location by stanza.verse].
_____. *La vida de San Millán de la Cogolla*, ed. Brian Dutton. London: Tamesis, 1978 [location by stanza.verse].
EE = Alfonso X El Sabio. *Estoria de España*, ed. R. Menéndez Pidal. 1955. *Primera crónica general*. 2 vols. Madrid: CSIC. [location by chapter.page.column.line of edition]; also: ms E of the Cámara Regia (transcription Seminary of Medieval Spanish Studies, University of Wisconsin—Madison) [location by folio.column].

Heredia, Juan Fernández de (1310?-1396). *Florilegio.* ms (transcription Seminary of Medieval Spanish Studies, University of Wisconsin–Madison) [location by folio.column].

_____. *Crónica de Morea.* ms (transcription Seminary of Medieval Spanish Studies, University of Wisconsin–Madison) [location by folio.column].

b. Studies

Adams, Marianne. 1989. Verb second effects in Medieval French. In Kirschner and DeCesaris 1989.1-31.

Andersen, Henning. 1973. Abductive and deductive change. *Language* 49.765-93.

Bates, Elizabeth and Brian MacWhinney. 1987. Competition, variation, and language learning. In MacWhinney 1987a.157-93.

Blake, Robert J. forthcoming. Aspectos sintácticos del español antiguo: la prosa latinizada del Cartulario de San Millán. In *Actas del II congreso internacional de historia de la lengua española*, ed. M. Cano Aguilar.

Bossong, Georg. 1991. Differential object marking in Romance and beyond. In Wanner and Kibbee 1991.143-70.

Braine, Martin D. S. 1988. Modeling the acquisition of linguistic structure. In Levy et al. 1988.217-59.

Butt, John and Carmen Benjamin. 1988. *A new reference grammar of Modern Spanish.* London: Edward Arnold.

Cerquiglini, Bernard. 1989. *Éloge de la variante. Histoire critique de la philologie.* Paris: Seuil.

Clark, Eve V. 1987. The principle of contrast: A constraint on language acquisition. In MacWhinney 1987a.1-33.

Coseriu, Eugenio. 1967. Sistema, norma y habla. In *Teoría del lenguaje y lingüística general*, 11-113. 2nd ed. Madrid: Gredos.

De Mauro, Tullio. 1984. *Storia linguistica dell'Italia unita.* 2nd ed. Bari: Laterza.

Fodor, Janet D. and Stephen Crain. 1987. Simplicity and generality of rules in language acquisition. In MacWhinney 1987a.35-63.

Haider, Hubert and M. Prinzhorn (eds.) 1986. *Verb second phenomena in Germanic languages.* Dordrecht: Foris.

Hawkins, John. 1983. *Word order universals*. New York: Academic Press.

Hirschbühler, Paul. 1989. On the existence of null subjects in embedded clauses in Old and Middle French. In Kirschner and DeCesaris 1989.155-75.

Hock, Hans H. 1986. *Principles of historical linguistics*. Berlin: Mouton de Gruyter.

Hyams, Nina. 1986. *Language acquisition and the theory of parameters*. Dordrecht: Kluwer Academic/Reidel.

Jensen, Frede. 1990. *Old French and Comparative Gallo-Romance Syntax. Zeitschrift für romanische Philologie*, Beiheft 232. Tübingen: Niemeyer

Keniston, Hayward S. 1937. *The Syntax of Castilian Prose*. Chicago: University of Chicago Press.

Kirschner, Carl and Janet DeCesaris (eds.) 1989. *Studies in Romance Linguistics. (Selected Papers from the Seventeenth Linguistic Symposium on Romance Languages, Rutgers University, 27-29 March 1987)*. Amsterdam: Benjamins.

Langacker, Ronald W. 1987. *Foundations of cognitive grammar*. Stanford: Stanford University Press.

Lass, Roger. 1980. *On explaining language change*. Cambridge: Cambridge University Press.

Levy, Yonata and Izchak M. Schlesinger. 1988. The child's early categories: Approaches to language acquisition theory. In *Categories and Processes in Language Acquisition*, ed. Yonata Levy, Izchak M. Schlesinger and Martin D. S. Braine, 261-76. Hillsdale, N.J: Erlbaum.

Lightfoot, David W. 1979. *Principles of diachronic syntax*. Cambridge: Cambridge University Press.

Macken, Marlys A. 1987. Representation, rules and overgeneralization in phonology. In MacWhinney 1987a.367-97.

Mackenzie, David. 1986. *A manual of manuscript transcription for the Dictionary of the Old Spanish language*. 4th ed., Victoria A. Burrus. Madison: The Hispanic Seminary of Medieval Studies.

MacWhinney, Brian (ed.) 1987a. *Mechanisms of language acquisition (The 20th Annual Carnegie Symposium on Cognition)*. Hillsdale, N.J: Erlbaum.

_____. 1987b. The competition model. In MacWhinney 1987a.249-308.

188 Dieter Wanner

Martineau, France. 1991. Clitic climbing in infinitival constructions of Middle French. In Wanner and Kibbee 1991.235-51.

Menéndez Pidal, Ramón. 1944. *Cantar de mio Cid. I: Crítica del texto, Gramática.* Madrid: Espasa-Calpe.

_____. 1950. *Orígenes del español.* 3rd ed. Madrid: Espasa-Calpe.

Monaci, Ernesto. 1955. *Crestomazia italiana dei primi secoli,* ed. F. Arese. Rome: Società Dante Alighieri.

Newell, Allen, Paul S. Rosenbloom and John E. Laird. 1989. Symbolic architectures for cognition. In Posner 1989.93-131.

Pearce, Elizabeth H. 1990. *Language change and infinitival complements in Old French.* London: Croom Helm.

Pinker, Steven. 1987. The bootstrapping problem in language acquisition. In MacWhinney 1987a.399-441.

_____. 1989. Language acquisition. In Posner 1989.359-400.

Posner, Michael I. (ed.) 1989. *Foundations of cognitive science.* Cambridge, Mass: MIT Press.

Ramsden, Herbert. 1963. *Weak-pronoun position in the Early Romance languages.* Manchester: Manchester University Press.

Rivero, María-Luisa. 1986. Parameters in the typology of clitics in Romance and Old Spanish. *Language* 62.774-807.

_____. forthcoming. Clitic climbing and NP climbing in Old Spanish. To appear in *Current Studies in Spanish Linguistics,* ed. Héctor Campos and Fernando Martínez-Gil. Amsterdam: Benjamins.

Roeper, Thomas. 1987. The acquisition of implicit arguments and the distinction between theory, process, and mechanism. In MacWhinney 1987a.309-43.

Rumelhart, David E. 1989. The architecture of mind: a connectionist approach. In Posner 1989.133-60.

_____ and James L. McClelland. 1987. Learning the past tenses of English verbs: Implicit rules or parallel distributed processing. In MacWhinney 1987a.195-248.

Smith, Edward E. 1989. Concepts and induction. In Posner 1989.501-26.

Vance, Barbara. 1989. The evolution of pro-drop in Medieval French. In Kirschner and DeCesaris 1989.397-441.

Väänänen, Veikko. 1974. *Introduzione al latino volgare.* 2nd ed. Bologna: Pàtron.

Wanner, Dieter. 1979. Die Bewahrung der lateinischen Haupttonstelle im Romanischen. *Vox Romanica* 37.1-36.

_____. 1982. A history of Spanish clitic movement. In *Proceedings of the 8th Annual Meeting of the Berkeley Linguistics Society*, ed. M. Macaulay et al., 135-47. Berkeley: Berkeley Linguistics Society.

_____. 1987. *The Development of Romance Clitic Pronouns. From Latin to Old Romance*. Empirical Approaches to Language Typology, 3. Berlin: Mouton de Gruyter.

_____. 1989. The continuum of verb position typology in Romance. In Kirschner and DeCesaris 1989.443-77.

_____. 1990. Subjects in Old Spanish: Conflicts between typology, syntax and dynamics. Paper read at the XX Linguistic Symposium on Romance Languages, University of Ottawa, April 1990.

_____. 1991. Multiple clitic linearization principles. Paper presented at the Linguistics Symposium on Romance Languages XXI, Feb. 24-26, 1991. University of California, Santa Barbara.

_____. forthcoming. The Tobler-Mussafia law in Old Spanish. To appear in *Current Studies in Spanish Linguistics*, ed. Héctor Campos and Fernando Martínez-Gil. Amsterdam: Benjamins.

_____ and Douglas A. Kibbee (eds.) 1991. *New Analyses in Romance Linguistics. (Selected Papers from the XVIII Linguistic Symposium on Romance Languages, Urbana–Champaign, April 7-9, 1988)*. Amsterdam: Benjamins.

_____ and Elizabeth H. Pearce. 1981-83. Unpublished materials for a computerized concordance program for Old Florentine syntax. University of Illinois at Urbana–Champaign.

Wexler, Kenneth and Peter W. Culicover. 1980. *Formal principles of language acquisition*. Cambridge, Mass: MIT Press.

Wright, Roger. 1982. *Late Latin and Early Romance in Spain and Carolingian France*. Liverpool: Cairns.

Appendix

A tentative schema of classification

symbol	#morphology#	{phrases}	[clauses]	(level)
a	adverb	adverb P	adverb cl	(s)
b	strong personal pron.	oblique NP	-	
c	subord. conjunction	conjunction P	complement cl	(s)
d	determiner	direct object NP	-	
e	exclamation	exclamation P	exclamation cl	(r)
f	demonstrat. adj./pron.	-	fragmentary cl	(r)
g	gerund	gerundial P	-	
h	indef./neg. adj./pron.	-	wish cl	(r)
i	infinitive	infinitival P	-	
j	adjective	adjectival P	adjective complem. cl	(s)
k	coordination	coordinate P (opt.)	coord. conjunct (opt.)	s/r
l	negation	-	-	
m	comparative adverb	comparative P	comparative cl	(s)
n	noun	NP (caseless)	noun complem. cl	(s)
o	possessive adj./pron.	appositive NP	imperative	(r)
p	preposition	prepositional P	root cl proper	(r)
q	QU word	QU P	interrogative cl	s/r
r	finite vb. subjunctive	complex preposition	relative clause	(s)
s	subject pronoun	subject NP	subject complem. cl	(s)
t	y/*ende*	indirect object NP	direct discourse	(r)
u	numeral	numeral P	-	
v	finite vb. indicative	vocative NP	ordinary cl	(r)
w	clitic pronoun	predicative nominal	pseudo-root cl	(r)
x	auxiliary verb	dislocated NP	-	
y	proper name/toponym	passive PP	parenthetical/quote cl	s/r
z	past participle	participial P	-	

On Editing 'Latin' Texts Written by Romance-Speakers[1]

Roger Wright

University of Liverpool

Editors of early medieval texts need to be continuously aware of the difference between *Grammatica* as used by Germanic- (or Celtic-) speakers and as used by Romance-speakers in the Early Middle Ages. The theme of this article is that modern editors of such texts from Spain are too often inclined to act as if the authors were not Romance-speakers, and follow a depressing and unhelpful tradition of seeing the early medieval Romance/Latin relationship as being analogous to the Germanic/Latin relationship. It was not.

1. For Romance-speakers, *Grammatica* = writing

The differences derive from the fact that *Grammatica* was taught in different ways in different language communities. The historical origins of the difference need to be appreciated. All early medieval education was based on the teaching and learning of *Ars Grammatica*. The words *Ars Grammatica* were originally connected specifically with writing. The *Ars Minor* and *Ars Secunda* (or *Ars Maior*) of the fourth-century Grammarian Aelius Donatus were compiled for the benefit of people who spoke as their native language fourth-century vernacular Latin; what philologists of some schools call 'Proto-Romance'. These works, plus the commentaries based on them, became the basis for linguistic education for centuries afterwards. The fifth-century grammarians, such as Consentius, Pompeius, Servius and Sergius, worked within the same atmosphere, still essentially considering the formal registers of a language

[1] This is the revised text of a lecture given at the Warburg Institute, University of London, in June 1990, and also at the University of Oslo, Norway, in September 1990. I am grateful for comments made by participants at these occasions.

which they and their readers already spoke. These grammarians were
thus, in modern terms, not specialists in the teaching of Latin as a foreign
language, but specialists in linguistics, with particular reference to the
demands of writing. In sixth-century Italy, Cassiodorus maintained, in his
work on language, a similar focus on deciding which were the supposedly
'correct' forms to be used in written texts; his grammatical works were
intended to help copyists at Vivarium, who were also native speakers of
the language. In sixth-century France, Caesarius of Arles tried hard to
encourage his flock to be literate in the language which they already had.
In the seventh century, the first chapter of Isidore of Seville's
Etymologiae was essentially a derivative grammar based on the fifth-
century African commentators on Donatus. He too, and his successors
such as Julián de Toledo, were teaching their readers about the smart and
formal way to operate and analyse the language they already spoke, that
is, seventh-century Spanish Early Romance/Late Latin (in this period we
can as justifiably call their language the one as the other).

The grammarians mentioned hitherto, and others, were writing for
the benefit of students who were native speakers of the language in
question, training them in the arts of writing, reading, and to some extent
analysing, the language they already had. The students could already be
expected to pronounce it, use the normal grammar of speech, and know
the basic vocabulary, and did not need to be taught that; features which
had by and large slipped out of spoken Latin, however, such as many of
the noun inflections, did need to be taught, which is why so much of the
Grammarians' attention lay precisely there. But all, including the
Grammarians, spoke the language of their time and place, and the
techniques of writing professionally (*Ars Grammatica*) were aimed at
producing respectably traditional-looking forms of that same language.
Recent historical research suggests that in early medieval Romance
communities few people could write, more could read, and almost
everybody (then as now) could understand written texts read aloud with
care. To the Romance speaker, Latin texts were not in a foreign
language.[2]

---

[2] These arguments were developed at greater length in the first two chapters of Wright
(1982).

2. For non-Romance speakers, *Grammatica* = another language

The teaching of Latin-as-a-foreign-language only began, naturally enough, where there was a community of non-Latin speakers who wished to learn to read written Latin texts. It is in eighth-century England that we begin to see a change in the nature of grammarians' texts; everything about Latin had to be taught there from scratch, for the students there had no advance native expertise.[3] The Anglo-Saxon scholars had some knowledge of the works of the Visigothic writers of Spain, and also some personal contacts with speakers of Early Romance from France and Italy. It is possible that there were native Romance-speakers around in Anglo-Saxon England who were able to demonstrate personally (in *Grammatica* classes) linguistic features that were taken for granted in the preexisting continental works of linguistics. This could be parallelled today, if a non-English-speaking community wished to learn English but only had the works of English-speaking theoretical linguists such as Halliday to guide them; the books are not totally useless for the purpose, but the students would need considerable extra guidance from native speakers who already know the language well, or they do not even get to square one. Yet the influence of Early-Romance speakers in Anglo-Saxon England was, so far as we can see, not decisive in the establishment of the nature of Anglo-Saxon Latin. In pronunciation, for example, the phonology of eighth-century Anglo-Saxon Latin owed more to the phonology of Anglo-Saxon than it did to the phonology of the native speakers of any part of the former Roman Empire. We can deduce this, at least, from the nature of the alliterative and rhyming techniques of Early Medieval Insular virtuoso poetry.

There were other Anglo-Saxon intellectuals with pedagogical linguistic interests, but the key initial figure is Bede. He kept a notebook of useful points that had come up in his pedagogical experience, covering orthography, grammar, inflectional morphology, derivational morphology, lexis and semantics, and even phonetics, although it seems only in connection with syllable-division in the choir. This work is practical and pedagogical, although essentially addressed to other teachers rather than to his students, and collectively has the air of being an aid to the 'Latin

---

[3] The best work on the use of *Grammatica* in non-Romance countries is Law (1982). As she shows in another study (1987), these Grammarians were actively reshaping the received tradition for their own community's different needs.

as a foreign language' teacher. When he adapts details from his sources, he does so for the practical purposes of his own community. It is unfortunate that this work has come to be given the misleading title of *De Orthographia*, for it is not especially concerned with spelling.[4] Bede established personally a tradition of eighth-century Insular Latin learning, which was in a number of ways rather different from that current in contemporary Romance-speaking Europe. Eighth-century written texts followed the same models, and ostensibly the same grammar, wherever they were written. But in the case of Germanic-speakers, including in due course those on the Continent speaking varieties of Germanic other than Anglo-Saxon, they were writing a foreign language that was self-evidently not their own vernacular. They were bilingual; and this foreign language was uniquely defined for them by the Grammarians (and their commentators).

They had to learn everything from teachers. This included pronunciation. The way the Anglo-Saxon speaker learnt and was taught to pronounce was on the basis of written texts. They knew, as they learnt, the written form of a word right from the first moment that they encountered it. The teachers offered it to them in written form, and they based their pronunciations on that preexisting written form. This had one significant consequence in particular; in the Germanic-speakers' *Grammatica* classes, every written letter in a word gave rise to a sound. There were to be no silent letters. This was a natural consequence of the general inability of the Early Medieval Grammarians, just like first-year language students today, to distinguish letters from sounds. Not only that, but each written letter (or digraph) was meant to give rise to the same sound in every circumstance, wherever it appeared in the written form. Thus, in the British Isles, the spelling determined the pronunciation. This is, of course, completely the opposite of what all people (including speakers of Early Romance) do with their own native language, where they pronounce the words first in speech, and only write them much later, if at all. Isidore's clientèle knew their language anyway, having learnt it in the ordinary manner as children, whether or not they ever learned later to read or write. Morphological features such as the paradigms demonstrating the endings of nouns (*declinationes nominum*), however, would have been useful in both traditions; in seventh-century Spain they were needed, and

---

[4] Dionisotti (1982:122) sees it as 'a reference work for the Library'.

explicitly taught, because they were largely unused in speech, but encountered in reading and needed for writing.

3. Early Romance

It is worth reminding ourselves of what the linguistic situation of seventh- and eighth-century Western Romance-speaking Europe was like. It was (mutatis mutandis) rather like that of Modern English or Modern French; a huge geographical area whose language, Early Romance, contained within it a wide variety of linguistic alternatives; there were alternative items of vocabulary, different grammatical ways of expressing the same idea, different phonetic ways of pronouncing the same word, but it still remained in essence a single speech-community.[5] All such wide single speech-communities have within them enormous variety, not only geographical but also stylistic, sociolinguistic, contextual, and even variation between young and old, male and female, rich and poor, etc. Such variation within a single language is not only normal but useful for all sorts of practical purposes (what linguists now call 'pragmatics'). A large number of innovating linguistic features had arisen over the centuries, in the way they always do, for no spoken language has ever been fixed, unchanging and static, not even fourth-century Latin. Some of the old Classical forms and constructions were no longer in active use. But it seems reasonable to deduce that the old linguistic features had in several cases not yet dropped out entirely; they would still be understood by those listening to written texts being read aloud, and even active seventh-century Romance speech, for example, could well have included both the old-fashioned accusative and infinitive constructions and the new *quod* plus indicative constructions which seem in retrospect to have neatly taken their place, both the old-fashioned genitive endings of nouns and the new-fashioned equivalents with the preposition *de*, both old words such as *equus* and new words such as *caballus*. In general, then, the Romance language of the time contained both old and new grammatical features, but only the reconstructably evolved phonetics; writing and talking involved statistically different proportions of the relevant competing morphosyntactic and lexical forms (as in modern

---

[5] On this see several studies in Wright (1991a) and McKitterick (1990), Herman (1988), Banniard (1989).

English) rather than any rigid apartheid between literate and illiterate, which (as Harvey and others have pointed out) is otherwise unattested and thoroughly improbable on many grounds.[6] This was essentially the nature of Iberian Romance until the second millennium.

When speakers from this pulsating, lively, versatile, flexible, rich, complex, but monolingual Early Romance speech community came to learn to write — if they ever did, for most of them did not — they were hit at once by the artificial restrictions of the old Donatus tradition. Early Medieval Romance was — to the eternal disappointment of all Romance philologists — not permitted to appear neat on parchment as in an exact phonetic transcription. Prescriptive Grammarians, then as now, are always restrictive. They always interpret their function as that of specifying as 'correct' in a written context just some, out of the wide existing variety, of the forms, expressions, constructions and words available in the wider community. They see their job in moral terms; variations are not merely formal versus informal, innovating versus archaic, characteristic of one geographical area rather than another, and so on, but — in writing, at least — as 'correct' or 'incorrect'. Whereas Latin for the non-Romance speaker was uniquely defined by the *Grammatica*, the Romance-speaker's language had a much wider range of usage of which the *Grammatica* only prescribed a sub-section as being acceptable in writing. The same happens today; native English-speaking university lecturers in Spanish-as-a-foreign-language usually have a considerably narrower idea of what is permissible Spanish than the native Spanish-speaking *lectores* who are their colleagues. As Franco (1985) has pointed out, for example, the rules that we teach students concerning the need to use *estar* rather than *ser* in locative senses are not always followed by native speakers (who can at times be heard saying *¿dónde es ... ?*).

This debilitating tendency to see a moral order in grammatical details hamstrings later generations of Romance-speakers who depend, when writing, on the earlier grammarians' prescriptions which have by then become traditional. The eighth-century spoken Romance community in general, and continuing to the twelfth century in the Iberian Peninsula, is alive and sophisticated, capable of communicating and interacting orally as well then as people are now, but Romance-speaking scribes were told in their training that in writing they ought to follow the

---

[6] See Harvey (1990), Herman (1990), Alarcos (1982), Wright (in press, b).

traditional prescriptions and only include on paper those linguistic features that had been blessed as 'correct' in the fourth century A.D. (with in practice the addition of some declensional subtypes of ecclesiastical words taken from Greek). This limitation was by then doubly restricting, because several of these forms deemed 'correct' in the Late Empire had largely disappeared from most active speech four hundred years later (ablative cases of nouns, synthetic passives, etc.), and the proportion of available eighth-century variants that coincided with the fourth-century moral perceptions was lower than it had been originally. And yet, in Romance Europe, people did succeed in writing; the 'Renaissance' of Visigothic Spain had made Spain the most educated area of the seventh century, and its intellectual traditions continued, both in nominally Christian and nominally Moslem Spain, to flourish well into the tenth century, producing a large number of written works, some of which survive. Collins deduced that tenth-century Leonese society was just as dependent on documentation as that of tenth-century Catalonia, despite the fact that Catalonia was, and León was not, an area where the Carolingian Latin-Romance distinction operated.[7]

4. The practical problem

Here we get to the serious practical problem. The original works of Isidore, Ildefonso, Eugenio de Toledo, Julián de Toledo, Eulogio de Córdoba, Álvaro de Córdoba, the ninth-century Asturian historians, and so on, were written by speakers of Early Romance; their speech was more versatile than were the written forms that they were taught were acceptable, and, although they knew their *Grammatica*, features of their ordinary speech habits are at times observable in the early manuscripts, including such erudite productions as those of the greatest scholar of the age (Isidore) and the texts of the mozarabic liturgy. So we find there, for example, *se* used instead of synthetic passives, prepositions used instead of case endings, theoretically neuter plural nouns used as the feminine singulars that they had become in speech, theoretically third-conjugation verbs used with the fourth-conjugation endings that they had often acquired in speech, etc., etc. The writers had been taught according to an already ancient tradition about which features of speech could and could

---

[7] Collins (1985); cp. also, Collins (1989).

not be included, but as time had gone on more and more normal spoken features theoretically could not be written, and they were not always successfully kept out of the texts.

The problem is that subsequent editors have misunderstood the essential distinction that we need to make. These Early Medieval Romance-speakers were writing the language they already spoke, following ancient restrictions; unlike the Germanic-speakers, they were *not* trying to write in a foreign language. Those modern editors, from Ambrosio de Morales in the sixteenth century, who 'corrected' the voluminous original work of Eulogio de Córdoba out of all authenticity, up to the recent editors of Isidore's *Etymologiae* who scorn the readings of the early manuscripts, do an enormous disservice to scholarship, assuming that these Romance-speakers had been taught Latin-as-a-foreign-language in the same way as the Germanic-speakers were, and that the Romance-speakers were trying to write in the restrictive foreign language rather than in an archaic but nevertheless 'correct' style of their own language which they had been led to believe was morally preferable. In short, I would plead with all editors of early medieval texts from Romance Europe — as do most of the contributors to the special issue of *Speculum* for January 1990 (on 'The New Philology'), and Law (1982) — *not to emend their early manuscripts at all.* Oroz Reta's comments at the start of his recent edition of the *Etymologiae* are little short of grotesque:

> ... creemos que el texto isidoriano que ofrece la Bibliotheca Oxoniensis, en muchos pasajes, podía corregirse sin dificultad ... en modo alguno podíamos pensar en realizar un estudio o análisis de los numerosísimos códices isidorianos ... para ofrecer un texto más puro y correcto ... hemos tratado de uniformar las grafías variadas ... hemos corregido ... creemos que hay que uniformar ...

He is, in short, proud to have distorted the original and rendered his edition useless for linguistic research. There is, however, one scholar above all who has aimed to edit these texts professionally: Juan Gil of Seville. As an antidote to the above, note his comment:

> Normalmente, al editar la obra de un escritor visigodo, se suele modificar la grafía al uso clásico. Esta corrección, con todo, entraña no pocos peligros; falsea el aspecto externo de un texto, regulariza grafías que no regularizaron nunca sus propios autores, encubre fenómenos fonéticos y en ocasiones atenta contra los mismos usos ortográficos visigodos.

Gil is referring here not only to spelling but also to morphological features. This important article came out in 1973, but seems not to have had the effect it deserves.[8]

5. How the Romance West was lost

Unfortunately, nowadays, in the Romance-speaking world, people do not think of themselves as Latin-speakers any more, and (like Germanic-speakers) they do now think of Latin as a foreign language, different from their own Portuguese, Catalan, Venetian, etc. The way in which this conceptual distinction arose is at the forefront of debate in contemporary Romance philology. I have long expressed, and still hold, the view that this conceptual distinction began at the point where the two traditions clashed; where the Germanic view of Latin as a foreign language, whose grammar was defined uniquely by the prescriptions of Grammarians and untouched by the enormous vitality of eighth-century spoken Romance, came into startled contact with the versatility and liveliness of that speech; and recoiled in horror. That is, to be more precise, the appointment of Alcuin of York to reform the Carolingian education system. The distinction between Latin and vernacular was obvious to a Germanic-speaker, naturally, and Alcuin and his group wished to introduce that distinction into the education system of Romance Europe as well. So they presided over the conscious invention of a new conceptual distinction, between Latin and Romance, and Romance-speakers in at least some of the Carolingian cultural centres of the ninth and tenth centuries began to be taught, on Anglo-Saxon lines, Latin as a foreign language, with a grammar, a vocabulary, and even a pronunciation distinguishably separate from even the most formal styles of their own native language as spoken in France, Catalonia and Northern Italy. (Incidentally, I do not wish to be accused of fostering a 'great man' view of history; the consequences of Alcuin's prejudices were almost totally pernicious.) Eventually this invented conceptual distinction spread out of the Carolingian Empire into the rest of the Iberian Peninsula, Italy, and

---

[8] These quotations are from Oroz's edition of Isidore (1982:258-59) — of which Díaz y Díaz's Introduction is excellent — and Gil (1973:193), which is relevant for all texts up to the twelfth century (and sheds also an interesting light on the *Historia Roderici*, p. 223).

elsewhere, and in due course it came to seem so obvious and natural and normal that Dante, in his *De Vulgari Eloquentia*, thought it had always existed. But the distinction, even in France, took time to become generally accepted and spread beyond progressive Church circles; on the whole it seems that students in France were not generally taught to make a conceptual Latin/Romance distinction till after the millennium, still previously on the whole being taught to write in a particular style of the language they had rather than being taught from scratch a whole foreign language.[9] As suggested above, in Spain, this stage probably lasts until at least 1080 and for most purposes until after 1200; that is, in Spain, as in France, the eventual triumph of the dead hand of restricting Germanic pedagogy over the preexisting complex Romance monolingualism took a long time to be generally accepted. My own recent studies of the *Vita Dominici Siliensis* (of the 1080s) and the *Chronica Adefonsi Imperatoris* (c.1147) suggest that the Latin-Romance metalinguistic distinction which seems so obvious to us now, as if it had always existed, was not consciously felt then (and, as Niederehe pointed out, was not entirely clear even to Alfonso el Sabio).[10] This means that all texts from pre-12th century non-Catalan Spain, and quite possibly most of those from the 12th century as well, are in written Romance, rather than, as usually stated, corrupt and barbaric Latin.

I have discussed the implications of this reevaluation at some length elsewhere with reference to the *Chronicle of Alfonso III*. Fortunately this Chronicle (originally from the royal court of late ninth-century Oviedo) has been luckier in its modern editors than has poor Isidore; Bonnaz's edition (1987) is stultifyingly classicizing, but the editions of Prelog (1980) and above all Gil et al. (1985) are intelligently and accurately presented in such a way that we can watch how successive adaptations of the text gradually formalized an original that began essentially in written Romance.[11] In France, the textual evidence of pre-Reform compositions was often doctored ('emended') into apparent respectability by Carolingian and post-Carolingian scholars. They did this

---

[9] See McKitterick (1989), Van Uytfanghe (1989, 1991), and the long Introduction to Guerreau-Jalabert (1982).

[10] The references are to Wright (in press, a), Wright (1991b), and Niederehe (1987:102).

[11] Wright (in press, b) considers this in more detail.

themselves to the Benedictine rule, for example, as well as to many of the texts of the early Fathers of the Church, and to their own *Annales Regni Francorum*; and almost certainly to large numbers of other earlier texts that only now survive in post-Carolingian manuscripts. And from being taught that this 'correction' was what they were supposed to carry out, gradually students and editors came to be taught that the original writers must have got it 'right', and that everything which Donatus would not have approved of must have been introduced by careless copyists because they could not have been there in the original; hence Ambrosio de Morales' assumption that he was right to distort the evidence of his manuscript, as if Eulogio de Córdoba was a closet Anglo-Saxon, as if Eulogio had been writing a non-vernacular foreign language defined only by the *Ars Grammatica* tradition rather than writing a formal style of his own speech, such that Ambrosio de Morales presumed that all the non-Grammatical features must be the fault of incompetent manuscript copyists. But we know, particularly as regards twelfth-century Spain (and later), that copyists were more likely to distort their originals by making 'corrections' of their pre-Reform originals, rather than by introducing errors. There is no need for us to do the same.

6. After the separation

We have seen that before 800, and in many cases later, Romance-speakers, if they were taught to write at all, were taught how to write acceptably the language which they already spoke, according to an ancient tradition which ruled out of acceptability a large number of features of their speech. Germanic speakers, on the other hand, were taught only that limited and limiting tradition, Latin as a foreign language, not usually including knowledge of how the language was actually spoken at the time. After 800 the two systems coexist in Carolingian France until eventually — perhaps after a couple of centuries in several places — the view of Latin as being a foreign language became normal; in due course this conceptual separation became normal in the whole Romance-speaking world. In Spain the definitive dissociative process accompanied the invention and general spread of undisguised vernacular writing and the Latin-teaching reforms consequent on the Lateran Council of 1215 and the Council of Valladolid of 1228.

It was a Pyrrhic victory. For it was precisely in places where Latin was taught and learnt and conceived of as a separate language from native vernacular that works were also written in a new form based on that vernacular; this explains why works in Germanic vernaculars seem to appear in written form before those in French, Provençal, Catalan, Sicilian, Castilian, etc. But this apparent precedence of Germanic texts is a mirage. Before the change in perspective in Romance areas, Romance indeed had a written form, but to us, looking back from much later, that form appears to be 'Latin'. The texts in consciously reformed non-traditional spelling and morphology that we call now 'Old French', 'Old Provençal', 'Old Castilian' (etc.) emerged from centres of expert Latinity only after this metalinguistic change, in places (such as St Amand, Fleury, San Millán, Palencia, Toledo, San Fernando's chancery, etc.) where it seems probable that Latin had recently started being taught and learnt as a foreign language from the normal Romance vernacular, and as a result the vernacular came in due course to appear to need a new separate written guise. It cannot be pointed out too often that the earliest 'Romance' texts were in fact elaborated by expert Latinists in progressive cultural centres; the reason for that was that nobody else saw any point in making such a distinction until Latin (*Grammatica*) was generally conceived of as being a different language from normal speech. It is time to discard forever the ridiculous idea, still apparently current, that early texts in written vernacular form were produced by and for the illiterate; on the contrary, by definition, the illiterate could not write at all, and those that could read or write would (as in the modern English-speaking world) find a phonetic script harder to use than the traditional forms. (The practical mechanics of the changeover in the Iberian Peninsula have been illuminated by Emiliano (1988, 1991)). Eventually, in this new guise, written medieval Romance languages were able to capture their own oral spontaneity, vitality and life (as we see in their literature) — which had been there in speech all along, but impermissible in writing —, whereupon the dead hand of reformed *Grammatica* could be left to the pedants.

7. An Unscientific Analogy

Consider the following analogy. In the year 2000 a reform of the United States education system is entrusted to a politically powerful group of Arabs, who have only learnt English as a foreign language uniquely defined by the Grammar books, use in speech as a result only the most formal grammar, and pronounce every written letter (such as to be often unintelligible to the natives), but write it according to the same rules as the English-speakers in the U.S.A. The Arab scholars' leader (Mohammed Al-Kwin) is empowered to insist that everyone in the best universities should speak as he does (at least, in formal situations), and indeed, within a century or so this artificial system comes to be normal in U.S. higher education. This system, already normal in the non-English speaking world, effectively excludes the majority of English-speakers in the U.S. from understanding what used to be merely the written form of their own language. So eventually someone thinks of the idea of writing spoken U.S. English according to a reformed writing system — for, say, oaths sworn in court, sermons, popular poems. The new vernacular writing systems are taken up in the rest of the English-speaking world, until eventually, after another century, the distinction between English-as-a-foreign language (*Grammar*) and regional vernaculars (formerly seen as variants of English, but now separately called e.g., Australian, Indian, British, etc.) comes to seem natural everywhere. Meanwhile Arab and Arab-trained scholars rewrite the text of the works of American writers of pre-2000, in order that they can fit their preconceptions of how they 'ought' to have been written (excising *didn't* for *did not*, *gonna* for *going to*, *thru* for *through*, etc.).

Under such circumstances, would it be right for subsequent scholars to regard the surviving original versions of works by J. D. Salinger, Philip Roth, etc., as being in barbarous *Grammar* rather than merely in the written mode of their own vernacular? Would it not be preferable to edit them without such emendation? Let us not, therefore, in the real world do the same to early Spanish medieval texts, for they too were originally in the written mode of their author's vernacular.

8. Nine Conclusions

1. All Spanish texts from before 1080, and most from before 1200, need to be edited without any emendation at all from the earliest manuscript(s), rather than changed as a result of what anachronistic preconceptions lead editors to think 'ought' to have been written instead. This applies not only to Histories, but all varieties of legal documents, including *fueros*,

Church Councils (such as the 1055 Council of Coyanza), hagiography, and indeed everything else. Ideally, facsimiles of the manuscripts would be available (as the latest editors of Merovingian documentation realize: see the comments of Ganz and Goffart, 1990), but they are often not clear enough in themselves. Conversely, García Larragueta's (1984:123-46) attempt at a typescript facsimile of the *Glosas Emilianenses*, for example, clarifies Olarte Ruiz's photographic facsimile (1977), but would be misleading on its own (in that it resolves some abbreviations and is not free of misprints).

This is in no way a revolutionary suggestion. It is, for example, what is prescribed by the *Asociación de Lingüística y Filología de la América Latina* for its forthcoming publications of documents. Quoting Gil again (1973:208): 'la tarea es difícil; pero la única manera de cumplirla es respetar al máximo — no me cansaré nunca de repetirlo — las grafías de los manuscritos'.

2. This fidelity should include a resistance to any temptation to resolve abbreviations at all, for in practice the way abbreviations are resolved begs many questions. Abbreviations were intended to be recognized, but the unit to be recognized was meant to be the lexical word rather than the omitted letters; that is, for example, whether we resolve *nro* as *nostro* or *nuestro*, or *tēs* as *testis* or *testigo* (etc.), our decision probably results in giving a misleading impression.

3. Since the texts in question are written in the formal version of Spanish Romance, rather than a barbarously unsuccessful attempt at another language entirely, we should stop insulting their language and their authors. We cannot seriously explain the language of the Rotense version of the Chronicle of Alfonso III simply with the theory that the Asturians were all barbarously stupid and corrupt; for we know from historical research how enterprising and resourceful ninth- and tenth-century Asturians actually were. Similarly, the present nature of the *Fuero de Valfermoso de las Monjas* is better described as the result of a serious attempt at formalizing the vernacular than of a crass attempt at writing another language entirely.

4. Etymologists should realize that all the texts in question are evidence for Spanish vocabulary. It is inappropriate that Corominas and Pascual should adduce the first attestation of a Spanish word (in their ety-

mological dictionary) as of necessity being one that is spelt incorrectly in cases where the same word 'correctly' spelt is attested earlier. *Camisa*, for example, is given by Corominas and Pascual (1980:787) a first documentation date of 899, despite being attested as *camisiam* in Isidore's *Etymologiae* XIX.21.1.

5. The computerized dictionaries should therefore extend their corpus further back in time also. Not to do so is misleading. For example; the fact that *rege* appears in the late tenth-century *Nodicia de kesos* and also in countless documents and histories, etc., should not be hidden from the enquiring philologist who might otherwise think that the thirteenth-century invented the lexical word itself rather than merely the orthographic form *rey* (and *rei*). Oelschläger (1940) glimpsed this truth.[12]

6. Likewise, the exciting CD-ROM project of all old Spanish texts (ADMYTE), sponsored by Professor Faulhaber, would ideally start earlier than it will, since its initial cut-off point depends on an anachronistic dichotomy.

7. Ideally, also, the Madison medieval Spanish publication enterprises should include all such texts (before, let us say, St Martin of León) as within their brief.[13] A chronological line has, however, for practical reasons to be drawn somewhere: I suggest 500 A.D.

8. Let us altogether appreciate that (from the point of view of the authors) there is a greater linguistic continuity between the *Chronicle of Alfonso III* and the Chronicles of Alfonso X than between the former and Lucas of Tuy, despite its greater textual similarity with Lucas; that is, both Alfonsos (or their ghosts) formalized their vernacular in the currently prescribed manner.

9. It is thus up to the philologist to work out how notaries in (for example) tenth-century Galicia, speaking in the way that we can

---

[12] Wright (1982:173) reprints the *Nodicia*; *rei* is the form used in what may be the first official document in 'written Romance', that is, the Treaty of Cabreros of 1206.

[13] For St Martin of León, and why he deserves to be considered exceptional, see McCluskey (1989).

reconstruct tenth-century Galicians did, in practice learnt to write their texts in the way they did (in particular as regards orthography and morphology). By a strange coincidence, that is exactly what I am currently investigating.

References

Alarcos Llorach, Emilio. 1982. *El español, lengua milenaria*. Valladolid: Ámbito.

Banniard, Michel. 1989. *Genèse culturelle de l'Europe: Ve - VIIIe siècle*. Paris: Du Seuil.

Bonnaz, Yves. 1987. *Chroniques asturiennes (fin IXe siècle)*. Paris: CNRS.

Collins, Roger. 1985. *Sicut lex Gothorum continet:* Law and charters in ninth- and tenth-century León and Catalonia. *English Historical Review* 100.489-512.

_____. 1989. *The Arab Conquest of Spain, 710-797*. Oxford: Blackwells.

Corominas, Joan and José A. Pascual. 1980. *Diccionario crítico etimológico castellano e hispánico*, vol. 1. Madrid: Gredos.

Dionisotti, Carlotta. 1982. On Bede, Grammars and Greek. *Revue Bénédictine* 92.111-41.

Emiliano, António. 1988. Contribuição grafemática para o estudo do leonês medieval; análise da variável grafémica [ie] nos Foros de Alfaiates. In *Actas del I congreso internacional de historia de la lengua española*, ed. Manuel Ariza, Antonio Salvador and Antonio Viudas, 103-14. Madrid: Arco.

_____. 1991. Latin or Romance? Graphemic variation and scripto-linguistic change in medieval Spain. In Wright 1991a:233-47.

Franco, Fabiola. 1985. A deeper look at the grammar and some implications of SER and ESTAR + locative in Spanish. *Hispania* 68.641-48.

Ganz, David and Goffart, Walter. 1990. Charters earlier than 800 from French collections. *Speculum* 65.906-32.

García Larragueta, Santos. 1984. *Las glosas emilianenses*. Logroño: Instituto de Estudios Riojanos.

Gil, Juan. 1973. Para la edición de los textos visigodos y mozárabes. *Habis* 4.189-234.

_____, Moralejo, José Luis and Ruiz de la Peña, Juan I. 1985. *Crónicas asturianas*. Oviedo: Universidad de Oviedo.

Guerreau-Jalabert, Anita. 1982. *Abbo Floriacensis: Quaestiones grammaticales*. Paris: Les Belles Lettres.

Harvey, Anthony. 1990. Retrieving the pronunciation of Early Insular Celtic Scribes: Towards a methodology. *Celtica* 21.178-90.

Herman, József. 1988. La situation linguistique en Italie au VIe siècle. *Revue de linguistique romane* 52.55-67.

_____. 1990. *Du latin aux langues romanes*. Tübingen: Niemeyer.

Isidoro de Sevilla. 1982. *Etimologías, edición bilingüe preparada por José Oroz Reta, con introducción general por Manuel C. Díaz y Díaz*. Madrid: Biblioteca de Autores Cristianos.

Law, Vivian. 1982. *The Insular Latin Grammarians*. Ipswich: Boydell and Brewer.

_____. 1987. Grammars and language-change: An eighth-century case. In *Latin vulgaire - Latin tardif*, ed. József Herman, 133-44. Tübingen: Niemeyer.

McCluskey, Raymond. 1989. The genesis of the *Concordia* of Martin of León. In *God and Man in Medieval Spain*, ed. Derek W. Lomax and David Mackenzie, 19-36. Warminster: Aris and Phillips.

McKitterick, Rosamond. 1989. *The Carolingians and the Written Word*. Cambridge: Cambridge University Press.

_____ (ed.) 1990. *The Uses of Literacy in Early Medieval Europe*. Cambridge: Cambridge University Press.

Niederehe, Hans-Josef. 1987. *Alfonso X el Sabio y la lingüística de su tiempo*. Madrid: SGEL.

Oelschläger, Victor R. B. 1940. *A Medieval Spanish Word-List*. Madison: University of Wisconsin Press.

Olarte Ruiz, J. B. 1977. *Glosas emilianenses*. Madrid: Ministerio de Educación y Ciencia.

Prelog, Jan. 1980. *Die Chronik Alfons III*. Frankfurt: Lang.

Van Uytfanghe, Marc. 1989. Les expressions du type *quod vulgo vocant* dans des textes latins antérieurs au Concile de Tours et aux Serments de Strasbourg: témoignages lexicologiques et sociolinguistiques de la 'langue rustique romaine'? *Zeitschrift für romanische Philologie* 105.28-49.

_____. 1991. The consciousness of a linguistic dichotomy Latin-Romance in Carolingian Gaul: The contradictions of the sources and of their interpretation. In Wright 1991a:114-29.

Wright, Roger. 1982. *Late Latin and Early Romance in Spain and Carolingian France.* Liverpool: Cairns.

_____. (ed.) 1991a. *Latin and the Romance Languages in the Early Middle Ages.* London: Routledge.

_____. 1991b. La metalingüística del siglo doce español y la *Chronica Adefonsi Imperatoris.* In *Actas del II congreso internacional de historia de la lengua española,* 793-800. Madrid: Arco.

_____. in press, a. El latín y el ladino (siglos XI-XII). In *Actas del XIX congreso internacional de lingüística y filología románicas.* La Coruña: Barrié de la Maza.

_____. in press, b. Textos asturianos de los siglos IX y X: ¿latín bárbaro o romance escrito? *Lletres asturianes.*

Ysopete-Zaragoza, 1489

hic liber confectus est
madisoni .mcmxci.